Stories from a migrant city

Manchester University Press

Stories from a migrant city

Living and working together in the shadow of Brexit

BEN ROGALY

Manchester University Press

Published by Manchester University Press
Altrincham Street, Manchester M1 7JA
www.manchesteruniversitypress.co.uk

British Library Cataloguing-in-Publication Data
A catalogue record for this book is available from the British Library

ISBN 978 1 5261 3174 4 hardback
ISBN 978 1 5261 3173 7 paperback

First published 2020

Typeset
by Toppan Best-set Premedia Limited
Printed in Great Britain
by TJ International Ltd, Padstow

Contents

Preface

> You'd go dancing, you'd go to the nightclubs and things and you'd be dancing with a guy and he'd say, 'Oh there's nothing happening in Peterborough and in London we do this, and in London we do that!' And I'd say, 'Oh the road you came in on, you can just turn your car around, you can go out on it again! Lovely to see you ...' But it used to wind me up that, you know, I'm happy you've got a job and I'm happy you've got a house and I think you're lovely because I'm obviously dancing with you *but* stop saying [chuckles] that London's better. (Fiona Dawson)[1]

> Because the Italians for the daughters, oh the daughters they mustn't talk to a young man if the mother and father didn't know anything about it. And we moved here and [my husband, who was Italian] kept saying, 'Oh no we ain't staying there, with all them ...' He used to call them foreigners. I didn't. To me everybody's equal. But to him, 'No,' he says, 'We ain't having it,' he says, 'No way. We're moving. She's not having a foreigner...' and all this and all that, ooh all the rigmarole. (Alicia Vendenthoren)

In the UK's 'Brexit' referendum on European Union (EU) membership held in June 2016, 'immigrants' and 'immigration' were central to debate. After the event, it was 'immigration' that was understood by many to have lain at the heart of the majority Leave vote. A central and explicit cause of this was the 'freedom of movement' of people across borders *within* the EU. Often implicit, and subject to much hype and innuendo, was the idea that large-scale immigration of non-EU nationals, particularly Muslim men, was likely if the UK remained within the Union. Racialisation of black and brown citizens of the New Commonwealth in the 1950s and 1960s as 'immigrants', culminating in Enoch Powell's infamous 'rivers of blood' speech in 1968, had turned 'immigration' into a racialised signifier, even though the majority of international migrants entering Britain in the 1950s were white.[2] And it is because of this association that darker-skinned British people are still routinely asked the notorious 'Where are you from?' question by white people self-identifying as 'locals', followed, if the response is not considered sufficiently far-flung, by 'No, where are you really from?'[3]

The extracts I started with from Fiona and Alicia complicate this way of thinking. Both were resident in the English city of Peterborough in 2011, when they recorded life history interviews with me. Just a few years on from the 2007–08 financial crisis, the subsequent bailout of the banks and the start of what would become a decade of government austerity and falling real wages, this was a time when 'immigrants', along with unemployed benefit recipients, were increasingly being framed in sections of the print media as responsible for the country's ills. The narrative applied to the hundreds of thousands of non-British EU nationals who had travelled to the UK for work since the accession of eight central and eastern European countries to the EU in 2004.[4] It also referred to people who had entered the country from outside the EU, in spite of what became officially labelled as the creation of a 'hostile environment' for immigrants and the further tightening of already restrictive immigration policies for nationals of non-EU countries.

Yet Fiona's ambivalence about newcomers to the English provincial city of Peterborough in the above quotation focuses on the arrival of mostly white British *Londoners* during a period in the 1970s when the expansion of Peterborough through the building of satellite New Towns was at its height. Alicia, who had moved from Belgium to live with her English mother-in-law in the countryside just to the east of Peterborough twenty-five years earlier, and whose second husband had come from Italy to work in the brick manufacturing industry in the city, relates, without irony, how her Italian husband portrayed newer arrivals from South Asia as 'foreign'. It seems that being an 'immigrant' was becoming easier to disaffiliate from for Italian people who had previously experienced racialisation and were now constructing themselves as white and 'local'. In contrast, Sabriya, a Kurdish woman who moved to Peterborough from Iraq in 2007, celebrates the city's international mix:

> [In Kurdistan] there is no different people. Not like England. What I like in England is here you can find a good mix of people … Because where I live here, if you see my neighbours, if I told you my neighbours, one is from Poland, one is from India. There is from Portugal I think, the other is from Italy. It's mixed! (Sabriya Hama)

Far from a 'local'/'migrant' binary based on bounded ethnic and/or national identity categories, therefore, these examples suggest a range of residential movements, over varying distances, both within and across the borders of the nation-state.[5] The length of time someone stayed in a new location following a move also varied. Travelling Showman Charles Wood remembered a regular pattern of short-duration moves during his 1950s childhood. He emphasised his dislike for the periods when his family would stop in one place for a week or more:

> We would be here … from October until Christmas, at Peterborough in a yard. And they just pulled the caravans in the yard and lived in the caravans until like I say, Christmas, and we'd do Norwich Christmas Fair and then King's Lynn Mart and then Wisbech … then Peterborough, then we'd go on to Wanstead Flats, and then we'd go into the other side of London, like I say, Dartford and then round there. So no, I mean what I used to hate was … well I say hate, I didn't like, was when we used to go to different places and they'd put me in school for a week!

This book makes four key interventions. The first is to argue that a rethink of how the terms 'immigration', 'migration', 'immigrant' and 'migrant' are imagined and conceptualised is long overdue. Moreover, a biographical approach that moves away from a local/migrant dichotomy could help to unite people on the basis of common humanity, and also draw the sting from popular nationalist renditions of 'white British' as the familiar norm around which other people's identities should be defined.

The second, equally important, intervention of this book is to contest the idea that being at ease with racialised difference is characteristic of a so-called 'cosmopolitan elite', out of touch with 'ordinary' (often a euphemism for 'white') working-class life. On the contrary I argue not only that there is an economic and political elite which uses its power to *reinforce* axes of racialised difference (for example through promoting negative images of Muslims in the print media and online), but that, in certain spaces and at particular times, non-elite people of all backgrounds show themselves to be at ease with such difference.[6] The 'cosmopolitan elite' vs 'indigenous white working class' argument is dangerous because it reproduces and perpetuates a racialised hierarchy, the logic of which is that being both 'white' and working-class automatically qualifies a person as native and entitled to national belonging,[7] whereas, by implication, black, Asian and minority-ethnic people are excluded from working-class identity, and thus, in an environment characterised by racisms, remain doubly marginalised. There is a geography to this framing too – a cosmopolitan orientation is portrayed as *metropolitan:* more likely to be found in residents of big cities than in those who live in small cities, towns or rural areas. Further, because of the association of 'cosmopolitan' with 'elite', responsibility for the rampant growth in inequality of wealth and income, falling real wages and the crisis in housing (especially in the south-east of England) which makes both renting and buying feel unaffordable to a generation of young adults, is displaced from purveyors of neoliberalism and austerity and becomes racialised. Rather than making visible the causes of contemporary economic injustices, the promoters of the idea of a 'cosmopolitan elite' obscure them by pointing the finger at 'immigrants', a term which, as we have seen, is assumed by many to include British black and Asian people and other racialised minorities. This also plays to a politics that reproduces, and draws down upon, imperial nostalgia. As Stuart Hall put it,

> Few strategies are so successful at winning consent as those which root themselves in the contradictory elements of common-sense, popular life and consciousness. Even today, the market/free enterprise/private property discourse persists cheek-by-jowl with older conservative attachments to nation, racial homogeneity, Empire and tradition. 'Market forces' is good for restoring the power of capital and destroying the re-distributionist illusion. But in moments of difficulty, one can trust 'the Empire' to strike back.[8]

Fiona, Alicia, Sabriya and Charles, and the dozens of other Peterborough residents whose narratives are drawn on in *Stories from a migrant city*, recall individual experiences of *provincial* life in England in the late twentieth and early twenty-first centuries that, taken together, show how ordinary it is to be at ease with difference.[9] This is not a romantic portrayal. There are negotiations and conflicts, including physical and psychological violence. For example, Alicia speaks of how 'foreigners' moving into the area where she and her family lived caused them to move to another part of the city. Like other studies of non-elite cosmopolitanism in contemporary Britain,[10] *Stories from a migrant city* shows how it exists alongside ongoing racisms.

The book's third intervention is to further push back against contemporary reactionary analyses and prescriptions through its use of Doreen Massey's concept of place. Place here, following Massey, is seen as relational, multi-scalar, porous and built on the sediments of the past.[11] No single provincial city can be said to be like any other or stand in for all non-metropolitan places in the national territory as a whole – a point made powerfully in Joe Kennedy's *Authentocrats*.[12] However, as I will explain in Chapter 1, in-depth engagement with a particular place can allow for understandings of more general processes. Throughout the book I will return to two major questions about place posed by Massey: 'to whom does this place belong?' and 'what does this place stand for?' These questions invite an approach which is both analytical and political, something in keeping with Massey's orientation as well as my own.[13]

Place is considered at the levels of neighbourhood and of city. Contestations over a particular neighbourhood in the early 2010s are shown to have anticipated the emphasis in the national referendum debates over Brexit on 'taking back control'. Here again immigration, and who comes to be seen as an 'immigrant' (and who does not), are crucial to the outcome. Through a local-level investigation of 'to whom the place belongs', the book brings to light recent arrivals' lack of political representation. Alongside this it shows how whiteness is drawn on as a source of power and a way of legitimising assertions of 'localness' for those seeking to resist change in the demographic composition of the area. Behind this analysis lie questions about the nature of citizenship and, in particular, whether the notion of *urban* citizenship can or should be advocated as a means of enabling a city's residents to live alongside each other with mutual respect and dignity, even in the face of divisive and hierarchical *national* (and international) discourses and policies.

A relational view of place must include the effect of the place on places beyond. In addition to the oral history narratives at its core, *Stories from a migrant city* also reflects on four books written by Peterborough residents and published towards the end of 2016. This engagement with Peterborough's effect on the wider world brings the discussion back to the question of 'what does this place stand for?', and connects it with that of 'to whom does this place belong?' through a consideration of the denigration of the cultural products of 'ordinary places'.

Understanding changes in capitalist work through the workplace stories of current and former workers is the fourth key intervention made in the book. The predominant forms of capitalist employment for new arrivals to Peterborough changed over the period between the 1950s and 2010s. They included manufacturing, especially in the earlier decades,[14] food production and processing throughout and, increasingly in recent years, warehouse employment. The decade following the 2007–08 financial crisis saw a continuous year-on-year decline in average real wages for workers across the UK. Workers like Agnieszka Sobieraj, interviewed in the summer of 2017, complained of increasingly stringent sets of demands at food factory and warehouse workplaces – such as ever-higher targets, tightly policed breaks and job insecurity. Here, she recalls working conditions in a fruit-processing factory soon after her arrival in Peterborough from Poland in the 2000s.

> Then on the line as well you find people with similar sense of humour, you laugh I think. Actually, I remember this as a great time, the atmosphere, because we were in such a bad situation, it was summertime, we were wearing a lot of winter clothes because in the factory the temperature like fridge temperature, eight degrees, runny nose, I don't know, they're not nice some of the people who work there, they weren't nice, and you just try to do something in opposite just to keep yourself alive and happy, and I remember atmosphere was great.

Stories from a migrant city builds on John Berger and Jean Mohr's seminal *A Seventh Man*,[15] using an expanded concept of the workplace that incorporates journeys, recruitment and dwelling spaces, as well as sites where work was performed. Like Berger and Mohr, I explore the interplay between the changing political economy of capitalist work and individual worker subjectivities. As the extract from Agnieszka Sobieraj's interview suggests, this provides insights into workers' agency, creativity, humour and resistance in ever harsher workplaces. At the same time, the book provides an account of racial capitalism:[16] in Peterborough in the 2010s, people racialised as 'migrants' staffed many agency-supplied warehouse and industrialised food supply jobs. The biographical approach reveals continuities (the use of agencies, temporary working and being bussed to work outside the city) and changes (the intensification of work and ever more 'agile' workplace requirements)[17] in relation to workplace experiences remembered as far back as the 1950s.

Stories from a migrant city thus critiques hegemonic narratives of nation and belonging and re-examines capitalist work through engagement with people's stories about life and work in one small provincial city. The book is organised around a reframing of 'immigration' and key questions about place as viewed from the Brexit era. Each of the first five chapters opens with a quotation (and in most cases more than one quotation) from one of the narrators' stories. The first chapter begins by locating the book within a wider body of work exploring bottom-up approaches to cosmopolitanism and the related concept of conviviality. It sets up the idea of the Brexit era as defined by the period of austerity since the 2007–08 financial crisis and fed into by longer-term processes including neoliberalism, de-industrialisation, and the residue of colonialism.[18] The chapter also critiques the deeply divisive and reactionary analyses that emerged on the back of the referendum and introduces the reader to Peterborough and to the research project that led to this book. It finishes with a summary of the remaining chapters.

Notes

1 The name Fiona Dawson is a pseudonym. *Stories from a migrant* city includes a mixture of pseudonyms and real names according to the preferences of the people being quoted.
2 Gurminder K. Bhambra, 'Brexit, Trump, and "methodological whiteness": on the misrecognition of race and class', *The British journal of sociology*, 68:S1 (2017), S214–S232.
3 Reni Eddo-Lodge, *Why I'm No Longer Talking to White People about Race* (London: Bloomsbury, 2017); Nikesh Shukla (ed.), *The Good Immigrant* (London: Unbound, 2016).
4 The enlargement of the EU in 2004 involved the accession of a total of ten new countries. The UK, Ireland and Sweden were the only existing EU member states that waived temporary restrictions on labour market access for nationals of the eight central and eastern European countries. Nationals of the other two 2004 accession countries, Malta and Cyprus, already had access. Bulgaria and Romania joined the EU in a further enlargement in 2007; this time the UK limited labour market access using quotas for particular sectors.
5 This understanding of migration as inclusive of residential moves *within* nation-state boundaries thus differs from that used in two excellent, collaborative works that have been inspirations for this book: Hannah Jones, Yasmin Gunaratnam, Gargi Bhattacharyya, William Davies, Sukhwant Dhaliwal, Kirsten Forkert, Emma Jackson and Roiyah Saltus, *Go Home? The Politics of Immigration Controversies* (Manchester: Manchester University Press, 2017), p. xvi; and Les Back and Shamser Sinha *et al.*, *Migrant City* (London: Routledge, 2018), p. 4.
6 This is not the same as claiming that racisms are solely created by elites. For an important corrective to such an argument, see Satnam Virdee, 'Racialized capitalism: an account of its contested origins and consolidation', *The sociological review*, 67:1 (2019), 3–27.

7 Akala, *Natives: Race and Class in the Ruins of Empire* (London: Two Roads, 2018). For an extensive and insightful analysis of hierarchies of belonging, see Amy Clarke, 'National lives, local voices: boundaries, hierarchies and possibilities of belonging' (PhD dissertation, University of Sussex, 2018).

8 Stuart Hall, 'The neo-liberal revolution', *Cultural studies*, 25:6 (2011), 713.

9 Sivamohan Valluvan, 'The uses and abuses of class: left nationalism and the denial of working class multiculture', *The sociological review*, 67:1 (2019), 36–46.

10 Anoop Nayak, 'Purging the nation: race, conviviality and embodied encounters in the lives of British Bangladeshi Muslim young women', *Transactions of the Institute of British Geographers*, 42:2 (2017), 289–302; Sarah Neal *et al.*, *Lived Experiences of Multiculture: The New Social Relations of Diversity* (London: Routledge, 2017); Sivamohan Valluvan, 'Conviviality and multiculture: a post-integration sociology of multi-ethnic interaction', *Young*, 24:3 (2016), 204–221.

11 Jamie Peck *et al.*, 'Out of place: Doreen Massey, radical geographer', in Brett Christophers *et al.* (eds), *The Doreen Massey Reader* (Newcastle upon Tyne: Agenda Publishing, 2018), pp. 1–38.

12 Joe Kennedy, *Authentocrats: Culture, Politics and the New Seriousness* (London: Repeater, 2018).

13 Doreen Massey, *World City* (Cambridge: Polity Press, 2007); Doreen Massey, *Landscape/Space/Politics: An Essay* (2011), available online at: http://thefutureoflandscape.wordpress.com/landscapespacepolitics-an-essay/ (accessed January 2019); Peck *et al.*, 'Out of place', p. 5.

14 Peter Tyler, Emil Evenhuis and Ron Martin, 'Case study report: Peterborough', Structural Transformation, Adaptability and City Economic Evolutions, Working Paper 10 (UK Economic and Social Research Council, Urban Transformations Initiative, 2018), available online at: www.cityevolutions.org.uk/working-paper-peterborough-case-study/ (accessed January 2019).

15 John Berger and Jean Mohr, *A Seventh Man: A Book of Images and Words about the Experiences of Migrant Workers in Europe* ([1975] London: Verso, second edition, 2010).

16 Gargi Bhattacharyya, *Rethinking Racial Capitalism: Questions of Reproduction and Survival* (London: Rowman & Littlefield International, 2018).

17 See Phoebe Moore, 'On work and machines: a labour process of agility', *Soundings*, 69:69 (2018), 15–31.

18 See Danny Dorling and Sally Tomlinson, *Rule Britannia: Brexit and the End of Empire* (London: Biteback, 2019).

1

Introduction: non-elite cosmopolitanism in the Brexit era

> [My song's] about the battles that people face in the city and in general really, all over the world. It's about what I face and other young people as well … The first line is: 'As I walk on this earth I start to feel the hurt …' So it's like as soon as you get here you sort of feel the pain and the hurt that people around you face as well as yourself. So that's mainly what it's based on, myself … I don't actually think I mention anything specific in the track about me. I try and generalise it so that if it does get released it helps other people.

The poet and rapper Donna Stevens was describing one of her songs to me. A white woman born in Zimbabwe, Donna had lived in London and the English West Midlands before moving to Peterborough with her parents seven years previously, in 2004. Donna's global sense of connectedness and her care for other people and for the world were palpable. Her words strongly suggest a cosmopolitan disposition.

Yet, in stark contrast to the association frequently made by right-wing media commentators and nationalist politicians, they were not spoken by a member of any elite. At the time of our conversation Donna was living on benefits, having recently lost her job as a youth support worker at Peterborough City Council. This was, after all, a period of central government austerity following the financial crisis of 2007–08 and the subsequent bailout of the banks. Local authorities suffered some of the most drastic spending cuts.[1] Donna could not afford the bus fare to the city centre and, in spite of health issues, would walk the one and a half hours each way instead.[2] A central argument of this book is that a non-elite cosmopolitan disposition and the acts and practices that flow from that should be listened to rather than dismissed. Moreover, they present a challenge to the often taken-for-granted understanding of Brexit-era England: that the 2016 referendum result was a revolt by people and places that were 'left behind' by decades of de-industrialisation and neoliberalism. This over-simplified explanation ignores other ways in which class inequality and racisms contributed, for example through machinations of super-rich Leave campaign funders,[3] and through the inclination of *white middle-class* people based in the south of England to vote for Brexit.[4] By challenging the standard narrative, the book helps to signpost the way to a more hopeful future politics.

Non-elite cosmopolitanism and conviviality in provincial England

The word 'cosmopolitanism' is derived from the Greek *kosmopolitês*, which means 'citizen of the world'. It has been argued about for centuries both by philosophers and by those who seek practical ways of enabling people to live together in peace. At its core is the idea that 'all human beings, regardless of affiliation, do or can belong to a single community which should be cultivated'.[5] Cosmopolitanism is thus defined here as, at the same time, actually existing, a political possibility and something that *should* be. It is simultaneously analytical and normative.[6]

Although Diogenes, who first proposed *kosmopolitês*, was an 'outcast, exile, slave and criminal' in the Greek society of his time,[7] the normative content of 'cosmopolitan' has been used in elitist ways through an association with rich travellers, cognoscenti who know better and, at the extreme, whose ideas should be imposed on people too ignorant to understand.[8] It was this problematic, classed, notion of cosmopolitanism that the then British Prime Minister, Theresa May, alluded to in her attempt to burnish the desired credentials of her Conservative

Party with the 'working-class', 'just-about-managing' people she assumed to have made up the bulk of support for the Leave side in the referendum. 'If you are a citizen of the world, you are a citizen of nowhere', she declared, preceding this with the connected assertion that 'those who still believe Britain has made a mistake in voting to leave the EU are just patronising members of a liberal metropolitan elite'.[9]

When these statements are taken together, there is no doubting the association May was making between 'elites' and 'cosmopolitanism'. This connection was reflected in the approval the speech drew from elements of the print media in the UK, which have for many years been known for their nativist, anti-migrant and anti-Muslim headlines. In a similar vein, during his visit to the UK in July 2018, the US President Donald Trump spoke of immigration being a major problem because it was 'changing the culture' of Europe. Notwithstanding the absurd implication that any 'culture' ever exists without change, Trump's anti-cosmopolitan comments deliberately conveyed a pejorative racialised use of 'immigrant' and 'immigration' to mean people of colour, and especially Muslims, regardless of their citizenship or country of birth. This rhetorical use of 'immigration' and associated terms resonates with much media and political discourse in the UK. So white British nationals moving *from* the UK have often referred to themselves as expatriates;[10] while white English-speaking immigrants *to* the UK, especially those with money, have not always been seen as 'immigrants'. The legacy of immigration from New Commonwealth countries following the end of the Second World War led to an identification of immigrants as people of colour.

This raises the question of who has the power to regard themselves as the norm against which other people are judged.[11] Even more problematically, this can apply to countries as well as people. Cosmopolitanism itself has been regarded as a normative ideal that can justifiably be imposed on others through use of arms. In recent decades, cosmopolitanism has thus been used to justify the bombing and invasion of sovereign countries and to obscure a critical reckoning with colonial history, including the wars over decolonisation in the 1950s and 1960s. Paul Gilroy critiques the way war became legitimised in the UK after 9/11 via 'the cosmopolitan idea of humanitarian intervention' and the notion that 'women, homosexuals and other vulnerable groups [should be] liberated from the medieval claws of Islamist barbarism'.[12] Gilroy shows how in the opening two decades of the twenty-first century, the UK justified its armoured humanitarian interventions through memorialising the anti-Nazi war of 1939–45, purveying an image of being enlightened, liberal, cosmopolitan and defined by the battle against the fascism of the 1930s and 1940s. He also makes the point that while 'the Second World War is omnipresent ... the decolonization conflicts that followed it have been actively overlooked in accounts of renewed fighting in some of the very same places'.[13]

Yet Gilroy does not follow this critique by abandoning cosmopolitanism as an ideal. On the contrary, in the face of renewed nationalism which seeks to 'reinstate the cultural differences between "us" and "them"' and which 'appeals to a primal likeness', Gilroy sees an urgent need for 'critical theories of cosmopolitanism [to] be renewed'.[14] He argues that anti-fascist thinking needs to explicitly engage with the history of colonisation and decolonisation. In his words, 'sustainable pluralities ... will have to become comfortable with their obvious postcolonial provenance'.[15] He cites Fanon's *Wretched of the Earth*: '"For Europe, for ourselves and for humanity, comrades, we must make a new start, develop a new way of thinking, and endeavour to create a new man"' (sic).[16]

Stories from a migrant city responds to this call by listening out for an anti-racist, non-elite cosmopolitanism. As with Tariq Jazeel's definition of the word, 'cosmopolitanism' is used here in three different ways: as an analytical and descriptive category; as a normative ideal; and as political possibility. It is with regard to the last of these that I have been inspired by the work of Doreen Massey. Massey identified the potential for 'common anger' among people displaced by moving from place to place – those seeking asylum, or employed in working-class occupations, rather than elite, wealthy migrants – and people who have been displaced because the area around them has become unrecognisable and they would be unable to move even if they wanted to.[17] In such shared adversity, I will argue, lies the potential for an alliance that, refusing elite-driven attempts to divide it, looks upwards at the causes of key crises in Brexit-era England: declining real wages, deteriorating employment conditions, intensified workplace management regimes, cuts to public services, benefit cuts and the housing crisis.

Such a possibility was evident in the response among survivors and other residents to the horrific Grenfell Tower fire of June 2017. This included a monthly silent memorial walk,[18] to which all were welcome as an expression of solidarity. This is a London-based illustration of some people's inclination and capacity to see the human in each other and to confront the causes of inequality and oppression.

Massey's theorisation of place contains cosmopolitan thought within it, seeing place as porous, extroverted and always connected to other places elsewhere, rather than being bounded or fixed. Key in Massey's formulation is the role of stories. Much of the material in this book draws on stories recorded during biographical oral history interviews by me or my co-researcher Kaveri Qureshi with residents of a provincial English city. The book also draws out stories from the published works of four residents of that city. Finally, it is a story that emerges in relation to my story, on which a little more shortly. Responding to Gilroy's call for critical theories of cosmopolitanism to be renewed, as well as to Fanon's for new thinking and a new start, requires a collective effort by many people. This book aims to contribute, not through theorising per se, but through stories.

A further caveat is required. Non-elite cosmopolitanism is not itself a *new* idea. Pnina Werbner asked whether a 'non-elite cosmopolitanism' was possible two decades ago,[19] while others have since then, not necessarily in direct response to Werbner, written on 'subaltern', 'ordinary', 'working-class', 'vernacular' and 'visceral' cosmopolitanisms. No two of these are identical to each other, although they have a considerable amount in common. Minhao Zeng's excellent review covers many of these works, subsuming them within the concept of 'subaltern cosmopolitanism' and exploring 'how this concept has helped scholars theorize the social and political agency of a wide range of peripheral subjectivities and broaden the possibilities of resistance and empowerment against hegemony of various kinds'.[20]

The starting point for *Stories from a migrant city* is that non-elite cosmopolitanism consists of cosmopolitan dispositions, acts and practices that often sit alongside, and are inter-related with, divisive, nationalist and racist ones. Even if they are outnumbered by the latter they provide a progressive politics of possibility. A crucial intervention of this book is to explore these dynamics through stories from an ordinary, *provincial* place that contrasts with the global cities, including London, where many studies of non-elite cosmopolitanism have been located.[21] Yet, in the spirit of Massey, the non-elite cosmopolitanism explored here is equally based on the connections *between* places. Moreover, I agree entirely with Joe Kennedy that no one provincial place can stand in for the English provinces in general.[22]

In researching *Stories from a migrant city*, I have thus listened out for signs of a more hopeful politics than one based on hatred or contempt for other people categorised by 'race', ethnicity, faith, nationality, or migration history. In so doing, it is important to keep Les Back's 'metropolitan paradox' firmly to the fore. Such politics are not the product of utopias.[23] They emerge out of and exist within local contexts where racisms of various kinds are *also* rife, as well as in relation to a longer British national history of racisms, including as tools in its pursuit of global domination through colonialism and slavery, as so devastatingly analysed by Akala.[24] Moreover, as Cedric Robinson has shown, racisms have long formed part of people's lived reality *outside* conditions of economic unfreedom and colonial rule as well as within them. Importantly, through his concept of 'racial capitalism' Robinson has shown how capitalism has, since its inception, encouraged differentiated identities and put difference to use for its own ends.[25]

Zeng divides writings on subaltern cosmopolitanism into 'inward' and 'outward' oriented groupings. The inward-oriented ones typically refer to places, such as cities, and sometimes to towns and rural areas. The outward-oriented ones focus on what the US geographer Vinay Gidwani refers to as cosmopolitanism 'that enables connectivity between the disenfranchised'.[26]

One outward-oriented writer, de Sousa Santos, sees the possibilities for a 'cosmopolitanism of the oppressed' that can come about through linking grass roots initiatives in the Global South, giving the specific example of the World Social Forum.[27] De Sousa Santos's earlier work was an important inspiration for David Harvey's *Cosmopolitanism and the Geographies of Freedom*.[28] Making a similar distinction to Zeng (place versus internationalist conceptions of subaltern cosmopolitanism), Harvey contrasts Iris Marion Young's classic work *Justice and the Politics of Difference*, and its focus on the city, with de Sousa Santos's international approach. Both Young and de Santos emphasise the importance of connections between social movements. For de Sousa Santos,

> Whoever is a victim of local intolerance and discrimination needs cross-border tolerance and support; whoever lives in misery in a world of wealth needs cosmopolitan solidarity… the large majority of the world's population, excluded from top-down cosmopolitan projects, needs a different kind of cosmopolitanism.[29]

In the same spirit, Stuart Hall saw promise in 'the more open horizon pioneered by "cosmopolitanism from below"', without which, he adds, 'we will find ourselves driven either to homogenisation from above or to the retreat into the bunker and the war of all against all'.[30] Paul Gilroy has also advocated a cosmopolitanism from below. In *The Black Atlantic*, he shows the 'analytical limits of cultural nationalism and ethnic absolutism'.[31] For Gilroy the fight should not be for rights defined by ethno-national groupings and categories but against a racism that defines people according to such groupings and disavows that 'Blacks are hybrid people with as much claim to the Western heritage as their former slave masters'.[32] As he puts it in *After Empire*:

> There are other stories about 'race' and racism to be told apart from the endless narrative of immigration as invasion and the melancholic blend of guilt, denial, laughter, and homogenizing violence that it has precipitated. Those emancipatory interruptions can perhaps be defined by a liberating sense of the banality of intermixture and the subversive ordinariness of [the UK's] convivial cultures in which 'race' is stripped of meaning and racism, as it fades, becomes only an after-effect of long-gone imperial history rather than a sign of Europe's North American destiny.[33]

Conviviality, or being at ease with difference,[34] is closely related to bottom-up, non-elite cosmopolitanism.[35] These do not exist separately from racisms or histories of colonialism but rather in relation to them.[36] The analytical project of holding conviviality and racisms in tension is skilfully (and critically) taken forward through research in London and Stockholm by Sivamohan Valluvan, and in Sunderland by Anoop Nayak.[37] Valluvan discusses Paul Gilroy's *After Empire* as part of a whole slew of literature on ordinary or everyday multiculture. With approval, he paraphrases Karner and Parker's argument that 'conviviality's everyday instantiation always sits adjacent to processes of ethnically construed "conflict"'.[38] In particular Valluvan seeks to distinguish conviviality from (i) 'liberal universalism' and its implications that difference is non-existent; (ii) an approach to 'integration' that entails subsuming difference; and (iii) a multiculturalism that reifies difference.[39] He thus returns approvingly, in this third distinction, to Gilroy's argument against the reification of boundaries defined by ethnicity and national identity.

In *After Empire* Gilroy explores conviviality in order to elaborate his aforementioned proposal for 'articulating cosmopolitan hope upwards from below rather than imposing it from on high'.[40] In a review, Tariq Jazeel describes *After Empire* as an attempt by Gilroy at a 'manifesto' – that is, a normative proposition – 'for a yet-to-come cosmopolitan ethic predicated on ambivalence and dis-identification with "national" or "raced" cultures'.[41] Returning to Valluvan and putting conviviality another way, it occurs when 'ethnic differences do not require accommodation, remaking or respectful recognition vis-à-vis the white majority, but should simply cease to require scrutiny and evaluation *in the first place*'.[42]

Valluvan gives a vivid example of this, situated in a specific place and time. He recalls the contrast made by Farima, one of the participants in his research, between an afternoon when Valluvan accompanies her and her friends as they spend time in cafés and out shopping, and her experiences at the white space of the University of Westminster:

> There is a difference in how people make choices about me. If I am Iranian, that's not the problem. But you can choose to see me like I am a problem or you can choose [not to]. To be treated fairly, until I mess up I guess. … Innocent till proven guilty. … The [white] people here, like Claire, they know how to behave and know they shouldn't joke about some things, … like not ask stupid questions about this and that.
>
> At Uni (Westminster) there were so many people who didn't seem used to being with other people. I found it hard kind of to be with them, but it was strange because I know loads of white

> people from [here]. But at Uni or over on the other side, like in [two neighbouring areas], there you have a different kind of white person ... you can tell that they are unsure about what my history might be. Like [wondering about] what I do and think. I don't want to be with people like that.[43]

Valluvan also illustrates how conflict can erupt very quickly even in an otherwise convivial atmosphere. His London example connects directly with Nayak's work in the provincial city of Sunderland with Bangladeshi young women.[44] Appreciating what has been written about conviviality, Nayak states that 'it affirms the value of "light-brush" encounters in the making and remaking of a progressive sense of place where difference constitutes the new norm'.[45] Yet Nayak stresses that he 'seek[s] to stretch the elastic concept of conviviality – almost to breaking point – to demonstrate how points of tension and rupture come to mark daily encounters'. The narratives of the young people he interviewed 'challenge the easy conviviality signalled in previous *metropolitan* research, through an explicit engagement with the politics of racism and nationalism'.[46]

Nayak's critique of some of the existing scholarship is beautifully put. For example, he writes that 'the sonic melody of multiculturalism advanced through the convivial turn can risk deafening us to some of the scratchiness and bumpiness that lie in the grooves of many encounters with difference'. Such scratches and bumps (along with the violent racisms not alluded to in this metaphor) have their own temporality, resonating with Valluvan's examples of how place and also particular moments in the day or in a life matter in whether and how much conviviality is experienced. While Valluvan shows conviviality to be negotiated, similarly for Nayak it 'is not a given, but the result of ... struggles'.[47] Understanding the contingency of such struggles requires us to be attentive to other elements of temporality beyond the microvariations. It is to the particular temporalities of the Brexit era that I now turn.

The Brexit era

> [I]nsurgent nationalist mobilizations ... have recently been very successful at identifying senses of loss (of livelihoods and ways

> of life, of relative privilege, or conceptions of the future as progress, of stability) and feelings of disempowerment, disenchantment, abandonment and betrayal as fertile grounds that could be brought to voice around a cluster of key themes – restoration (Make American Great *Again*; putting the Great *back* into Great Britain etc.); authenticity (the people versus the cosmopolitan elite); unity (the people versus its others) and, in the Brexit moment explicitly, the promise of 'taking back control'.[48]

This book is being written at a time of national and international ferment and change. Populist nationalist regimes with 'strong-men' leaders, most of them associated with far-right politics, have come to power in the USA, Brazil, Hungary, the Philippines, Turkey, Italy and India. Russia is led by its long-established strong man Vladimir Putin. In 2016 the UK voted to leave the EU, a move campaigned for (for different reasons) by politicians of both left and right, with its largest and most determined base on the nationalist populist right. The terms of the UK's withdrawal from the EU and its future relationship with the block are currently under negotiation. If, as seems likely, it goes ahead, Brexit may have taken place by the time this book is published. Because the Brexit era is therefore a time of great national uncertainty it led authors of books being published in 2018 to include caveats that things could change dramatically between the time of writing and the date of publication.[49] The same is true one year later for *Stories from a migrant city*.

Investigative journalists continue to ask searching questions about the amount of funding secured for the Leave campaign, its sources and the role of targeted, but largely unregulated, social media advertising. Where answers have been successfully obtained they reveal proximate, surface-level causes of the majority vote to Leave in June 2016.[50] To understand the deeper changes that led to the electoral revolt requires a conjunctural analysis, an approach that seeks to determine the inter-relation between political, economic and ideological change.[51] It also requires an answer to questions of 'when?' and 'where?'[52] Conditions in the UK had deteriorated for many since the 2007–08 financial crisis, and the subsequent bailout of major banks in 2008 led to drastic public spending cuts, including through caps on welfare benefits and the reduction or closure of public services. Real average wages declined year-on-year for a decade, while young adults found themselves increasingly priced out of the market for renting accommodation, and home ownership became an ever more distant dream. As John Clarke explains, however, there is no simple periodisation of the temporalities of the conjuncture of the Brexit moment: what counts is the articulation between the period of austerity from 2008 onwards and much longer-duration economic, political and ideological change.[53]

The British manufacturing industry had been decimated in the 1980s under Thatcherism, while, through a range of other measures, including the violent policing of the miners' strike in 1984–85, the power of the state had been relentlessly brought to bear to crush trade union power.[54] Over the forty years between Margaret Thatcher's first election victory and this book's publication, a new common sense was manufactured promoting the idea that the market allocated resources better than the state and that this applied to the public sector as well as the private sector. Neoliberal 'common-sense' provided a rationale for the deregulation of the financial sector and employment protections;[55] the privatisation of utilities and formerly public services; and cuts to central government spending, including the decimation of grants to local government.[56] Meanwhile the legacies of British colonialism were not critically confronted. Instead, ignorance and selective amnesia were nurtured, for example through the cultivation of a nostalgic view of empire and the continuing suppression of full information regarding the violence through which colonial rule was enforced. These factors together allowed foreign wars pursued using a colonial logic to continue to find legitimacy among the majority of the public, just as a related logic was used to govern black and minority-ethnic Britons as well as newly arriving migrants in the UK.[57]

In 1968 Powell's notorious 'rivers of blood' speech touched a deep vein of racism towards black and brown immigrants and their descendants. This never went away; it was later tapped into by Thatcher, for example, and according to Danny Dorling '[w]ithin the UK, immigration was the demographic fixation of the 2010–16 period'.[58] *Stories from a migrant city* challenges head on the use of 'immigration' as a metaphor for racial difference – in particular the presence of black and brown people and increasingly, since 9/11, of Muslims. A crucial companion to the highly racialised notion of 'immigration' and 'immigrant' was its opposite, the notion of an 'indigenous' 'white working class'. Both were used as important signifiers by the Leave campaign in the 2016 referendum.

The construction of 'indigenous white working-class' victimhood has carried force in the Brexit era. For example, it has been articulated with renewed vigour by the far-right anti-Islam leader Stephen Yaxley-Lennon (also known as Tommy Robinson) following explicit pronouncements of political and financial support from individuals and organisations in the USA associated with various versions of white supremacist politics, including Steve Bannon. Yet its selectivity along ethnic lines distorts the contemporary demographics of the British working class. As the aftermath of the horrific tragedy of the Grenfell Tower fire on 14 June 2017 has continued to make plain, the working-class residents of the tower – as of much of London – were 'multi-faith, multi-national, Black, Asian, Arab, "other" as well as white'.[59] Cuts to public services, especially the fire service, the 'slow violence' of decisions made by the local authority and the cladding manufacturer to cut corners on manufacture and procurement, and the deregulation and outsourcing of safety inspections and enforcement contributed to the fire spreading and thus to the high death toll.[60] These cuts were part of the aforementioned more general policy of austerity that intensified following the 2008 bank bailout but had their roots in the Thatcher-era marketisation. The cuts hit working-class people and others hard, especially women and racialised minorities within the working class.[61]

A second key problem with the focus on 'indigenous white working-class' victimhood lies in its use as part of class-based explanation of England's unambiguous vote to Leave in 2016. Crucially, it was found in survey analysis after the referendum that a greater proportion of Leave votes were cast by middle-class than by working-class people.[62] In as much as the vote to Leave was driven by anti-migrant, anti-minority and/or anti-Muslim sentiments, these were middle class and elite at least as much as working class. They were brought to a head by the Leave campaign's use of imagery suggesting the imminent arrival of brown-skinned, male, implicitly Muslim, refugees and migrants, and the relentless demonising of racialised outsiders and migrants more generally by elements of the print media and their associated internet-based platforms. Continuity is evident here with Stuart Hall's characterisation in 1979 of 'those three popular ventriloquist voices of the radical right, the *Mail*, the *Sun*, and the *Express*',[63] although carefully targeted advertisements on social media during the 2016 referendum campaign bypassed existing election regulations applicable to the print and broadcast media, and marked a major and potentially decisive break with the past in terms of the medium and degree of overtly racist fear-mongering.[64]

In the UK, the post-referendum increase in racist attacks against Muslims and people of colour highlighted how the rhetoric of ending the free movement of mainly white EU nationals that was deployed by the Leave campaign only thinly veiled the campaign's attempts to tap into latent Islamophobia and racism.[65] A photograph of people, mostly men of colour and implicitly mostly Muslim, crossing the border between Macedonia and Slovenia in October 2015 was notoriously weaponised by the same campaign. This played on long-standing tropes deployed not only by the far right but also by 'mainstream' parties and many UK newspapers suggesting that Islam itself, and by implication Muslims, represented a threat to European values.

England thus faces twin challenges simultaneously: first to fight back against the ill effects of neoliberal policies and practices that have created and perpetuated a vast gulf of inequality in how people live their lives within the country, and secondly to confront, critically, the legacies of colonialism and slavery, and how these play out in different ways in anti-migrant xenophobia and anti-Muslim and other racisms. It might be expected that the major UK political party of the left, the Labour Party, would be well placed to take on these two challenges, especially as, at the time of writing, the leadership of Labour is avowedly anti-neoliberal, anti-austerity and anti-racist.

However, the most recent Labour government of 1997–2010, notwithstanding valuable investments in health and education spending, both continued the previous Conservative regime's neoliberal approach to the economy and advocated and carried out the invasion of Iraq as a junior partner to the USA, with the consequent loss of hundreds of thousands of Iraqi lives and 182 British ones. Moreover, nationalist and internationalist ideologies have battled within the party since its inception.[66] In the late twentieth and early twenty-first centuries, Labour's nationalist thinking – for some racialised as white – has been associated with the 'Blue Labour' movement.[67] Some Labour politicians' proposition of restrictionist immigration policies, along with their signalling of the party's understanding of experiences of austerity, deteriorating working conditions and heightened job insecurity since 2007–08, were particularly aimed at *white* long-term resident working-class people.[68]

Joe Kennedy brilliantly traces the slow acceptance in Britain of the popular Blue Labour narrative that there is a 'white working class' whose members are 'more interested in missile systems and the Queen's wellbeing, and particularly in holding on to ethno-regional identity, than any philosophy of economic redistribution'.[69] These are the people referred to as the 'forgotten' and, so the narrative goes, 'what really needs to be "listened" to in order to un-forget these people is their anger at being culturally sidelined by multiculturalism'.[70] Part of the conjuncture of the Brexit era is that this has come to be seen as 'common sense'. As Kennedy suggests,[71] 'the boldest statement of the argument regarding the "forgotten"' is made by the author David Goodhart, whose 2017 book *The Road to Somewhere* was, according to Goodhart's acknowledgements section, influenced by Blue Labour thinking.[72]

The Road to Somewhere, published before the 2017 general election, attempts a general explanation of the majority vote to leave the EU the previous year – one that does not allow for a non-elite cosmopolitan disposition such as that of Donna Stevens, with whose words this chapter opened. Goodhart set out to explain to 'the political class' that the referendum result reflected a sharp national division of worldviews. In short, people he refers to as 'Somewheres' were, at long last, able to push back against the dominance of 'Anywheres', the group, 'citizens of the world' indeed, to which his intended readership mostly belong. For Goodhart the two groups map in approximate and complex ways onto two ideological perspectives, to which he gives the corresponding labels 'Somewhere' and 'Anywhere'. While he recognises a range of views in each case, Goodhart's central point is that Somewheres are unhappy with the pace and extent of 'cultural change' since the 1960s, in particular with the growing ethnic diversity of Britain, the legacy of multicultural policies and mass immigration

– the latter being a multi-purpose term that served as a euphemism for the former two.

Tom Smith, a white British Peterborough resident and Labour Party activist, speaking to me six years before *The Road to Somewhere* was published, held views that chimed with Goodhart's characterisation of a Somewhere ideology and explicitly racialised it:

> I also want the Labour Party to realise the importance of the ordinary white English working man and the fact that they've been neglected, I think they should be running this country for the benefit of all the people who live here, now that includes white, black, martians, you name it. But it's no good keep taking the piss out of English workers and expecting them to suffer.

In contrast to Somewheres, Goodhart argues, Anywheres are comfortable with 'cultural change' because they are mostly university graduates, and, therefore, under the UK's residential university system, much more likely to live away from the place in which they grew up.[73] The vote for Brexit, as Goodhart would like his readers to understand it, was a 'revolt' by Somewhere people against the dominance of policies and social trends with which Anywheres are comfortable.

Reality is of course more complex, and Goodhart's generalisations are both misleading and divisive. For example, as we have already seen, Donna, not a university graduate, expressed what Goodhart would see as an Anywhere worldview. Yet her memory of how it felt to move to Peterborough suggests a Somewhere attachment to an earlier phase of her life in London; this would not have been surprising for a teenager faced with moving away from familiar surroundings. Goodhart's binary categories and his defence of people he believes to be Somewheres thus hold no place for the feelings of loss experienced by those who have moved or the possibility that people he defines outside the English 'mainstream' (on which see more below) might also have a strong attachment to place and a lifestyle based on community, family and religion.

Goodhart pays too little attention to the common inheritance among working class people of the devastation of de-industrialisation, and the fallout of the 2007–08 banking crisis, regardless of ethnic or national heritage or migration history.[74] His use of 'we' and 'us' is insidious. Goodhart is particularly concerned that those whom he sees as further removed in cultural terms from what he calls 'the mainstream' should not receive equal treatment or status in the national polity.[75] Although he does not define what 'mainstream' is in the UK context, he implies that nationals of eastern and central European EU countries are further removed from it than nationals of western and southern European ones, as are not only international migrant people of colour from Africa and Asia but, at some points in the book, their descendants too, regardless of their citizenship.[76]

Without attending to the racialised selectivity in his argument, Goodhart continues: for him, trust and familiarity are reduced by high levels of immigration and ethnic diversity,[77] 'especially when the people arriving come from places that are culturally distant; absorbing 100,000 Australians is very different to 100,000 Afghans'.[78] Among other things, this assumes that the Australians are 'white' and the area they are 'absorbed' into is mainly 'white' too. Such deeply problematic assumptions form part of what Emejulu has called the 'hideous whiteness of Brexit',[79] a phenomenon partly disguised by some social scientists' erroneous identification of Leave voters as primarily 'white working class'.[80]

The explicit concern in *The Road to Somewhere* with immigration to the UK from the Global South portrays a hierarchical view towards humankind, something which would have been anathema to Donna Stevens: 'Newcomers, *especially* refugees and *people from developing countries*, often draw out more than they pay in at least in the period after arrival and do not always have the same sense of allegiance to a country's norms or its national story – an indifference that was actively encouraged by first wave multiculturalism in the 1970s and 1980s. This makes many people feel uneasy.'[81] Goodhart does not expand on or try to justify his assertion that newcomers 'from developing countries' are likely to be less committed to the 'norms' and 'national story' of the country they arrive in than people coming from other countries. Like the statement that this can make 'many people feel uneasy' this implicitly continues the theme of lending greater priority to white than to black, Asian and other ethnic-minority citizens.[82]

Donna was having problems with the benefits system at the time of my interview with her in 2011. These concerned the failure of the system to ensure she received the right amounts of benefits on time rather than any sense of having been deprioritised in favour of black or Asian people or more recent migrants.[83] Conscious that others in her family held different views, she was forthright in her pro-migrant and anti-racist perspectives.

> I think there is a lot of people here, but I believe that if you come here to make a better life and to work and have a nice life with your family there's no reason that you can't be here. But I do think it should apply to everywhere in the world, if you are prepared to work and have a nice life and start a life with your family you should be able to live there ... And one thing my [music] manager said he likes about me is that I absolutely hate racism, I hate it and it's the worst thing in the world for me, because a lot of my friends are black and because I'm South African as well ...

Goodhart's treatment of Islam and Islamism is illustrative of the way he approaches racisms in the book and of his exclusive sense of 'us'. In a section on 'integration' that pushes a strongly assimilationist perspective, Goodhart turns to Muslims and, using the label 'Islamism', criticises 'some younger Muslims' for 'combining piety with enjoyment of many of the freedoms of liberal British society'.[84] This reads to me like a Somewhere ideology – and suggests that Somewhere-isms are seen by Goodhart as worthy of understanding and support if one is non-Muslim but not if one is Muslim.

Thus Goodhart's 'mainstream' has had enough of ethnic diversity, is 'wary' of Muslims (and is therefore not Muslim),[85] and is more culturally 'distant' from some immigrants than from others. Rather than *explaining* the referendum result, Goodhart promotes a hegemony in terms of what he himself calls 'national fellow citizen favouritism',[86] and a racialised hierarchy. In two books released in 2018, the authors Roger Eatwell and Matthew Goodwin, along with Eric Kaufman, sought to add academic legitimacy to this perspective across a broader historical and geographical canvas. These works were published on the same day by separate imprints of the high-profile trade publisher Penguin Random House and received widespread favourable coverage in the British print media.[87] Together with Goodhart, their authors (perhaps inadvertently?), provide fodder for the contemporary resurgence of the anti-Muslim far right in Britain. The English Defence League mustered only between one and two thousand supporters for its rally in Peterborough in December 2010. Most came from outside the city.[88] Having dwindled in numbers for part of the intervening period, the English Defence League combined with allied far right and anti-Muslim organisations to hold its biggest rally in decades in June 2018 in protest at the imprisonment of its founder Stephen Yaxley-Lennon for contempt of court, a crime to which he had pleaded guilty. At the time of writing this book the danger of successful mass organising by the far right continues to grow, while leading figures in the Conservative Party have adopted some of their rhetoric.[89] The sudden emergence and rapid growth of the Brexit Party in 2019 built on the profile of its demagogic leader Nigel Farage,[90] who has close links to far-right leaders across the world.[91] Farage burnished his credentials for this role in the 2016 referendum as the leader of the Leave campaign responsible for some of its most racist, especially anti-Muslim, messaging.

While Goodhart's stated intention is to champion Somewheres, whom he identifies as being without influence over the direction of society, his 'analysis' attempts to link cosmopolitanism and the 'metropolitan elite'. As set out earlier in the chapter, I argue that this is a 'straw person' argument which has the divisive effect of undermining ordinary, non-elite expressions of cosmopolitanism such as Donna's. Goodhart's position here, like that of Eatwell and Goodwin, flies in the face of multi-ethnic solidarities among working-class people, which, in spite of their elusiveness,[92] are the most effective route to redressing social, economic and political injustice for all workers. And, as Satnam Virdee has argued so convincingly, in British history it has often been racialised outsiders who have taken the lead in such struggles.[93]

Seeing non-elite cosmopolitanism through the lens of Peterborough

> Before it was Peterborough people. Like I say, when I go back to when I first settled down here, everybody knew everybody. We used to go to the nightclub and everybody knew everybody. But 90 per cent of people know me because it goes back to my

> generation when we was all jack-the-lads and we was all earning a living, and then all of a sudden the [New Town Development Corporation] come in, then we got foreigners come in, shall we say. Same as when I come and settled down in Peterborough. I got on the Conservative Committee, and you couldn't say, 'Why don't we do that?' 'You Cockney boy, you know it all don't you?' You had to *suggest* … 'What do you think about so-and-so?' And in the next meeting they'd go, 'We thought about this …' [Laughs.] (Charles Wood)

When we last met Charles Wood, he described the nomadic life he had lived as a child in the 1950s, and his dislike of his Travelling Showmen's family's week-long stops when he would have to go to school, often in Peterborough. Here Charles candidly highlights the resonances between his own earlier outsiderhood and that of the tens of thousands of Londoners who moved to Peterborough in the 1970s and 1980s when the New Town satellite areas of the city were built. By now a 'local', no longer nomadic and an active member of the Conservative Party, Charles remembered being frustrated that he had to hold himself back from speaking his mind in the presence of the newcomers.

Listening to people's biographical oral histories complicates ideas about who is 'local' and who is a 'migrant'. In itself this fulfils a key purpose of this book. Yet it also contributes to the book's other main aim: to refuse the automatic association of a cosmopolitan disposition with elites, by listening out for non-elite conviviality and other cosmopolitan acts and practices, however fleeting, even as they coexist and are intertwined with various forms of racism. If conviviality is being at ease with difference, the capacity to see otherness in oneself – as Charles Wood does here – surely makes this more likely.

In the next chapter we will see how, ever since the end of the Second World War, businesses in and around Peterborough have sought to recruit international migrant workers to do low-skilled, low-paid, repetitive, dangerous or unhealthy work. These have ranged from London Brick Company in the 1940s, 1950s and 1960s through the canning firm Farrows in the 1960s to the distribution giant Amazon in the 2010s. Indeed, even before the Second World War Irish people were hired for work in Peterborough and its hinterland, harvesting crops and building railways.[94] Peterborough's location on the main railway line connecting London with the north, like the commonality for many of its residents – whether British-born or from outside the UK – of being connected to places elsewhere, is among the reasons why the city is a helpful illustration of Doreen Massey's theory that places are porous, lively and extroverted, rather than fixed and bounded.[95]

Massey insists on attending to how places relate to each other as well as how the local is influenced by the national and international, and vice versa. If Massey's *World City*, for example, is ostensibly a book *about* London, it is also 'an extended meditation from, through, and *out of* London, a search for alternative, disruptive and progressive political-geographical imaginaries, beyond the entrenched hegemony of neoliberal globalisation'.[96] Following this approach, I argue that the provincial city of Peterborough can provide insights for understanding Brexit-era England.

An earlier classic book of Massey's, *Spatial Divisions of Labour*, emphasises the *specificities* of the socio-political, economic and institutional underpinnings of particular places. It is important, for example, not simply to try to read off from the local to the national, to see Peterborough as a metaphor for the Brexit-era English provinces. Joe Kennedy has acerbically attacked some writers for doing just this. He is unapologetic about his attention to the particular through his own case study of Darlington. Indeed he rightly points out that a whole swathe of London-based writers and journalists visited rural and provincial England after the 2016 referendum seeking evidence to fit the narrative that people in 'left-behind places', overwhelmed by 'cultural change', were key to understanding the significant majority of voters in England who backed Brexit. Kennedy's critique centres on the implication of these writers' generally brief trips outside London that any one provincial, majority-Leave-voting part of England can stand in for any other.

The criticism faced by Massey following the original publication of *Spatial Divisions of Labour* in 1984 and the subsequent 'localities' research project was exactly the opposite: she was seen as overemphasising the importance of local factors.[97] Yet, as Andrew Sayer argued at the time, Massey's detractors were too insistent on the value of statistical analysis of national trends. For Sayer, studying 'the particular or the unique' includes investigating its relation to 'some aspects of the whole or other parts of the system', and can therefore enable broader, more general insights.[98] Attending to context does not necessarily mean a parochial focus on the local. The 'context may be simultaneously local, national and global',[99] or, as Kennedy puts it, '[g]lobal shifts in the mode of production are experienced in ways mediated by national factors; national shifts are mediated by local factors.'[100]

My background and the genesis of the research

The book's focus on non-elite cosmopolitanism in provincial England might seem unlikely for someone who grew up in a privileged background in metropolitan north London in the 1970s. Both my parents were white: my mother was a UK-born Christian from an upper middle-class background, my father was a lower middle-class secular Jew. When they met in the early 1960s, he had recently arrived from South Africa, where his father worked as a travelling record company representative and his mother as a clerk; they had divorced when my father was a child. Yet for me, as a teenager in the second half of the 1970s, reggae and punk and their conjoining in Rock Against Racism were key politicising forces.[101] This was a time of intensified racism, manifest most notoriously in the active presence of the National Front, and opposition to it. It was also a turning point, a conjunctural moment, a move from the politics of redistribution and social democracy to one dominated by neoliberalism and Thatcher's authoritarian populism.[102]

My friends at the time – both male and female, black and white – crossed the middle-class/working-class divide. I knew that, among them, I was privileged partly because of my mother's family background and partly because of my father's successful career as a journalist. This unsettled me, which probably played a part in my insistence as a teenager on returning from private to state education, my choices of music, the style I adopted, the company I sought for travelling to watch Arsenal with at Highbury every other Saturday and my anti-racist politics. As I got older I became more aware of the structural advantages conveyed by white, male and class privilege.[103] The first time I witnessed active struggle to redress race and class inequality was a morning spent with my father in the press area next to the picket line at Grunwick Film Processing Laboratories in Willesden on a day in the late 1970s when thousands of miners from south Wales and the north of England arrived in coachloads to support the strikers.[104]

Yet my earlier north London years were also formative in making me 'alive to the ludic, cosmopolitan energy and the democratic possibilities so evident in the postcolonial metropolis'.[105] I was excited in the late 2000s, long after I had moved out of London, to be approached to be co-supervisor of a doctoral research project on class, social mixing and social mobility in an area of Kentish Town, close to where I had grown up.[106] Economic inequality there, as elsewhere in London, had increased exponentially since the 1970s – and class relations were highly unequal even then. Subsequently, reading Akala's story of his childhood in Archway in the 1990s, I learned how the combination of racisms and class inequality as well as everyday multiculture had continued since my own youth.[107]

British colonial history formed the context not only for the metropolitan paradox of everyday multiculture and racisms,[108] but also, on an individual level, for my own life, including the moves made to the UK from South Africa by my father and from India by my Sikh Punjabi parents-in-law, in both cases in the 1960s. The racialised inequalities produced through colonisation and its aftermath made it unremarkable for me as a middle-class white UK national in my twenties and thirties to move to India for several years in the 1990s, first working on a PhD and subsequently doing post-doctoral research about the temporary migration of people for seasonal agricultural work and their employment relations. A similar move in the other direction would, on the other hand, have been highly unlikely. It was nevertheless through this period of living and working in India that I received an education in the history of British colonialism and resistance to it from friends and acquaintances I made and from others whom I came to know through my research.

Might this have given rise to my perspective in this book, on the one hand critical and challenging of inequality and its causes and, on the other, with due credit to Sivamohan Valluvan, driven to explore how cosmopolitanism might do work 'of the *ethical* sort', in relation to 'its resilient antagonist' communitarianism?[109] If it is impossible, as Gerard Delanty argues, to see cosmopolitanism entirely as a subject of study, to separate it from 'the normative vision of an alternative society',[110] then it is pertinent to be attuned to cosmopolitan sympathies in poetry and other forms of art.[111] *Stories from a migrant city* emerges from eight years of research based on such listening, including biographical oral history interviews with the rapper Donna Stevens, with whom this chapter started, and with seventy-five other individual Peterborough residents.

This research began in earnest in March 2011, at a time when the austerity policies that had followed the 2008 bailout of the banks had begun to bite, and it continued until 2018, including the aftermath of the 2016 UK-wide Brexit referendum. It set out to use oral history, ethnography, film, photography and theatre to explore the multiple and diverse place attachments and work and migration histories of Peterborough residents of all ethnic backgrounds, from people born in the city to people who had arrived very recently. Initially involving a team of seven academics and artists,[112] it engaged with the stories of over 100 residents, including the biographical oral history interviews, which mostly took place in people's homes, in some cases over more than one visit.[113] In addition to the residential fieldwork carried out by Kaveri Qureshi and myself for varying lengths of time,[114] other members of the team were engaged in arts activities, from young people's theatre inspired by the oral histories we had collected (Mukul Ahmed and Raminder Kaur), through individual photographs of narrators (Liz Hingley), to films co-produced with people who had experienced street homelessness in the city or lived in supported housing (Teresa Cairns and Dennis Doran). Subsequent work with food factory and warehouse workers in Peterborough in 2016 and 2017 entailed ten further oral history interviews, regular short-duration residential fieldwork visits to Peterborough and collaboration with the film-maker Jay Gearing and arts and community organisations in that city.[115]

Structure of the book

The overall aims of this book are to think again about who is considered 'migrant' and who 'local', and to listen out for non-elite cosmopolitanism and conviviality in Brexit-era England. The era comes at the end of four decades of neoliberalism and ten years of harsh austerity policies, which together have led, in Danny Dorling's words, to 'peak inequality'.[116] The era is also characterised – internationally as well as in the UK – by renewed mobilisations of nationalism and racisms, manifest both in mainstream politics and especially on the far right.

'Immigration' has been at the heart of this changing politics. In Chapter 2 I draw on biographical oral history interviews with three men resident in Peterborough, all of whom were born outside the UK and have South Asian heritage. All of them moved to England as children or teenagers, and all at some point in their lives worked in factories. The analysis of these three narratives uses concepts developed in the field of critical mobilities studies to challenge the way in which migration is often discussed. It shows first how biographies of spatial mobility – people's life geographies – cannot be understood separately from racisms and from class and gendered inequalities. Secondly, it insists on undoing the taken-for-granted hierarchy in understandings of migration that often automatically gives greater importance to international moves than to shorter-distance ones. Thirdly, the chapter shows how fixity – not moving residence – exists in relation to mobility, a conceptual development which opens new possibilities for political alliance between people who are displaced by moving residence and those who are displaced because the place around them has become unrecognisable.

Chapter 3 builds on this politics of potential through a focus on the workplace. Among a number of significant changes in capitalist work in the UK and elsewhere in Europe and North America in the years leading up to the 2016 referendum, there has been an increase in employment through agencies, zero-hours appointments, 'agile' management and supervision regimes, digital recording of productivity and the use of algorithms for allocating labour. In and around Peterborough the growing, packing and processing of food has a longer history of relying on seasonal, temporary and/or migrant workforces. The practice of gangmastering through much of the nineteenth and twentieth centuries included transporting people to where labour was temporarily needed, as the workplace of the day shifted from field to field and from landowner to landowner. Employment agencies supplying workers to contemporary businesses in Peterborough's industrialised food supply chain follow a comparable business logic, albeit on a larger scale and in the context of a much-changed food sector capitalism. The recent growth in warehouse employment on the edge of the city builds on a similar model of recruitment and management of workers for the tasks of picking, packing and despatching goods. This chapter explores the organisation and experience of work in all these sectors, drawing on oral history interviews with current and former workers, many of them non-British EU nationals. Some of these interviews were conducted in 2017, one year after the referendum. The chapter also examines the way workers' experiences in these sectors are shaped by the specificities of their workplaces. This sub-regional labour market, with an urban hub at its core where workers are housed, demands an extended understanding of workplace geographies that incorporates not only the places where labour is undertaken but also workers' homes, the spaces of recruitment and work-seeking and the car, van and bus journeys to work in the surrounding countryside. The chapter reveals these capitalist workplaces to be sites of discipline and control, in spite or because of which the often non-unionised, multi-ethnic, multi-national and multi-lingual workforces occasionally find means to resist, assert their dignity and experience solidarity and conviviality.[117] In Brexit-era discussions that problematise anti-racist struggle as potentially weakening action to reduce class inequality, this chapter poses a challenge, showing how addressing racial injustice is essential to fighting the inequalities and injustices of capitalist workplaces.

The fourth chapter moves from the workplace to the neighbourhood and the city. Following the 2016 referendum, the future status in the UK of nationals of other EU countries became the subject of intensified political debate. Meanwhile in several localities in England, EU nationals from central and eastern Europe were subject to xenophobic attacks, as part of a wider post-referendum spike in racist abuse which some perpetrators may have felt was legitimised by statements of leading figures in both the official and unofficial Leave campaigns and by parts of the corporate-owned media. This chapter is concerned with the contestations over place in which class, 'race' and the right to the neighbourhood and to the city are all at stake. It focuses on the life histories of people who either moved to or grew up in the Gladstone, Millfield and New England areas of Peterborough, parts of which have housed new international migrant arrivals since at least the 1940s. Stories of working-class lives in these neighbourhoods included inter-ethnic mixing, conviviality and racisms. The large-scale growth in arrivals of international migrants since the enlargement of the EU in 2004 has not been matched by political representation. Stereotypes have emerged about 'eastern Europeans' that ignore the diversity of subjectivities and identities among the more recent migrants and the fact that many of them are not actually from eastern Europe. Demands made by recently arrived international migrants for a voice in city governance and for housing and workplace justice can be seen as struggles over the nature of citizenship. In the context of the ongoing multi-scale quasi-colonial governance of 'difference' in Britain, such citizenship struggles need to be understood alongside (and in relation to) those of other working-class people, including long-term residents and migrants from elsewhere in the UK, and both ethnic minorities and the white British ethnic majority.

Throughout much of *Stories from a migrant city* I draw on biographical oral histories to argue that to understand what a place stands for – the important question Massey raises about London in *World City* – it is necessary to consider its relation to the multiple other places to which its residents are connected. In the fifth chapter I continue to explore this theme using a different source of stories: four books based on the lives of residents of Peterborough that were all published in the last quarter of 2016. The books vary from the part-fictionalised biography of a Holocaust survivor as narrated by an EU national and former food factory worker currently resident in the city, through a South Asian cookery book that links Peterborough, Bradford and Pakistan, to the product of a year-long artist's residency at The Green Backyard in Peterborough and a book of reunion photographs taken across a gap of thirty years that has received worldwide media coverage. Taken together, the four books evoke city residents' connections across space and time. They show how the ever-shifting present in the city is made, at least in part, by the geographically wide-ranging pasts of its people. They also hint at the opposite: how the work, actions and objects produced by and with Peterborough residents affect, influence and shape other places. While the books are produced by professionals, each of them contains elements of 'professional amateur' creativity,[118] and of the non-elite cosmopolitanism that sits alongside racism and xenophobia in the city.

In the concluding chapter I return to my central aim of rethinking the terms of the immigration debate and the lines of division drawn up and frequently repeated by dominant elements of the print media and by certain politicians. Ironically, the framing of society as divided between a disaffected working class (either implicitly 'white' or named as such) and a 'cosmopolitan elite' is a narrative constructed by writers who are often themselves part of an elite. This chapter challenges the premise of the divisions that they claim to be reporting on or analysing but in fact, inadvertently or otherwise, promote. Instead it brings together shared histories of mobility and fixity; workplace experiences that produce solidarity across boundaries of ethnic, national, linguistic and faith identities; and struggles for urban citizenship for all residents of a particular place. Being forced to move or stay put is in both cases structured by class inequalities and racisms. As Massey has argued, this can provide the seeds of 'common anger'.[119] Moreover, migration is within the experience of people defined as 'locals' or 'us' rather than an action undertaken by a separate category of 'them'. While some commentators buy into the terminology of nativism through their adoption of the notion of a disaffected 'white working class', I argue against such ethnicisation of class. Racisms continue, rooted in colonial history, and promulgated, individually and collectively, by middle-class people and rich elites as well as by some working-class people. Alongside and entangled with such politics, the stories drawn on in this book also collectively portray universal elements of human experience, and thus enable a vision of common humanity that can be a resource for future struggles for equality and justice. It is with one oral history narrator's recollection of cosmopolitan everyday life in a working-class locality of Peterborough that the next chapter begins.

Notes

1 Tom Crewe, 'The strange death of municipal England', *London review of books*, 38:24 (2016), 6–10.
2 A distance of 2.6 miles (4.1 kilometres).
3 See, for example, Anushka Asthana with Carole Cadwalladr and Eva Wiseman, 'Arron Banks, the man who bankrolled Brexit', podcast, *The Guardian*, 2018, available online at: www.theguardian.com/news/audio/2018/nov/09/arron-banks-man-who-bankrolled-brexit-podcast-today-in-focus (accessed January 2019).
4 Danny Dorling, *Peak Inequality: Britain's Ticking Time Bomb* (Bristol: Policy Press, 2018).
5 Tariq Jazeel, 'Review essay: spectres of tolerance: living together beyond cosmopolitanism', *Cultural geographies*, 14:4 (2007), 617.
6 Gerard Delanty argues that discussion of cosmopolitanism always and inevitably contains an element of normativity. See Delanty, 'The cosmopolitan imagination: critical cosmopolitanism and social theory',

The British journal of sociology, 57:1 (2006), 25–47; Greg Noble struggles to pull out the analytical category from the normative ideal ('Cosmopolitan habits: the capacities and habitats of intercultural conviviality', *Body & society*, 19:2–3 (2013), 162–185).

7 Nina Glick Schiller and Andrew Irving, 'Introduction: what's in a word? What's in a question?', in Nina Glick Schiller and Andrew Irving (eds), *Whose Cosmopolitanism? Critical Perspectives, Relationalities and Discontents* (Oxford: Berghahn, 2015), p. 1. Diogenes lived from 412 to 323 BC.

8 Nina Glick Schiller and Andrew Irving (eds), *Whose Cosmopolitanism? Critical Perspectives, Relationalities and Discontents* (Oxford: Berghahn, 2015).

9 Theresa May, Conservative Party Conference Speech, October 2016, *International Business Times*, available online at: www.ibtimes.co.uk/brits-are-well-travelled-open-minded-global-citizens-damn-brexiteers-that-want-change-us-1587348 (accessed January 2019).

10 Sarah Kunz, 'Expatriate, migrant? The social life of migration categories and the polyvalent mobility of race', *Journal of ethnic and migration studies*, available online (early view), DOI: 10.1080/1369183X.2019.1584525 (accessed April 2019).

11 Uma Kothari, 'Global peddlers and local networks: migrant cosmopolitanisms', *Environment and planning D: Society and space*, 26:3 (2008), p. 501.

12 Paul Gilroy, 'Cosmopolitanism and conviviality in an age of perpetual war', in Nina Glick Schiller and Andrew Irving (eds), *Whose Cosmopolitanism? Critical Perspectives, Relationalities and Discontents* (Oxford: Berghahn, 2015), p. 232.

13 Ibid., p. 232. See also Gurminder K. Bhambra and John Narayan, 'Introduction: a new vision of Europe: learning from the south', in Gurminder K. Bhambra and John Narayan (eds), *European Cosmopolitanism: Colonial Histories and Postcolonial Societies* (London: Routledge, 2017), pp. 1–14, on the obscuring of imperial and colonial history in the EU's self-identity as representing cosmopolitan values.

14 Gilroy, 'Cosmopolitanism and conviviality', p. 234.

15 Ibid., p. 237.

16 Frantz Fanon, *The Wretched of the Earth*, trans. Richard Philcox (1961; New York: Grove Press, 2005), p. 239. Gilroy, 'Cosmopolitanism and conviviality', p. 240. Julian Go argues that Fanon's call for 'decolonization in order to transcend the … contradictions of colonialism and realize a new humanism' evoked a 'postcolonial cosmopolitanism' (see his 'Fanon's postcolonial cosmopolitanism', *European journal of social theory*, 16:2 (2013), 213). Similarly, rejecting the hypocrisy and contradictions of a cosmopolitanism that 'appeal[s] to the tradition of the liberal internationalism of empire',

Partha Chatterjee finds a promising cosmopolitics in anti-colonial nationalism ('Nationalism, internationalism and cosmopolitanism: some observations from modern Indian history', *Comparative studies of South Asia, Africa and the Middle East*, 36:2 (2016), 320–334).

17 Doreen Massey, *Landscape/Space/Politics: An Essay* (2011), available online at: http://thefutureoflandscape.wordpress.com/landscapespace-politics-an-essay/ (accessed January 2019); see also Nina Glick Schiller, 'Whose cosmopolitanism? And whose humanity?', in Nina Glick Schiller and Andrew Irving (eds), *Whose Cosmopolitanism? Critical Perspectives, Relationalities and Discontents* (Oxford: Berghahn, 2015), pp. 31–33; Mohsin Hamid, *Exit West* (New York: Penguin, 2018).

18 See www.facebook.com/events/317740485351527/ (accessed January 2019).

19 Pnina Werbner, 'Global pathways: working class cosmopolitans and the creation of transnational ethnic worlds', *Social anthropology*, 7:1 (1999), 17–35.

20 Minhao Zeng, 'Subaltern cosmopolitanism: concept and approaches', *The sociological review*, 62:1 (2014), 140. See also Yi'En Cheng, 'Educated non-elites' pathways to cosmopolitanism: the case of private degree students in Singapore', *Social & cultural geography*, 19:2 (2018), 151–170.

21 Sivamohan Valluvan, 'The uses and abuses of class: Left nationalism and the denial of working class multiculture', *The sociological review*, 67:1 (2019), 36–46.

22 Kennedy, *Authentocrats*.

23 Les Back, *New Ethnicities and Urban Culture: Racisms and Multiculture in Young Lives* (London: University College London Press, 1996).

24 Akala, *Natives: Race and Class in the Ruins of Empire* (London: Two Roads, 2018).

25 Cedric J. Robinson, *Black Marxism: The Making of the Black Radical Tradition* (London: Zed, 1983). See also Lisa Tilley and Robbie Shilliam, 'Raced markets: an introduction', *New political economy*, 23:5 (2017), 534–543; Gargi Bhattacharyya, *Rethinking Racial Capitalism: Questions of Reproduction and Survival* (London: Rowman & Littlefield International, 2018).

26 Vinay K. Gidwani, 'Subaltern cosmopolitanism as politics', *Antipode*, 38:1 (2006), 18; cited by Zeng, 'Subaltern cosmopolitanism', p. 140. This was the ethos that led to the setting up of the 'Creative Interruptions' research project (through which some of the research behind this book was funded), led by Professor Sarita Malik of Brunel University. See 'Creative Interruptions: grass-roots creativity, state structures, and disconnection as a space for "radical openness"', available online at: https://creativeinterruptions.com (accessed April 2019).

27 Bhambra and Narayan, 'Introduction', pp. 1–14.

28 David Harvey, *Cosmopolitanism and the Geographies of Freedom* (New York: Columbia University Press, 2009).

29 Bonaventura de Sousa Santos, 'Beyond Neoliberal Governance: The World Social Forum as Subaltern Cosmopolitan Politics', in B. de Sousa Santos and C. Rodriguez-Gravito (eds), *Law and Globalization from Below* (Cambridge: Cambridge University Press, 2005), cited in Harvey, *Cosmopolitanism and the Geographies of Freedom*, p. 95.

30 Stuart Hall in conversation with Pnina Werbner, 'Cosmopolitanism, globalization and diaspora', in Pnina Werbner (ed.), *Anthropology and the New Cosmopolitanism: Rooted, Feminist and Vernacular Perspectives* (Oxford and New York: Berg, 2008), pp. 345–360.

31 Paul Gilroy, *The Black Atlantic: Modernity and Double Consciousness* (Cambridge, MA: Harvard University Press, 1993), paraphrased in R. D. Kelley, 'Foreword', in Cedric J. Robinson, *Black Marxism: The Making of the Black Radical Tradition* (1983; revised edition, Chapel Hill: University of North Carolina Press, 2000), p. xix.

32 Kelley, 'Foreword'.

33 Paul Gilroy, *After Empire: Multiculture or Postcolonial Melancholia* (London: Routledge, 2004), p. 166.

34 Following Amanda Wise and Selvaraj Velayutham, 'Conviviality in everyday multiculturalism: some brief comparisons between Singapore and Sydney', *European journal of cultural studies*, 17:4 (2014), 407.

35 In her research on international migrant workers' cosmopolitan practices in Singapore Amanda Wise considers what it takes for such practices to 'become bedded into dispositional qualities involving a convivial sensibility that is not so much about "loving of difference", but open to difference'. Amanda Wise, 'Becoming cosmopolitan: encountering difference in a city of mobile labour', *Journal of ethnic and migration studies*, 42:14 (2016), 2291.

36 Amanda Wise and Greg Noble, 'Convivialities: an orientation', *Journal of intercultural studies*, 37:5 (2016), 423–431; Clare Rishbeth and Ben Rogaly (2018) 'Sitting outside: conviviality, self-care and the design of benches in urban public space', *Transactions of the Institute of British Geographers*, 43:2 (2018), 284–298; Back, *New Ethnicities and Urban Culture*.

37 Sivamohan Valluvan, 'Cosmopolitanism and intelligibility', in Nina Glick Schiller and Andrew Irving (eds), *Whose Cosmopolitanism? Critical Perspectives, Relationalities and Discontents* (Oxford: Berghahn, 2015), pp. 74–82, and Sivamohan Valluvan, 'Conviviality and multiculture: a post-integration sociology of multi-ethnic interaction', *Young*, 24:3 (2016), 204–221; Anoop Nayak, 'Purging the nation: race, conviviality and embodied encounters in the lives of British Bangladeshi Muslim young women', *Transactions of the Institute of British Geographers*,

42:2 (2017), 289–302. For another example of critical non-metropolitan work on conviviality, see Katharine Tyler, 'The suburban paradox of conviviality and racism in postcolonial Britain', *Journal of ethnic and migration studies*, 43:11 (2017), 1890–1906.

38 In Valluvan, 'Conviviality and multiculture', p. 205.

39 Ibid., p. 211.

40 Gilroy, *After Empire*, p. 74.

41 Jazeel, 'Review essay', p. 620.

42 Valluvan, 'Conviviality and multiculture', p. 219, emphasis in original.

43 Ibid., p. 201.

44 Nayak, 'Purging the nation'.

45 Ibid., p. 291.

46 Ibid., p. 293, emphasis added.

47 Ibid., pp. 291 and 296.

48 John Clarke, 'Finding place in the conjuncture: a dialogue with Doreen', in Marion Werner *et al.* (eds), *Doreen Massey: Critical Dialogues* (Newcastle-upon-Tyne: Agenda, 2018), pp. 210–211, emphasis in original.

49 Les Back and Shamser Sinha *et al.*, *Migrant City* (London: Routledge, 2018), p. 9; Kennedy, *Authentocrats*, p. 211.

50 Anushka, 'Arron Banks'.

51 Conjunctural analysis (as developed by Althusser and Gramsci) was practised by Stuart Hall and Doreen Massey, including in their collaborative work with Michael Rustin, *After Neoliberalism? The Kilburn Manifesto*. Stuart Hall, Doreen Massey and Michael Rustin, *After Neoliberalism? The Kilburn Manifesto* (London: Lawrence & Wishart, 2015).

52 As John Clarke shows brilliantly in his reflections on conversations with Doreen Massey, which were still ongoing at the time her death in 2016; Clarke, 'Finding place in the conjuncture'.

53 Ibid., pp. 203–204.

54 Jay Emery, 'Belonging, memory and history in the north Nottinghamshire coalfield', *Journal of historical geography*, 59 (2018), 77–89.

55 Hall, Massey and Rustin, *After Neoliberalism?*

56 Crewe, 'The strange death of municipal England'.

57 See video interview, 'Owen Jones meets Akala: the black on black violence narrative is rooted in empire' (March 2019), available online at: www.youtube.com/watch?v=soim1n4nFaQ (accessed April 2019).

58 Dorling, *Peak Inequality*, p. 9.

59 Robbie Shilliam, *Race and the Undeserving Poor: From Abolition to Brexit* (Newcastle upon Tyne: Agenda Publishing, 2018), p. 171.

60 Stuart Hodkinson, *Safe as Houses: Private Greed, Political Negligence and Housing Policy after Grenfell* (Manchester: Manchester University

Press, 2019); Lowkey, 'Grenfell: from micro to macro and back again', lecture given at the University of Sussex, March 2019, available online at: www.youtube.com/watch?v=JLyZ8QVEBco (accessed April 2019).

61 Ruth Pearson, 'A feminist analysis of neoliberalism and austerity policies in the UK', *Soundings*, 71 (2019), pp. 28–39.

62 Dorling, *Peak Inequality*, p. 70. As Jay Emery points out, it is nevertheless important to note the historical geographical dimension of the Leave vote in England and in particular its disproportionate association with areas characterised by low pay, high unemployment and a tradition of manufacturing employment ('Geographies of de-industrialization and the working-class: industrial ruination, legacies, and affect', *Geography compass*, 2018, available online (early view) at: doi/pdf/10.1111/gec3.12417 (accessed April 2019).

63 Stuart Hall, 'The great moving right show', in *Selected Political Writings: The Great Moving Right Show and Other Essays*, ed. Sally Davison *et al.* (1979; London: Lawrence & Wishart, 2017), p. 182.

64 Digital, Culture, Media and Sport Committee, report, 29 July 2018, available online at: https://publications.parliament.uk/pa/cm201719/cmselect/cmcumeds/363/36302.htm (accessed January 2019).

65 Satnam Virdee and Brendan McGeever, 'Racism, crisis, Brexit', *Ethnic and racial studies*, 41:10 (2017), 1802–1819.

66 Satnam Virdee, *Racism, Class and the Racialized Outsider* (New York: Palgrave Macmillan, 2014).

67 Shilliam, *Race and the Undeserving Poor*, pp. 136–144.

68 Satnam Virdee, 'Racialized capitalism: an account of its contested origins and consolidation', *The sociological review*, 67:1 (2019), 3–27; Shilliam, *Race and the Undeserving Poor*; Valluvan, 'The uses and abuses of class'.

69 Kennedy, *Authentocrats*, p. 81.

70 Ibid., p. 82.

71 Ibid.

72 David Goodhart, *The Road to Somewhere: The Populist Revolt and the Future of Politics* (London: Hurst and Company, 2017), p. vii. The critique of *The Road to Somewhere* in this chapter draws on Ben Rogaly, 'Brexit writings and the war of position over migration, "race" and class', *Environment and planning C: Politics and space*, 37:1 (2019), 28–33.

73 Goodhart, *The Road to Somewhere*, p. 23.

74 Omar Khan and Faiza Shaheen, *Minority Report: Race and Class in Post-Brexit Britain* (London: Runnymede, 2017).

75 Goodhart, *The Road to Somewhere*, p. 131.

76 For example, on p. 128 (in the quoting of an 'eloquent short parable' by Franz Timmermans regarding the lack of 'integration' of the 'children (and grandchildren)' of 'many migrants'), p. 131 (in the critique of

writers who 'give no special weight to the ethnic majority') and p. 132 (in the apparent favouring of an arrangement of 'neighbourhood demography so that people from the ethnic majority can retain a sense of ownership of the area').

77 Goodhart's reference to 'trust and familiarity' draws on the work of Robert Putnam for whom they are key concepts.

78 Goodhart, *The Road to Somewhere*, p. 22.

79 Akwugo Emejulu, 'On the hideous whiteness of Brexit: "Let us be honest about our past and our present if we truly seek to dismantle white supremacy"', *Verso*, 28 June 2016, available online at: www.versobooks.com/blogs/2733-on-the-hideous-whiteness-of-brexit-let-us-be-honest-about-our-past-and-our-present-if-we-truly-seek-to-dismantle-white-supremacy (accessed January 2019).

80 Gurminder K. Bhambra, 'Brexit, Trump, and "methodological whiteness": on the misrecognition of race and class', *The British journal of sociology*, 68:S1 (2017), S214–S232.

81 Goodhart, *The Road to Somewhere*, pp. 121–122, emphasis added.

82 See Bhambra, 'Brexit, Trump, and "methodological whiteness"'.

83 See Ben Rogaly, 'Class, spatial justice and the production of not-quite citizens', in Bridget Anderson and Vanessa Hughes (eds), *Citizenship and Its Others* (Basingstoke: Palgrave Macmillan, 2015), pp. 157–176.

84 Goodhart, *The Road to Somewhere*, p. 130.

85 Ibid. See Sayeeda Warsi, *The Enemy Within: A Tale of Muslim Britain* (London and New York: Allen Lane, 2017), for an excellent critique of liberal commentators defining Muslims as outside the mainstream.

86 Goodhart, *The Road to Somewhere*, p. 228.

87 Roger Eatwell and Matthew Goodwin, *National Populism: The Revolt Against Liberal Democracy* (London: Pelican, 2018); Eric Kaufman, *Whiteshift: Populism, Immigration and the Future of White Majorities* (London: Allen Lane, 2018).

88 Ben Rogaly and Kaveri Qureshi, 'Diversity, urban space and the right to the provincial city', *Identities: global studies in culture and power*, 20:4 (2013), 423–437.

89 See Sayeeda Warsi's critique of the then Foreign Secretary Boris Johnson's comments on the niqab in 2018, available online at: www.theguardian.com/politics/2018/aug/08/tory-peer-accuses-boris-johnson-of-making-hate-more-likely (accessed January 2019).

90 See Richard Seymour, 'Nigel Farage is the most dangerous man in Britain', *New York Times*, 28 May 2019, available online at: www.nytimes.com/2019/05/28/opinion/nigel-farage-brexit.html,= (accessed June 2019).

91 See, for example, Peter Walker and Paul Lewis, 'Nigel Farage discussed fronting far-right group led by Steve Bannon', *The Guardian*, available online at: www.theguardian.com/politics/2019/may/22/nigel-farage-discussed -fronting-far-right-group-led-by-steve-bannon (accessed June 2019).

92 On which see chapter 6 of David Roediger, *Class, Race and Marxism* (London: Verso, 2017) and David Featherstone, *Solidarity: Hidden Histories and Geographies of Internationalism* (London: Zed, 2012).
93 Virdee, *Racism, Class and the Racialized Outsider.*
94 Julie Cameron, 'Postwar European integration: how did a brick shortage change Peterborough?' (MA thesis: Birkbeck College, University of London, 2012).
95 Doreen Massey, 'A global sense of place', *Marxism Today*, June 1991, 24–29.
96 Jamie Peck *et al.*, 'Out of place: Doreen Massey, radical geographer', in Brett Christophers *et al.* (eds), *The Doreen Massey Reader* (Newcastle upon Tyne: Agenda Publishing, 2018), p. 27. Doreen Massey, *World City* (Cambridge: Polity Press, 2007).
97 David Harvey, 'Three myths in search of a reality in urban studies', *Environment and planning D: Society and space*, 5:4 (1987), 367–376; Neil Smith, 'Dangers of the empirical turn: some comments on the CURS initiative', *Antipode*, 19:1 (1987), 59–68.
98 Andrew Sayer, 'Behind the locality debate: deconstructing geography's dualisms', *Environment and planning A*, 23:2 (1991), p. 298; cited by Gillian Hart, 'Becoming a geographer: Massey moments in a spatial education', in Marion Werner *et al.* (eds), *Doreen Massey: Critical Dialogues* (Newcastle upon Tyne: Agenda Publishing), p. 79.
99 Sayer, 'Behind the locality debate', p. 289.
100 Kennedy, *Authentocrats*, p. 90.
101 Paul Gilroy, *There Ain't No Black in the Union Jack* (Chicago: University of Chicago Press, 1987), pp. 162–164.
102 Hall, *Selected Political Writings*, p. 174.
103 Kalwant Bhopal, *White Privilege: The Myth of a Post-Racial Society* (Bristol: Policy Press, 2018).
104 See Sundari Anitha and Ruth Pearson, *Striking Women: Struggles and Strategies of South Asian Women Workers from Grunwick to Gate Gourmet* (London: Lawrence & Wishart, 2018); Joe Rogaly, *Grunwick* (London: Penguin, 1977).
105 Gilroy, *After Empire*, p. 154; see also Valluvan, 'Cosmopolitanism and intelligibility'.
106 Debbie Humphry, 'Moving on? Experiences of social mobility in a mixed-class north London neighbourhood' (PhD thesis, University of Sussex, 2014).
107 See Akala, *Natives*. In contrast to me, Akala grew up in a lone-parent working-class household. Other recent research on Kentish Town by Sophie Watson – in her case specifically the Queens Crescent locality – emphasises the *work* that goes into *making* multiculturalism – by which I understand her to mean cosmopolitan dispositions

and practices – and draws attention to its precariousness. Sophie Watson, 'Making multiculturalism', *Ethnic and racial studies*, 40:15 (2017), 2635–2652.

108 Back, *New Ethnicities and Urban Culture*.

109 Valluvan, 'Cosmopolitanism and intelligibility', pp. 78–79.

110 Delanty, 'The cosmopolitan imagination', p. 32.

111 Jahan Ramazani, '"Cosmopolitan sympathies": Poetry of the First Global War', *Modernism/modernity*, 23:4 (2016), 855–874.

112 I led the 'Places for All?' research project team made up of Mukul Ahmed, Teresa Cairns, Denis Doran, Donna Hetherington, Liz Hingley, Raminder Kaur, Keely Mills, Kaveri Qureshi and Jabeen Maqbool. The project was funded by the UK's Arts and Humanities Research Council from 2011 to 2013 (see www.placesforall.co.uk, accessed January 2019). As I will explain in Chapter 4, the 'Places for All?' project was part of the wider Citizen Power Peterborough programme, and urban citizenship struggles were also a key theme of the research.

113 The rest of the stories were drawn from key informant interviews, oral histories of specific events and transcripts of eighteen interviews with Peterborough residents carried out in 1999 by other researchers in a separate project for BBC Radio Cambridgeshire and deposited with the British Library as part of the Millennium Memory Bank.

114 See Rogaly and Qureshi, 'Diversity, urban space and the right to the provincial city'.

115 I conducted this later part of the research as Co-Investigator on the 'Creative Interruptions' project, led by Sarita Malik at Brunel University and funded by the UK's Arts and Humanities Research Council from 2016 to 2019. My role in it included researching and co-producing the film *Workers* with Jay Gearing (2018, 42 minutes; available online at www.creativeinterruptions.com/workers, accessed January 2019), and collaboration with Metal Peterborough (where I was Writer-in-Residence), Peterborough Racial Equality Council and Gladstone Community Association. See Jay Gearing and Ben Rogaly, '"Workers": life, creativity and resisting racial capitalism', *The Sociological Review Blog*, 8 March 2019, available online at: www.thesociologicalreview.com/blog/workers-life-creativity-and-resisting-racial-capitalism.html (accessed April 2019).

116 Dorling, *Peak Inequality*.

117 Some workforces were also *multi-status* in the sense that they included workers with varying immigration statuses.

118 Harriet Hawkins, *Creativity* (London: Routledge, 2017), p. 71.

119 Massey, *Landscape/Space/Politics*.

2

'India's my heart, and I know I'm an Indian': histories of mobility and fixity

Introduction

> You would walk down the street and first of all you would smell all the different foods that were coming out, you walked past that house there'd be saag coming out, saag just wafted out like that. [Chuckles.] And then you'd walk past someone else's house and there'd be some Polish food and then you'd walk past the Marcus Garvey Centre, there'd be Bob Marley playing, reggae. And as children all my friends were like Yugoslavian, Chinese, Italian, we all played football together. So we didn't even know that there was any difference, and I remember thinking that there was no difference between us at all, everyone got on, there was never any trouble. I remember that the only time there was any trouble was when the National Front decided to march down Cromwell Road … I think they postponed it on the day because there was a lot of people who were just standing on the street saying if they come then we'll see what happens. But I think they didn't [come], but that was the only time I can remember any angst … I found out later on that there was this thing, it was called Paki-bashing, if they were driving round and they saw an Indian guy by himself they would just jump him, and my dad did get jumped a couple of times. But we were too young to notice; we were just playing football and having fun, and then

> standing out in the street with everyone else when we didn't even know who the National Front were. (Ron Singh)

It was 20 June 2011. Three of us were sitting in the front room of the house where I lodged in Queens Road, Fletton, the area in the southern part of Peterborough where most of the city's brickyards had once been located, and where many of the mainly Italian former brickyard workers still lived. I shared the house with Paul, a white British Peterborough-born man in his late forties (around the same age as me), who was not at home. Ron Singh, who had grown up in Peterborough and lived there all his life, was taking part in a biographical oral history interview. My colleague Kaveri Qureshi, who had recently joined me in Peterborough, was conducting Ron's interview (and a couple of others) with me as a way of aligning our approach before interviewing people solo. Kaveri lodged with a Pakistani-heritage family north of the river, on Lincoln Road. This was in the Millfield area, which straddles Lincoln Road for part of its length and which, at the time of the interview and subsequently, was home to a relatively high proportion of international migrants and racialised minorities. Immediately to the south, between Millfield and the city centre, lies Gladstone, which had been the area of first settlement for international migrants arriving in the city since at least as far back as the 1940s.[1] Cromwell Road, where Ron grew up in the 1970s, was one of two key arteries running through Gladstone. Ron likened the Millfield of 2011 to his memory of Cromwell Road:

> I get the same sort of feeling in Millfield now, I mean you just look at someone, you don't know what they are, so you just take the person for what they are when they talk to you, how they are when they meet you …

He then moved to discuss how he first remembered hearing racist verbal abuse on a primary school trip outside Peterborough; at the time he did not realise that the abuse was aimed at him as much as his Pakistani-heritage classmates:

> I was thinking about this the other day, the first time I ever experienced any racism was our teacher at St Mark's who was a really

> nice guy, Mr Kind his name was … I think maybe his thinking was … because we were such a multicultural class, different nationalities in the class. And he must have thought I never see any different colours at a football game, and I'll take my class to a football match. So we went to watch Bristol City versus Norwich … It was a school trip and we went [to Norwich]. And I remember sitting [at the side of] the pitch, we were sitting about the halfway mark, like this, and we were only ten years old, and we got called the P word all through the game by all the people behind us, and our teacher must have been mortified, because he just couldn't have seen that one coming. And I remember thinking why are they calling the Pakistani kids all these names. Why are they picking on them? [Chuckles.] And not knowing that we were all up for it, so I felt really sorry for my Pakistani friends …

In 1976, when it came to applying to secondary school, Ron's parents were determined to avoid sending him to the school his brother had been to – outside the area they lived in – partly because of the relentless racism his brother experienced:

> my brother had gone to a school called Eastholm, and at the time Eastholm was the hardest school in Peterborough, and it was full of racial problems. [It was] in Eastfield, and it had a really bad reputation; my brother didn't have a good time there at all, he was basically pulled into a fight every day and he didn't like it. So he was a pretty cool guy, hard as nails, but a pretty cool guy and it just didn't work for him.

Ron had been offered a place at Eastholm having applied unsuccessfully to a different school as 'we lived just on the wrong side of the street'. His parents refused to allow him to go, so it was decided that he would go to Orton Longueville, a recently amalgamated comprehensive school in the Ortons – an area located around the two historic villages of Orton Longueville and Orton Waterville. The Ortons had been selected as the second of three New Town areas around Peterborough, and they were still under construction when Ron entered secondary school in 1977. Thousands of homes were built in the Ortons in the

1970s and 1980s to house newcomers to the city, most of whom were white British and from London:

> Now I hadn't even heard of Orton Longueville School because it was too far to go on my bike ... And when we went there it was a real, real turn-off, because at the junior school, St Mark's [on Gladstone Street, parallel to Cromwell Road], it was so mixed and so cosmopolitan and everyone was mates, you never had a fight there, you just played football and played with the tennis ball and it was brilliant. And then my cousin and I went to Orton Longueville, it was completely opposite, we were the only Indian kids there, plus we had turbans on, plus my name now is Ron, but at school it was Roopinder so they couldn't even say that name, so it just got changed to something else. I was really, really small and I was the youngest, and the worst thing I'll tell you, sometimes parents do things with the best intentions, but they just don't realise what kids are like: Because my uncles are doctors, so we got sent to school with brown leather doctors' briefcases.

Ron's recollection of being one of only two brown boys in a predominantly white secondary school in the Ortons contrasted with his memories of conviviality at home in Cromwell Road, where his parents at one point established a private cinema:

> [the cinema] used to be a large contingent of Pakistani people, but also the Indian families would come over, because it was a bit like a day out; after the temple you'd go to the cinema. I think it got blitzed in about six months after video came out, because that just put a stop to anything like a cinema because why pay ...[Chuckles.] Because I remember you'd go down someone's house, there'd be twenty people watching *Kabhi Kabhie* on video. And so the cinema died out then. But as kids we would go and watch ... and no subtitles in those days, we couldn't speak any Hindi or understand any Hindi.

Film songs were part of a rich diversity of music that Ron remembered hearing both at home and in the Gladstone area as he grew up, and which influenced the fusion style of the band Kissmet, which he formed with his brothers in the 1990s.

> I think this is partly where we get our musical diversity from, because my dad loves his Hindi films and he's one of these who … And I couldn't understand them, but then we listened to the A track in the car and *Qawwali* would come on and would go ah-ah-ah. But at the same time my mum would be sitting listening to Elvis. And somehow, it's another one of these crazy things, a song would come on [singing 'I saw her today, yes, her face was the face I loved'], how do I know the words to that song? 'Needles and pins'. [Chuckles.] It's just really strange. So you'd get snippets of what my mum was listening to as well, so. And for us, at the same time Dad would be listening to his Hindi music, and then you'd walk … past the Marcus Garvey Centre, reggae's blasting out all day long, and walk past the mosque and some of the people when they're reading at the mosque, they've got amazing voices. I don't know what they're saying, but I knew it sounded really good. So we were just bombarded with all these different genres influences, languages, cultures.

In 1984, when Ron was eighteen, his family moved to a large house in the countryside beyond the northern limits of the third New Town area, Werrington. This had been possible because Ron's father, Sotindra Singh Panchi, who we will hear more about later in the chapter, had made money from his businesses. Ron recalled enjoying the new spaciousness at Werrington but also emphasised that the conviviality he remembered from his childhood was confined to the particular area he lived in – Gladstone – rather than the city of Peterborough as a whole. Yet there were changes afoot because Cromwell Road, like the rest of the Gladstone area, was adjacent to the city centre, which was undergoing a complete transformation. As part of the New Towns building programme, much of the historic centre of the city was demolished. In its place the new Queensgate shopping centre was built. It finally opened in 1978.

> I think our world was just Cromwell Road, and it all changed as well. It could've been because I was at that age, but when Queensgate came

> along, because my dad had quite a few businesses in Peterborough, I think he had about five different shops or something … There was the cinema, then he had a TV hi-fi shop in the middle of the town, then they had a chip shop, and like a wholesale goods shop, then a few other things that were going on at that time. And they knocked a few of them down to make Queensgate, and that was when we first started venturing a bit further than our street, so I was about twelve, thirteen. I remember walking across Queensgate as it was rubble, as it was a building site, and the guard told us, 'bugger off you little Paki …'. [Chuckles.] Everybody said it, I remember. The guys were putting the double yellow lines down in the street, and my cousin was so stupid, he said, 'Put your finger in that.' And I went, 'All right then.' I put my finger in and it burnt my finger like … flames coming off. And all I remember is the bloke who was pushing the thing going, [chuckles] everybody said, 'Bugger off you little Pakis.' We just ran … So that was the thing you see, Cromwell Road and Gladstone Street, you never got any of that, everyone was mates, everything was cool. Then you'd go to Woodston, or West Town which is just over the bridge, and you'd get called silly names, so you just wouldn't go there.

Ron Singh was speaking with us in what I am referring to as Brexit-era England – a time and place of austerity economics, an increasingly restrictionist immigration policy, ever harsher rhetoric about people officially categorised as immigrants and the ramifications of that rhetoric for the wider racialised group that broad swathes of the white British public regard as 'immigrants'. Ron's positive portrayal of conviviality in the Gladstone area and the way he connected it to his emerging awareness and experience of racism speak both to our understanding of the time when he took part in the interview (the early 2010s) and to the time being remembered (in the 1970s and 1980s). Ron's story also evokes some of the multiple places elsewhere to which Peterborough residents are connected through migration (e.g. London, South Asia, Italy) and music. Such connections are seen to be historically specific: Peterborough underwent dramatic change during the period when its satellite New Town areas were being constructed in the 1970s and 1980s. And there is a geography to these changes that is not confined to Peterborough's relation with places beyond the city: they occurred unevenly across the contrasting areas *within* the city and the relations *between* these areas mattered too. Like every city, Peterborough was and is a place of places.

Ron told his story as someone who had lived in Peterborough all his life. However, he does not fit the image of an archetypal Somewhere in the deeply flawed Somewhere/Anywhere national division of worldviews proposed by David Goodhart as an explanation of the 2016 referendum on EU membership. Though not an immigrant himself, Ron is after all the *son of immigrants from the Global South* (a category that comes low down in Goodhart's racialised hierarchy).[2] Moreover, he is totally comfortable with multiculturalism and ethnic diversity. Yet precisely because Ron has not moved residence apart from within Peterborough and its immediate hinterland, he is also able to contribute to an understanding of how places change around people who do not move. In the rest of this chapter I want to think more about how dynamic stories of place such as Ron's can help rethink the terms of the contemporary immigration debate.[3]

Bridget Anderson begins her excellent book *Us and Them? The Dangerous Politics of Immigration Control* with what she calls 'the migration fairy story' in which a poor man sets off to find work across the border in a 'wealthy kingdom'. Anderson then states the aim of *Us and Them* as being 'to disrupt this story and the categories that underpin it'.[4] My purpose in this chapter is similar. In keeping with the aims of the book, I seek to move the terms of the immigration debate away from conceptualising society as divided into 'local people' and 'migrants'. This framing can itself deafen us to everyday conviviality and non-elite cosmopolitan dispositions and practices and make it harder to perceive the potential for anti-racist struggle to contribute to reducing class-based inequalities.

I will draw attention to the way in which racisms, class inequalities and gender relations shape how much power any individual has over whether or not to choose to make a migration journey. Of equal importance is how much these and other relations of inequality structure what happens during the time the individual remains at the place they moved to.

The chapter thus continues Anderson's disruption of some standard tropes of contemporary migration stories. It takes its lead from Doreen Massey's conception of place. Massey, like Anderson, challenges the idea of a binary division between 'us' and 'them'. For Massey, it is not only those seen as migrants but long-term residents like Ron Singh too whose dynamic stories are part of what links a 'place to places beyond' in a 'particular constellation of social relations'.[5] Such stories show that to understand geographical mobility it is equally important to grasp the social relations that produce its opposite: fixity.[6]

I will argue in this chapter that the notions of mobility and fixity and their inter-relationship make the 'new mobilities paradigm' a conceptually agile container for studies of the migration of people, in contrast to currently prevalent framings in migration studies, which usually leave the terms of the immigration debate unchallenged. However, in contrast to Anderson and Massey, I base my argument largely on an analysis of transcripts from biographical oral history interviews like the one with Ron Singh from which I have already quoted extensively. In relation to some standard tropes of transnational migration studies, I argue that biographical narratives contain a built-in historical perspective that, by situating international cross-border moves across an individual's whole life, has its own disruptive power. Thus, looking back, someone who may once have migrated across international borders does not necessarily see that as the most significant moment in their life; someone's past moves *within* a nation-state may have greater significance to them than their moves *into* it; someone who moves at one point can also be stuck, reluctantly immobile, at another. These observations raise questions about the circumstances when it might be appropriate to categorise someone as a 'migrant' or its opposite, a 'local' person. I further argue that a biographical oral history methodology can reveal how both the representations and materiality of mobility and fixity are imbued with, and reproduce, class inequality and racisms.

In the next section of the chapter I review some key insights of the mobilities paradigm regarding the contingency and meaningfulness of spatial movement *per se*, of which international migration is just one kind of event.[7] I then go on to discuss how biographical oral history can be used to explore the connections between spatial mobility/fixity, on the one hand, and structural inequalities on the other, at multiple scales. This section returns to the Peterborough stories themselves, presenting three in-depth case studies of middle-aged men with South Asian heritage, all of whom crossed international borders to move to the UK as minors. A discussion follows of the implications of these cases, taken together, for how migration is imagined. The fourth section concludes the chapter.

How the idea of mobilities can change the way we think about migration

Mobility is now well established as a lens through which to analyse the social world, moving away from a prior ontological predisposition to dwelling and stasis.[8] The mobilities paradigm encompasses much more than the spatial movement of human beings, including, for example, the movement of atoms, commodities and air. However, it should not be inferred from this that mobility encompasses everything.[9] The mobilities theorist Pete Adey points out that mobility is distinguished from mere movement by its meaningfulness. '[T]o ignore the way movement is entangled in all sorts of social significance is to simplify and strip out the complexity of reality as well as the importance of those meanings.'[10]

At the scale of the individual, the mobilities paradigm enables a subject-based approach that prioritises how people characterise their own mobility and fixity.[11] Contrary to some prominent critiques,[12] studies of mobilities need not necessarily be celebratory of movement; indeed, explicitly *critical* mobilities works do the opposite, challenging the ways in which caricatures and stereotypes emerge of 'the manner in which people of different gender, class, ethnicity, wealth, age, sexuality or nationality are expected to occupy particular mobile subject positions, and erasing the differences of those same individuals'.[13]

Nevertheless, comparative reviews of migration studies and the insights of the mobilities paradigm raise questions about the limitations of both,[14] and about how much the mobilities paradigm does in fact contribute anything that was not there in migration studies already.[15] Waters is critical of the claim that migration studies tend to ignore fixity but concedes that in '[e]arly work on diasporas and transnationalism [in migration studies] … a valorization of movement was most certainly occurring, which gave little credence to the fact that people could at once be physically mobile *and* anchored … in particular places.'[16] Fortier concurs: 'much of the migration and transnationalism scholarship ... has largely neglected those who stay put'. Indeed, she applies the same critique to 'much mobilities research.'[17] However, my concern here is with the analytical *potential* of the concepts (rather than existing practice) and, in particular, how the insights of mobilities research, if not the precise, often rather academic, language, might be useful for challenging the dominant terms and assumptions of the immigration debate.

Power and inequality are central in understanding why some people do not have as many mobility/fixity options as others. As Massey showed in her work on power-geometry, 'some people are more in charge of [mobility] than others; some initiate flows and movement, others don't; some are more on the receiving end of it than others; some are effectively imprisoned by it'.[18] So *not* moving can, at particular times and places, be forced, free or a mixture of both.[19]

So much for fixity. The openness of the 'mobilities' concept also avoids the scalar hierarchy that emerged in migration studies, whereby longer distance moves of residence have been assumed to be more important than shorter ones.[20] The term 'migration' is regularly used to mean *international* migration without the qualifying adjective.[21] Indeed, the specialised lexicon involving terms like 'transnationalism' and 'integration' appears to take for granted who 'migrants' are and how they may be distinguished from 'locals'.

An important corrective here has come from studies of translocalism.[22] Once seen as a subset of transnationalism, the concept of translocalism has now evolved to 'include migration in all its forms ... translocal geographies are multi-sited and multi-scalar without subsuming these scales and sites within a hierarchy of the national or global'.[23] Translocalism is thus a significant analytical move because it displaces international border-crossing as a taken-for-granted component of the geographies of migration. Brickell and Datta also stress the inclusion in studies of translocalism of people 'who are "immobile" and often viewed as parochial'.[24]

Translocalism thus offers a language regarding migration and the connections between people across space, which parallels some of the key advantages offered by the mobilities paradigm. In this chapter, however, I argue that because the conceptual apparatus of the mobilities paradigm explicitly attends to the relationship between movement and moorings or fixity at a number of scales,[25] it is better placed to explore the simultaneity between the two in relation to the migration of people, just as it is also uniquely engaged with the connection between migration and other mobilities.

In his study of workers in Japanese inns, Chris McMorran revealed how the simultaneity of mobility and fixity can extend to a single individual at one point in time.[26] He draws on the stories of three co-workers he encountered during a year-long workplace ethnography. He shows 'how some employees with "nowhere to go" besides [a specific type of inn] get stuck in a dead-end job, while simultaneously cherishing the freedom the [inn] provides, including freedom from domestic abuse'. McMorran thus combines analysis of paid work and workplaces with the family lives that workers have left behind. His argument is for a more nuanced analysis of how 'people's mobility at one scale can co-exist with their immobility at another',[27] and hints at the importance of both classed and gendered processes in producing mobility and fixity.

The mobilities paradigm also explicitly incorporates analysis of the inter-relation between different kinds of mobilities, for example that between the long-distance migration of bodies and *everyday* mobilities, such as daily commutes. '[W]e should be wary of neglecting forms of mobility that are enduring, predictable, habitual, repetitive and of brief duration and short distance.'[28] Collins's research with construction workers in Singapore exemplifies this. He explored the relationship between the workers' visa status and their mode of travel around the city.[29] Workers' everyday mobility was tightly constrained by the length and intensity of the working day as well as by low pay, all produced by the immigration regime that restricted who they were permitted to work for. Thus people who from one perspective were internationally mobile, from another had their daily urban mobilities reduced to travelling to and from work on employer-provided buses.

Writing different mobilities and fixity together can contribute to better understanding of the relation that both of them have to social class.[30] Class is conceptualised in this chapter both as an objective position in social space, indicated for example by occupation, education level, income or wealth, and as an identity or category which is subjectively experienced.[31] The class positions and subjectivities of international migrants are complex because of the simultaneous and dynamic interplay of class structures and meanings both in an individual's current place of residence and in their country of origin.[32] The same point can be extended to residential mobility within national space.[33] Further, the class position and experience of an individual needs to be understood both in historical context and as intersecting with the dynamics of other social divisions and relations, particularly gender and 'race'.[34]

Biographical oral history as a way of listening to stories of mobility ... and fixity

The interplay between mobility/fixity, social class, gender and racialisation is explored in this chapter through biographical oral histories of three middle-aged men with South Asian heritage who migrated to the UK between the ages of nine and twelve and who worked in factories for part of their adult lives. All were Peterborough residents when they were interviewed in 2011. This biographical approach responds to Cresswell's point that '[w]e cannot understand new mobilities without understanding old mobilities.'[35] I will return to the three men, the context of their international mobility and the figure of the 'Asian male factory worker' later in this section. First it is important to establish how biographical oral histories can enable a more nuanced, but still critical, analysis of mobility and fixity.

The use of biographical oral history methods with mobile subjects has a long-established pedigree.[36] One major review found that migration, both within and across the borders of nation-states, 'emerges as one of the most important themes of oral history research'.[37] A key strength of the oral history approach is that, while 'personal narratives are anchored in social history ... the uniqueness of the subject is valued ... [I]t produces a specific kind of knowledge ... one that is attentive to the diversity of experiences.'[38] This gives oral history potentially important roles both in furthering understanding and in politically contesting stereotypes regarding migration, identity, 'race' and class. Not only do '[o]ral testimonies ... have the potential to actually challenge the categories and assumptions of official history';[39] they can 'reshap[e] the ways in which migration is understood' as 'individual migrants and their descendants struggle with the labels of identification'.[40]

Such disruption of migration stories through addressing 'caricatures and stereotypes' connects with critical mobilities scholars' concern with the power of representation.[41] '[M]eanings given to mobilities make a difference. In fact they can make a big difference. They can shape social relationships ... For some people, labels have an intrusive and permanent presence which will simply not go away.'[42] This chapter uses life histories to explore the disjuncture between representations of certain mobile subjects, and the embodied experiences of such people. This is important precisely because representations and experiences are not separate, but rather are intensely related to each other. Of central importance to this book is the relation between the often racialised ways in which the categories 'immigration' and 'immigrants', 'migration' and 'migrants' are used in the media, policy, political pronouncements and everyday life on the one hand, and the experience of people whose lives are being classified by these terms on the other.[43]

In what follows I will be drawing on biographical oral histories recorded with three Peterborough residents. Many of Peterborough's current residents (or their parents) were born outside the city. The population of the city rose from 86,000 in 1968 to 135,000 in 1988;[44] this period was the institutional lifespan of Peterborough's New Town Development Corporation – a time when, as already mentioned, it sought to attract migrants from London and elsewhere in the UK. There is also a long history of movement to settle in the city from surrounding rural areas, particularly the Fens to the east, and tens of thousands of international migrants from Italy, Pakistan, India, the Caribbean, Kurdistan, Portugal, central and eastern Europe and elsewhere have moved to Peterborough over the last seventy years, in most cases seeking work.

In contrast to migration-focused studies, we were as interested in the stories of people such as Ron Singh, who had been born in the city and never moved away, as we were in those of the most recent arrivals. Nor were we seeking to study a particular ethno-national group. The emotionality of oral history accounts related not only to the 'displacement' experienced by *migrants*,[45] but also to the experiences of both recently arrived people and long-term residents in relation to *fixity*, whether chosen or forced, and to experiences of displacement that occur when places change around people who have not moved residence.

It is no accident that of the seventy-six biographical oral histories, I have drawn on those of three people with South Asian heritage. As I implied in the first chapter of this book, my own relative fixity – a decade and a half working as an academic at the University of Sussex in England – was produced by earlier periods of temporary mobility between the UK and the Indian subcontinent to study the seasonal migration within India of agricultural workers.[46] Moreover, my earlier international mobility between the UK and India, shared with other, mostly white, UK-based academics was itself intimately entangled in the history of colonial relations between the two countries.[47]

The biographical oral history narratives drawn on in the rest of this chapter enable the disruption not only of commonly used tropes regarding migration, but also of intersectional stereotypes regarding class, 'race' and masculinity. If snapshots had been taken at single points in each of the three men's lives in Britain, they might have been categorised as 'factory workers', for each did indeed work in a factory for a number of years. 'Factory work' could serve to fix their class position, and it might have been expected that their subjective experiences of it had much in common.[48] The classed positionality and experiences of New Commonwealth immigrants to Britain between the 1950s and 1970s emerged out of a longer history of British colonialism,[49] which produced racialised hierarchies.[50] Objective class position involving, for many, reliance on hard, low-status work in the manufacturing sector was also a consequence of existing societal inequalities of 'material wealth, power and privilege',[51] with the vast majority of New Commonwealth immigrants among those at the bottom of the scale.

Yet contemporary analysis of the intersection of 'race' and class in the period posited the racialised incomers to a national society as not fitting into any class framework.[52] So New Commonwealth immigrants to Britain in the 1950s, 1960s and 1970s were viewed as an 'underclass' by one influential sociological study,[53] and by others as a separate 'class fraction' or 'class stratum'.[54] Those with South Asian heritage – born either in South Asia itself or in the diaspora, including east Africa – who moved to the UK were the largest group of arrivals from the New Commonwealth.[55] From 1948 until the passing of a series of new parliamentary acts in the 1960s and 1970s, people arriving from the New Commonwealth were legally citizens rather than 'immigrants'.[56] While most who came from South Asia itself were men, later joined by women and children, the 'Asians' who were expelled from Uganda by Idi Amin in 1972 moved to Britain as whole families.[57] A high proportion of South Asian men and women arriving in Britain found work in the manufacturing sector.[58] Many South Asians were 'at the bottom of the racial ladder [which] ensured their designation to the most unpleasant, physically taxing jobs that involved heavy lifting and other gruelling tasks'.[59] Racialised hierarchies in the workplace – a part of what some refer to as 'racial capitalism'[60] – are dealt with in more detail in the next chapter.

This context is common to the three men whose life histories are discussed in this chapter, but the three individual narratives have also been selected to exemplify diversity and thus contribute to disrupting commonly used migration categories by continuing the long-established scholarly tradition of problematising the category Asian / South Asian in Britain.[61] Moreover, Britain's society and economy, as well as its legislation on immigration and 'race relations', underwent profound change across the period from the mid-1950s to the early 1970s when the three men (then boys) moved to the UK.[62]

Apart from their different ages, the men have followed distinct employment trajectories and have contrasting histories of family relations. In each of the three stories, the man's relationship with and/or the absence of his father is telling. Family relations are thus key for these men's identities and occupational trajectories: all three biographical oral histories include stories of gender relations and masculinities.[63] As Katy Gardner showed in her work on older Bangladeshi migrants in east London, masculinities, and how they are narrated, are in flux over the life course;[64] gender is always wrapped up in intersectional relations with class, ethnicity and other social divisions.[65] In a study of Pakistani male former industrial workers in Britain, Ali Nobil Ahmad too insists on an intersectional approach, exploring 'the specific set of constraints that position Pakistani males as economically and politically marginalised and racialised subjects in British society, as well as beneficiaries of their power over women'.[66]

My focus in this chapter is not on gendered identities *per se* but on the complexity of the relationship between mobility and fixity and on the contingent connections between both of these, racialisation, racism and social class. At the same time, the stories raise questions about the very category 'migrant', suggesting that categorising people in this way should be done only with alertness to the particular discursive and political context. They also caution us against too easily boxing people into class categories, and are strongly suggestive of the significance of short distance and internal moves, and of fixedness-in-place, whether chosen or to some degree compelled.

Sotindra Singh Panchi moved to the UK from India in 1954, aged nine; Mam Bandali was the same age when he was expelled from Uganda in 1972, and Pakzaad arrived from Pakistan in 1966, aged twelve. For each of them, recalling childhoods, close family, places of short and long-term residence and significant journeys was emotionally charged. All faced adversity at certain points, including encounters with racism of varying intensity. None simply moved from one place in South Asia or east Africa to another place in Britain but rather their lives entailed both mobility and fixity at a number of scales.

Pakzaad

I interviewed Pakzaad in the English police station where he worked. He talked a lot about his father, with a feeling of longing and admiration and a lingering guilt that he had not been able to satisfy the ambitions his father had had for him. Tellingly he remembered exactly how long his father had served in the British army:

> he was based in north Africa, he was there for four years, eleven months and thirty days. That's what his discharge certificate says. I read it with my own eyes.

Pakzaad's father had sent his military earnings back to his wife; they used the money to build the family home a mile and a half from Jhelum city. It was, he said, 'a very spacious house like a lot of the houses are in the Punjab, large forecourt, had animals like buffalo and cow and goats and chickens and the like'. Pakzaad's mother's family were 'proper Punjabis ... rural people who have got lots of land and do proper farming'. In contrast, his father's family had lost much of their land, partly due to river erosion and partly because one of Pakzaad's not-too-distant ancestors 'sold a lot of his land and ate it … He loved meat and, whenever he felt like selling a bit of land, he'd basically enjoy himself'.

When twelve-year-old Pakzaad arrived in England in 1966, the first place he moved to live was Bedford, where his father had just been made redundant from his labouring job in the brickyards. The fourth of eleven children and eldest son of his parents, Pakzaad had been excited by the thought of travelling to England mainly, he recalled, because of the humiliation he received as a child at the hands of teachers who regularly caned and swore at students.

> And the irony is that, when I left Pakistan I didn't really think too much about leaving my mother and brothers and sisters … All I was thinking about was no more school …

The irony stemmed from his experience of the school he went to in 1960s Bedford, speaking no English and subjected to both racist bullying by other pupils and caning by teachers. In response bonds soon developed between Indian and Pakistani boys in spite of fresh memories of the 1965 Indo-Pakistan war.

> I was in Pakistan when [the war] happened … and I remember having to dig trenches in our garden … Nationalistic feeling was very strong in both the Indian boys and the Pakistani boys … The Pakistani boys, we had a superiority complex. But … because we were being targeted by the English boys and the Italian boys and the rest, we actually gelled together, and we forgot our differences. And the commonality was our skin colour, our language, because we all spoke in Punjabi, and it didn't matter that we were Pakistanis and Indians.

After just over a year in Bedford, Pakzaad's father found employment in St Ives in Cambridgeshire, a much smaller town thirty miles to the north-east, and they moved there together. Pakzaad had vividly depicted the actual process of travelling from Jhelum to Karachi and then by plane, 'puking up', from Karachi to 'very, very cold, very, very dark England'. The 'vomiting', he clarified, 'wasn't because I'd never been on a plane, but because of the sprays which the air hostesses were using, I had never been subjected to that kind of smell'. Having lived apart from his father for three years, he had been 'very, very pleased to see [his] father'.

Yet Pakzaad's narrative seemed to give his later short-distance teenage move from Bedford to St Ives at least as much significance as his move from Pakistan to England, both in terms of how he felt about it and also in terms of the access it turned out to give him to higher-quality school education that contained the possibility of intergenerational advancement in occupation and income. It was also significant that while unhappily stuck in Bedford, fixed in place, crying himself to sleep each night when he thought of the mother and sisters he missed, he had lived with a cousin of his father's, his English wife and their children, and with this level of immersion he learned English much faster.

In St Ives, befriended by another white English person, this time one of his teachers, Pakzaad gained admission, and free transport, to a sixth form in St Neots, where he studied for the A levels that would eventually take him to Newcastle University to read chemical engineering. This move happened in spite of racism experienced during his school days. Pakzaad had persevered, not wanting to disappoint his father:

> ... my father actually got me over here if you want to use that terminology ... because he wanted me to get a good education ... He didn't get me over, he didn't call me to England ... so that I could work in a factory and help him out with the family finances.

And though Pakzaad did come to work in an electronics factory for three years following his graduation it gained only the smallest mention in his narrative. Yet he expressed regrets about not having worked for a wage while at university. This was because his father, in Pakzaad's words,

> worked in two places, one ... where chickens were slaughtered and basically they just prepare them ... [the other] where they make large concrete underground pipes for sewers etc. In fact he was working there when he had an accident ... and his hand was crushed, so he wasn't able to open his hand again.

In 1984, Pakzaad, who at one stage had wanted to go to medical school, one of the most class-protected routes to economic security in the UK, ended up joining the police in Peterborough. He had had a long career but had been professionally frustrated at a lack of appreciation for his skills at mediating between different ethnic groups in the city, and was looking forward to early retirement.

Sotindra Singh Panchi

It was in the year of Pakzaad's birth, 1954, that nine-year-old Sotindra set off from Patiala to join his father in England. He travelled with his mother, his sister and an uncle. Sotindra's father, a university-educated writer, traded in goods for a living and was mobile across international borders, coming and going from England long before large numbers of Indian Punjabis moved over to England to settle. Sotindra remembers how his father would arrive on his visits home laden with new things, and regularly tried to coax Sotindra's mother and grandfather to join him in England. However, this was deemed impossible: they were immobile. Sotindra's grandfather refused to go because 'in England they don't use logs to cremate.'

Sotindra's father had done well financially in England. He would buy clothes and other items in London and sell them in prisoner-of-war and refugee camps elsewhere in the country:

> They were ready-made shirts, ties, runners, TV runners and so forth and bed-clothing and cloths like that, and they did very good business. And then when my dad came over, went back to India, I must have been only six or seven or something like that, I can remember he bought a brand new car, Vauxhall, I've got some photos somewhere …

Sotindra's family's class position was complex. They were comparatively rich but could not avoid manual work; his father was a university-educated writer but worked as a trader. Sotindra's wife Jagdesh, who had come to England as a very young child in 1948 and was present at the first sitting for Sotindra's life history interview (conducted jointly by Kaveri Qureshi and me) in 2011 at their substantial suburban house in Peterborough, chipped in, using repetition to emphasise the subtle class difference between her own family and Sotindra's:

> our parents were similar, university people, my husband's grandfather was a *country person*, whereas my grandfather had come to England, had business in England, so that's why my father was more confident to come over to England. So we came over in 1948, and the difference was our grandfathers. My grandfather was a business person, coming and going from England and India, and my husband's grandfather, bless him, he was a *country person*.

Like Pakzaad, Sotindra had a vivid, sensuous memory of the sea journey from India to England. Bread was baked on board the ship – a smell which still brought intense memories of the voyage back to him almost sixty years later.

> Either we had a third class or fourth class or whatever, I don't know, but [on the upper decks] there were upper market people having their lunches and whatever, and we were down below, and I can remember staying down there and playing out on the ship and so forth, and one time the boat was going like that and [my mother] had a chunni, the scarf, and it blew and because it was blowing I was trying to grab hold of it, and I was going down there and Mum was saying, 'No, no, no, let it go, let it go!' And there's me trying to get hold of it while the scarf went overboard!

It surprised Sotindra that when the boat docked at an Italian port, people on shore threw coins to the passengers. Thinking back, he believes they must have appeared quite ragged after the long journey and been perceived as poor – which was not his self-image.

Like Pakzaad, Sotindra would find himself moving within England while he was still a young teenager: a move which, for very different reasons, continued to exercise an affective hold over him as he remembered and narrated it. The family first lived in the small rural town of March, where Sotindra's father had started a poultry business. A visit to March that Sotindra and Jagdesh had made a few weeks before the interview brought back memories of being part of the local gang of mainly white English boys.

As he grew older Sotindra toured other towns as a member of March Amateur Boxing Club, and would run errands for elderly neighbours and help his father deliver chickens to the Italian brickyard workers who, in the 1950s, had begun to move to Peterborough in large numbers as part of an inter-governmental agreement. He recited some of the Italian patter he developed for this work to me and Kaveri Qureshi. The pleasure radiated by Sotindra as he remembered his moorings in March and these accompanying mobilities may have been heightened by the contrast with the disappointment he expressed over his parents' decision to move house to Peterborough when he was fifteen. It was, in particular, his desire to fly with the British Royal Air Force (RAF), a dream that had depended on continuing with the air cadets he had joined in March, that he felt was being torn apart. He holds his father rather than his mother responsible:

> It was a shock. It was such a shock! I complained. I can remember saying to Dad, 'But Dad, I'm joining this ... I'm getting my equipment soon and everything. What do I tell them? Why are we doing it? You didn't tell us that you was going to go to Peterborough.'

Suggesting a very different relation with his father to Pakzaad, Sotindra explained that in Peterborough he could not continue with the air cadets:

> I couldn't go – Father dictated everything. He was the guy in charge and we were just kids, and whatever he said went.

Sotindra's parents opened a grocery shop in 1960 to serve the Italian community and the growing numbers of Pakistanis who had also arrived seeking work in the brickyards and in Peterborough's food factories. In his late teens Sotindra followed his brother to a factory job at Towgood and Beckwith paper mill at Helpston. In contrast to Pakzaad, he described the intensity of the work there in detail:

> we used to see stars as we went to work and then when we came out ... we used to see stars coming back. So we never saw daylight 'cause we spent most of the time at work, twelve hours a day.

Sotindra's father did not object to the factory work his sons were doing, and Sotindra became known as one of the best workers in the paper mill. He left because of an experience of favouritism with racist undertones that blocked his own progress and any further social mobility that might have been found through that job:

> And then what happened, I left then, 'cause I was one of the top workers at Towgood and Beckwith, 'cause I worked there for six years and I became the top earner, but what had happened, there was an opening in Germany and my foreman at that time gave it to one of his blue-eyed boys and not me you see, 'cause I was qualified to do that job, to go to Germany to set up a machine. And because I didn't get the job I created a bit of a … a commotion about it, to say 'Look, it's grossly unfair!' to my foreman. And I called him names and said, 'You've got favouritism' and this, that and the other, and 'you've let me down 'cause it should have been me' and because I swore at him [laughs]. I was then taken into the big manager who was his brother. And he said to me, 'Look son, what you need to do is to apologise to him and everything will be forgotten and you can have your job back' and I said, 'No, what I said, I meant.' So therefore I got the sack.

Over the decades that followed, often operating jointly with his elder brother, and latterly with the next generation of the family, including his son Ron Singh, whose story opened this chapter, Sotindra developed a number of successful businesses in the city, which made him and his family relatively rich. As Ron mentioned, when the family's terraced house on Cromwell Road became too small they moved to a large detached one just outside Peterborough and beyond the furthest reaches of Werrington, then its latest New Town area. At one stage they also bought land in Portugal. A helicopter was used for one of his son's weddings.

Mam Bandali

Like Pakzaad's father, Mam's paternal grandfather had moved to Africa through British colonial networks, in his case as part of the labour force brought over by the British to build a railway. Mam himself, one of six children, was four years old when his father died in 1967 aged only thirty-seven. Forced out of Uganda along with all other 'Asians', Mam's family were moved around first from one former army barracks (in London), to another (in Lincolnshire) and subsequently to Scotland, where they stayed for just under two years. Interviewed late one evening by Kaveri Qureshi, Mam remembered being struck by the strangeness of London, the number of white faces, the cold and a 'horrific' journey up to Scotland:

> It was by coach and there were loads of families being moved to different towns from the refugee place so we were the last drop ...

But he also remembered the 'absolutely fantastic' house the family was given to live in there:

> We got there really late and there was two couples there to greet us, there was a house ready for us and it was fully done. There was sofas in there, there was beds made up, the fire was on because it was a cold night, the kitchen had food in it, there was pots and pans ... What had happened is we were the ... first ever foreign family to stay there. There was no black people, Chinese people, no nothing, so it was quite strange and we'd already made the newspapers before we'd arrived. So they'd all got together ... and donated all sorts of things to the house and it was fully kitted! [Laughs.] It was, you didn't need *anything*! You just walked into the house and this is yours. Ornaments, everything ...

However, worry about whether Mam's sisters would marry white men caused his mother and grandmother to consider a move. 'I've got photographs of my sisters in the seventies and they're all in miniskirts and platform shoes, you know? And [Mum] thought "Wow, this is not good."' Neighbours told them of Peterborough's New Town expansion and a local political leader's championing of Ugandan Asian refugees (on which see Chapter 4). Mam's family moved there in 1974, something his mother soon regretted as 'all of a sudden it wasn't the western culture; it was like the Pakistani lads and everything'.

Like Ron Singh, Mam remembered a complex mix of ethnic and national heritages at his primary school, including a large number of Italians.[67] You may remember Alicia's words at the opening of the Preface on her Italian husband's determination to move from Gladstone to Fletton because of a fear about potential interest in their daughter from the growing number of young men with South Asian heritage in the area. Yet Mam felt an affinity with the Italians' family-based sociality. As with Pakzaad's South Asian gang of boys, it was a case of common interests and conviviality arising out of adversity:

> The cultures were different but similar sort of thing ... The same you know, at your mother's dinner is dinner. If you go and knock for him, 'Come in, come in, sit down, eat.' If you go to an English friend's ... it's 'Can you come back? He's having his tea.' And you'd say, 'OK', and you'd come home and Mum says, 'Why aren't you at Kevin's house?' 'Oh, he's having his tea.' 'What do you mean? They didn't invite you in?' I said, 'No.' 'What?' [Laughs.] They don't understand it.

However, as we saw in Chapter 1, conviviality is contingent on particular times and spaces, and Mam's mostly sweet memories of primary school were combined with strongly negative memories of secondary school. Like Ron's elder brother, Mam went to Eastholm School. This was a formative time for him: the racism directed at him, and his resolute response to it, meant that the educational path up the social class ladder was being closed off:

> My first year [at secondary school], the first word that came out was 'Paki', and I thought, 'What's that?' And I had a lot of problems there ... I was spat on and I got into a lot of trouble, a lot of fights, stood my ground ... Luckily I came out on top most of the time.

Mam said he experienced prejudice and violence, not only from white English peers but from Pakistani communities in Peterborough, who did not, he said, 'consider [him] a Muslim Muslim, because I'm different, I've got tattoos and things like that and I've been brought up a different way ...' Yet he blamed himself for not studying, for fighting, taking drugs, drinking and going out with girls from a young age. At school Mam remembered being set apart from the rest of the class with a small group of 'special needs' children that was effectively left without support. The structures were working against him. Inequality was being produced and entrenched.

Mam eventually walked out of school after hitting a teacher, left with no qualifications and since then, in his own words, had been a 'wheeler and dealer'. This in no way sums up his varied working life, however. Like both Sotindra and Pakzaad he had worked in factories; like Sotindra he got to a position where in his own assessment he was one of the most prized workers. But in his adult life, Mam had been both more stuck, more unable to move away from Peterborough, than either Sotindra or Pakzaad, and, in his wheeling and dealing, more mobile than either of them.

At various different points Mam was a restaurant worker in Essex, a travelling market stall-holder specialising in women's clothing and a trader in jewellery between India and the UK:

> every month twice a month I used to fly from England to either Delhi or Bombay and I loved it, absolutely at that time, India's my heart, and I know I'm an Indian ... even though I felt like a tourist.

Mam got married in his late twenties and 'had one little girl and a second one on the way' when he and his wife broke up. Having grown up without a father himself he was determined to remain available to his daughters. The struggle for access, and then taking over their upbringing when his wife had been unable to, were the forces, along with a not unrelated lack of money, that he saw as having kept him in Peterborough. This period was most intense in the early 1990s when he was out of work. For Mam, the factory job he obtained in 1995 was a lifeline:

> So I found a job near Cambridge, Barhill, 1995 ... I travelled all the way there and it was £3.60 an hour, basic pay and I was cutting bits of metal. A very technical place, Cambridge is full

> of high tech and I used to make photonic lamps and laser lamps and you had to cut this tungsten wire. So I used to go there and still battle on and to fight to see my children.

This work turned out to be crucial for Mam and the source of a kind of greater economic security, at least in the short term.

> I got into the work and really started doing well there … and I became, from cutting wires and everything, to actually doing freehand glasswork … And from the glasswork I started to train how to become a glass blower and before I knew it I was there for ten years. I am blowing my own trumpet here … And I became a qualified scientific glassblower and became supervisor, resource manager, production manager.

Mam used various mobilities to get on, just as he simultaneously experienced an involuntary tie to place. At least for a period. He was still living in Peterborough and running a workers' café in 2019 after both his daughters had graduated from university, although he also expressed a desire for his ashes to be scattered in Uganda, to join his father's, after his death. In the meantime, his elderly mother's continued presence in Peterborough until her death in 2016, along with other strong relationships, kept him in the city.

Discussion

How 'immigration' is discussed and debated is central to this book. Pakzaad, Sotindra and Mam each arrived in Britain in a different decade. The end of empire, 'race' and immigration were all subjects of intense and shifting national debate over the 1950s and 1960s, culminating with Powell's notorious 'rivers of blood' speech in 1968. Yet the place-specificity of the men's small-town experiences as boys militates against any easy reading off of trends in racism and prejudice. Indeed, Mam's story resonates *both* (through his stories of schooldays in Peterborough) with the right-wing backlash against New Commonwealth immigration in the 1970s *and* with the welcoming reception that some Ugandan Asians experienced at the start of that decade.[68]

In Massey's terms, Peterborough, like other places, was the site of multiple stories and unfinished trajectories. In the 1970s, tens of thousands of mainly white Londoners moved to the city under the New and Expanded Towns programme. Yet the migration 'problem' continued to be represented in public discourse as caused by the presence of darker immigrants from the New Commonwealth. This could feed into embodied experience through the perpetuation of racialised hierarchies, manifestations of racial capitalism,[69] which, like Pakzaad's, Sotindra's and Mam's stories, had deep roots in British colonialism.

Pakzaad's silence about his own experience of factory work and the details he provided on his father's workplace injury and enforced retirement fit with the racialised hierarchy of job roles in British manufacturing in the 1960s and 1970s, with New Commonwealth immigrants being expected to accept greater danger at work than other workers, and the lowest-status roles.[70] Sotindra's story illustrates workplace racism, with a blocked promotion but also a pride in resistance, in this case through exit, which, coming from a relatively well-resourced family, Sotindra could afford. Both men thus encountered structural inequalities, but their subjective experiences and individual trajectories diverged. Class and 'race' intersected but not in predetermined ways. Mam's experience of factory work twenty years later was different again. Like Sotindra, Mam narrated the skills and responsibilities he developed with pride, but for him, factory work was critical for fulfilling his gendered identity. Because he had lost his own father as a small child, it was especially important to him to be there for his children in spite of the break-up of his relationship with their mother.

The individual men's life histories thus help to move away from the stereotyped figure of the 'Asian factory worker', just as they simultaneously illustrate the production and maintenance of structural inequalities through the intersection of class inequality and racialisation.[71] The combination of a historical perspective, attentiveness to place and the agility of the concepts of mobility and fixity reveal much about the men's class position over time, their subjective experience of class and how these were gendered, racialised and simultaneously location-specific and stretched across space.

In the context of the men's whole lives, international migration at one point and factory work for a few years at another were put into perspective as components of stories that contained diverse, often simultaneously experienced, forms of spatial mobility and fixity. Rather than celebrating spatial mobility, mobilities and fixity can be seen through these stories as integral to an understanding of both representations and embodied experiences of class, 'race' and gender, and the intersections between them.

For Mam, the move to Peterborough, explained as being due to his mother's fear of her daughters marrying white Scottish men if they stayed put, was painful to remember because he experienced a form of racism at school that involved abuse from both white British and Pakistani children. He was also separated off as part of a 'special needs' group.[72] Both of these experiences negatively affected his future class position. Mam makes sense of his story, in particular not getting on well at school, in terms of the moves he had made over a few formative years, whether as a forced migrant or when he was moved by his mother after arrival in the UK.

Fixity has a major role in the story. Mam spoke of his continued base in Peterborough as enforced, following the break-up of his marriage. And yet he expressed a positive affective tie to Peterborough because of his mother's presence there: he told me in 2012 that a highlight of his week was going over to his mother's on a Sunday afternoon and falling asleep on her settee. Nevertheless, Mam's fixity and his mobilities worked concurrently and were inter-related. It was his commuting to Cambridge for work, for example, that enabled his residential moorings in Peterborough.

The majority of immigrants (initially mainly men) from the Indian subcontinent who resided in Britain in the mid-1960s lived in six major conurbations.[73] Yet Pakzaad and Sotindra started their periods of residence in the UK in small towns, as did Mam through the dispersal of 'East African Asians' in the 1970s.[74] Not only was their mobility *within* the UK narrated as highly significant, but it was bound up with fixity. Pakzaad's enforced immobility in Bedford coincided with his immersion in English thanks to his residence with a native speaker, providing the grounds for educational success and future spatial mobility. Sotindra's positive experience of fixity in March was based on ongoing everyday mobilities. Indeed his later fixity in Peterborough and access to new mobilities – wedding helicopter, land purchase in Portugal – were enabled by businesses that profited from the international mobility of other immigrants.

Class representations and embodied experiences of class also interweave in Sotindra's narrative of the journey by ship from India to Europe in the 1950s. Here he encountered the decks with different levels of comfort arranged by class – a relatively wealthy boy in Indian terms experiencing being in a lower-class deck, a process akin to one on 'railways [that] reinforce class-based social distinctions through the categorization of travellers into first, second or third class'.[75] As a passenger on a ship sailing from India he also experienced being seen as poor by coin-throwing Italians at the port of arrival.

Conclusion

This chapter began by invoking Anderson's migration fairy story,[76] a figurative construction familiar in public discourse on immigration in much of the Global North. While the attention to transnationalism in migration studies has enhanced scholarly understanding of the stretched-out lives of international migrants and the people they are connected to, migration studies often shares with the fairy story a focus on international border-crossers and on the significance of cross-border moves and networks in people's lives. The effect of this is to create a scalar hierarchy in which long-distance and international moves of residence are by implication considered more significant than short-distance ones or moves within national borders.

Yet it was in writing on *internal* migration that Halfacree and Boyle rightly argued for a biographical approach to understanding the migration of individuals.[77] The authors held that this could help avoid the fetishing of migration itself, seeing it rather from the more distanced perspective of an individual's whole life. However, they paid insufficient attention to the power of representation so that, for example, working-class people in Britain could be summed up as relatively 'immobile'[78] – inadvertently confirming the popular association of working-class people with nativity and as threatened by a migrant other.[79]

This chapter has analysed the life histories of three non-elite people who at one point or another in their trajectories might have been seen as working-class, whether in terms of their class position (e.g. occupation) or their subjective experience of class. The biographical approach has another advantage in that it avoids boxing people into class categories: class remains mutable even in the face of massive structural inequality. Using concepts drawn from critical mobilities studies, the chapter has illustrated ways in which people may be involved across their lives, and at particular phases in it, in moves across space involving a variety of durations and distances. There is no necessary hierarchy in people's experience of spatial mobility: a short-distance move or a set of everyday mobilities may be remembered as just as meaningful to an individual as an earlier international move. The mobilities paradigm best enables these different mobilities to be analysed alongside each other and across time, and its explicit attention to fixity – times when people do not move – permits a closer analysis of power geometries that make it impossible for some people to make certain moves while it is easy for others, and that enable some to stay still and prosper while others must move.

A critical mobilities approach thus reveals relations of power across scales and social divisions, including social class and its intersection with 'race' and gender. Class is increasingly examined in transnational migration studies too,[80] and influential migration scholars have called convincingly for an intersectional approach.[81] Moreover, migration studies has frequently used an oral history methodology to understand better the subjective experiences of individual migrants.[82] This chapter has extended this through showing how mobilities and fixity inter-relate and often coexist at the same moment in time for the same person. Critical mobilities studies *both* focus attention on connections between mobility/fixity and structural inequalities *and* provide a more nuanced account of individual subjecthood that militates against caricatures and stereotypes that can themselves contribute to experiences of inequality and oppression. This challenges the dominant binary 'us' and 'them' framing of the immigration debate and especially the idea of a 'left-behind' group of non-migrants, racialised as white. In so doing it invites a listening approach that is attentive to experiences that transcend divides among working-class and other non-elite people. One key location of such experiences is at work, and the next chapter draws extensively on workers' recollections of employment in Peterborough's food factories and warehouses in the 2000s and 2010s. In it I will argue that the relatively large numbers of international migrant workers, many of them from the EU, who made up the majority of the workforce during this period were racialised *as migrants*. At the end of the chapter I will also draw on instances where the very adversity of intensive workplace regimes was a source of friendship and humour among workers across difference, showing how racial capitalism can ironically be the cause of conviviality, non-elite cosmopolitanism and even working-class unity.

Notes

1 Julie Cameron, 'Postwar European integration: how did a brick shortage change Peterborough?' (MA thesis, Birkbeck College, University of London, 2012).
2 See Chapter 1 for a critique of Goodhart's position.
3 The rest of the chapter is a revised version of Ben Rogaly, 'Disrupting migration stories: reading life histories through the lens of mobility and fixity', *Environment and planning D: Society and space*, 33:3 (2015).
4 Bridget Anderson, *Us and Them? The Dangerous Politics of Immigration Control* (Oxford: Oxford University Press, 2013), pp. 1–2.
5 Doreen Massey, 'A global sense of place', *Marxism Today*, June 1991, 28–29.
6 Doreen Massey, *Landscape/Space/Politics: An Essay* (2011), available online at: http://thefutureoflandscape.wordpress.com/landscapespace-politics-an-essay/ (accessed January 2019). Massey used the historical example of the enclosure of the English countryside to demonstrate the dialectical relation between mobility and fixity.
7 Kevin Hannam, Mimi Sheller and John Urry, 'Editorial: mobilities, immobilities and moorings', *Mobilities*, 1:1 (2006), 2.
8 Peter Adey, *Mobility* (London: Routledge, 2010), pp. 40–42.
9 Peter Adey, 'If mobility is everything then it is nothing: towards a relational politics of (im)mobilities', *Mobilities*, 1:1 (2006), 75–94.
10 Adey, *Mobility*, p. 35.
11 Chris McMorran, 'Mobilities amid the production of fixities: labor in a Japanese inn', *Mobilities*, 10:1 (2015), 83–99.
12 e.g. Thomas Faist, 'The mobility turn: a new paradigm for the social sciences?', *Ethnic and racial studies*, 36:11 (2013), 1637–1646.
13 Tim Cresswell and Peter Merriman, 'Introduction: geographies of mobilities – practices, spaces, subjects', in Tim Cresswell and Peter Merriman (eds), *Geographies of Mobilities: Practices, Spaces, Subjects* (Aldershot, Hants: Ashgate, 2011), pp. 9–10; see also Ola Söderström *et al.*, 'Of

mobilities and moorings: critical perspectives', in Ola Söderström, *et al.* (eds), *Critical Mobilities* (Lausanne: EPFL Press, 2013), pp. v–xxv.

14 Anne-Marie Fortier, 'Migration studies', in Peter Adey *et al.* (eds), *The Routledge Handbook of Mobilities* (London: Routledge, 2014), pp. 64–73.

15 Johanna Waters, "Mobilities", in Roger Lee *et al.* (eds), *The SAGE Handbook of Human Geography* (London: Sage, 2014), pp. 22–44.

16 Ibid., p. 26 (original emphasis).

17 Fortier, 'Migration studies', p. 66.

18 Massey, 'Power geometry and a progressive sense of place', in Jon Bird *et al.* (eds), *Mapping the Futures: Local Cultures, Global Change* (London: Routledge, 1993), p. 61.

19 Nick Gill, Javier Caletrio and Victoria Mason, 'Introduction: mobilities and forced migration', *Mobilities*, 6:3 (2011), 301–316.

20 Söderström *et al.*, 'Of mobilities and moorings'.

21 Ronald Skeldon, 'Interlinkages between internal and international migration and development in the Asian region', *Population, space and place*, 12:1 (2006), 17.

22 Katherine Brickell and Ayona Datta, 'Introduction: translocal geographies', in Katherine Brickell and Ayona Datta (eds), *Translocal Geographies: Spaces, Places, Connections* (Aldershot, Hants: Ashgate, 2011), pp. 3–22; Clemens Greiner and Patrick Sakdapolrak, 'Translocality: concepts, applications and emerging research perspectives', *Geography compass*, 7:5 (2013), 373–384.

23 Brickell and Datta, 'Introduction: translocal geographies', pp. 10 and 16.

24 Ibid., p. 10.

25 Sara Ahmed *et al.*, 'Introduction: uprootings/regroundings: questions of home and migration', in Sara Ahmed *et al.* (eds), *Uprootings/Regroundings* (Oxford: Berg, 2003), p. 1; Tim Cresswell, 'Towards a politics of mobility', *Environment and planning D: Society and space*, 28:1 (2010), 29.

26 McMorran, 'Mobilities amid the production of fixities'.

27 Ibid., p. 84.

28 Jon Binnie *et al.*, 'Editorial: mundane mobilities, banal travels', *Social and cultural geography*, 8:2 (2007), 166.

29 Francis Collins, 'Transnational mobilities and urban spatialities: notes from the Asia-Pacific', *Progress in human geography*, 36:3 (2012), 316–335.

30 Although some more celebratory mobilities writers have assumed spatial mobility to be inherently correlated with upward movement in social class position (Adey, *Mobility*, pp. 37–38).

31 See Fiona Devine *et al.* (eds), *Rethinking Class: Culture, Identities and Lifestyle* (Basingstoke: Palgrave Macmillan, 2005); Debbie Humphry,

'Moving on? Experiences of social mobility in a mixed-class north London neighbourhood' (PhD thesis, University of Sussex, 2014).

32 Philip Kelly, 'Migration, transnationalism and the spaces of class identity', *Philippine studies: historical and ethnographic viewpoints*, 60:2 (2012), 153–185.

33 e.g. Ben Rogaly and Daniel Coppard, '"They used to go to eat, now they go to earn": the changing meanings of seasonal migration from Puruliya District in West Bengal, India', *Journal of agrarian change*, 3:3 (2003), 395–433.

34 Floya Anthias, 'Social stratification and social inequality: models of intersectionality and identity', in Fiona Devine *et al.* (eds), *Rethinking Class: Culture, Identities and Lifestyle* (Basingstoke: Palgrave Macmillan, 2005), pp. 24–45; Linda McDowell, 'Thinking through work: complex inequalities, constructions of difference and trans-national migrants', *Progress in human geography*, 32:4 (2008), 491–507.

35 Cresswell, 'Towards the politics of mobility', p. 29.

36 See for example Victoria Lawson, 'Arguments with the geography of movement: the theoretical potential of migrants' stories', *Progress in human geography*, 24:2 (2000), 173–189; Kathy Burrell and Panikos Panayi (eds), *Histories and Memories: Migrants and their History in Britain* (London: Tauris, 2006); Alison Blunt, 'Cultural geographies of migration: mobility, transnationality and diaspora', *Progress in human geography*, 31:5 (2007), 684–694; Joanna Herbert, *Negotiating Boundaries in the City: Migration, Ethnicity, and Gender in Britain* (Aldershot, Hants: Ashgate, 2008); Becky Taylor and Martyna Sliwa, 'Polish migration: moving beyond the iron curtain', *History workshop journal*, 71:1 (2011), 128–146.

37 Alistair Thomson, 'Moving stories: oral history and migration studies', *Oral history*, 27:1 (1999), 24.

38 Herbert, *Negotiating Boundaries in the City*, pp. 7–8.

39 Joanna Herbert and Richard Rodger, 'Frameworks: testimony, representation and interpretation', in Richard Rodger and Joanna Herbert (eds), *Testimonies of the City: Identity, Community and Change in a Contemporary Urban World* (Aldershot, Hants: Ashgate, 2007), p. 7.

40 Thomson, 'Moving stories', pp. 25 and 28.

41 Cresswell, 'Towards the politics of mobility', p. 19.

42 Adey, *Mobility*, p. 38.

43 See Hannah Jones *et al.*, *Go Home? The Politics of Immigration Controversies* (Manchester: Manchester University Press, 2017).

44 David Brandon and John Knight, *Peterborough Past: The City and the Soke* (Chichester: Phillimore, 2001), p. 122.

45 Thomson, 'Moving stories', p. 35; Ben Rogaly and Becky Taylor, *Moving Histories of Class and Community: Identity, Place and Belonging in Contemporary England* (Basingstoke: Palgrave Macmillan, 2009).

46 Ben Rogaly and Susan Thieme, 'Experiencing space-time: the stretched lifeworlds of migrant workers in India', *Environment and planning A*, 44:9 (2012), 2089.

47 In addition to the short section on my background in the previous chapter, I have written briefly elsewhere on the classed and gendered reproduction of my academic position, and my immersion in British Punjabi culture through my long-term partner, children and extended family (Rogaly and Taylor, *Moving Histories of Class and Community*, pp. 24–26).

48 See Virinder Kalra, *From Textile Mills to Taxi Ranks: Experiences of Migration, Labour and Social Change* (Aldershot, Hants: Ashgate, 2000); Katy Gardner, *Age, Narrative and Migration: The Life Course and Life Histories of Bengali Elders in London* (Oxford: Berg, 2002); Ali Ahmad, 'Gender and generation in Pakistani migration: a critical study of masculinity', in Louise Ryan and Wendy Webster (eds), *Gendering Migration: Masculinity, Femininity and Ethnicity in Post-war Britain* (Aldershot, Hants: Ashgate, 2008), pp. 155–169; Kaveri Qureshi, 'Pakistani labour migration and masculinity: industrial working life, the body and transnationalism', *Global networks*, 12:4 (2012), 485–504.

49 Barnor Hesse and Salman Sayyid, 'Narrating the postcolonial political and the immigrant imaginary', in Nasreen Ali, Virinder S. Kalra and Salman Sayyid (eds), *A Postcolonial People: South Asians in Britain* (London: Hurst, 2006), pp. 13–31.

50 Avtar Brah, *Cartographies of Diaspora: Contesting Identities* (London: Routledge, 1996), p. 13.

51 Ibid., p. 26.

52 See Robert Miles, *Racism and Migrant Labour: A Critical Text* (London: Routledge, 1982).

53 John Rex, *Race, Colonialism and the City* (Oxford: Oxford University Press, 1973).

54 Annie Phizacklea and Robert Miles, *Labour and Racism* (London: Routledge, 1980); Stephen Castles and Godula Kosack, *Immigrant Workers and Class Structure in Western Europe* (Oxford: Oxford University Press, 1985).

55 Ceri Peach, 'Demographics of BrAsian settlement, 1951–2001', in Nasreen Ali, Virinder S. Kalra and Salman Sayyid (eds), *A Postcolonial People: South Asians in Britain* (London: Hurst, 2006), pp. 168–169.

56 Gurminder Bhambra, 'Viewpoint: Brexit, class and British "national" identity', *Discover Society*, 5 July 2016, available online at: https://discoversociety.org/2016/07/05/viewpoint-brexit-class-and-british-national-identity/ (accessed February 2019).

57 Sundari Anitha and Ruth Pearson, *Striking Women: Struggles and Strategies of South Asian Women Workers from Grunwick to Gate Gourmet* (London: Lawrence & Wishart, 2018).

58 Brah, *Cartographies of Diaspora*, pp. 2 and 35; Kalra, *From Textile Mills to Taxi Ranks*, p. 2.

59 Ali Ahmad, 'Gender and generation in Pakistani migration: a critical study of masculinity', in Louise Ryan and Wendy Webster (eds), *Gendering Migration: Masculinity, Femininity and Ethnicity in Post-war Britain* (Aldershot, Hants: Ashgate, 2008), pp. 156–157. However, as Jazeel emphasises in his study of upper-middle class Sri Lankans in Britain, some immigrants from South Asia maintained high socio-economic status. See Tariq Jazeel, 'Postcolonial geographies of privilege: diaspora space, the politics of personhood and the Sri Lankan Women's Association', *Transactions of the Institute of British Geographers*, new series, 31:1 (2006), 19–33.

60 See Cedric J. Robinson, *Black Marxism: The Making of the Black Radical Tradition* (London: Zed, 1983); and Gargi Bhattacharyya, *Rethinking Racial Capitalism: Questions of Reproduction and Survival* (London: Rowman & Littlefield International, 2018).

61 See e.g. Brah, *Cartographies of Diaspora*; Claire Alexander and Helen Kim, 'South Asian youth cultures', in Joya Chatterji and David Washbrook (eds), *Routledge Handbook of the South Asian Diaspora* (London: Routledge, 2013), pp. 350–362.

62 There was a shift from assimilation in the late 1950s and early 1960s to the 'race' relations paradigm of the late 1960s and 1970s, embodied in four Race Relations Acts and aimed at protecting existing residents from racial discrimination. At the same time immigration became increasingly racialised and restrictive through the Commonwealth Immigration Acts of 1962 and 1968 (Alice Bloch, Sarah Neal and John Solomos, *Race, Multiculture and Social Policy*, Basingstoke: Palgrave Macmillan, 2013, pp. 24–25 and 55–57).

63 See also Paul Thompson, 'Family myth, models, and denials in the shaping of individual life paths', in Daniel Bertaux and Paul Thompson (eds), *Between Generations: Family Models, Myths and Memories. International Yearbook of Oral History and Life Stories II* (Oxford: Oxford University Press, 1993), pp. 13–38.

64 Gardner, *Age, Narrative and Migration*.

65 See also Anthias, 'Social stratification and social inequality'.

66 Ahmad, 'Gender and generation in Pakistani migration', pp. 155–156.

67 Mam's primary school was in West Town, which was close to the Gladstone area, separated from it only by the tracks of the London–Edinburgh main line.

68 Tony Kushner and Katherine Knox, *Refugees in an Age of Genocide* (London: Routledge, 2001), pp. 270 and 273.

69 The concept of racial capitalism is explored further in Chapter 3.

70 Stuart Hall *et al.*, *Policing the Crisis: Mugging, the State and Law and Order* (1978; second edition, Basingstoke: Palgrave Macmillan, 2013); Castles and Kosack, *Immigrant Workers and Class Structure*, pp. 86–87; Ahmad, 'Gender and generation in Pakistani migration', pp. 156–157.

71 These processes, and the racial capitalism of which they are part, are explored further in Chapter 3, which draws on the biographical oral histories of workers in Peterborough's twenty-first-century food factories and warehouses.

72 Racialisation of children of colour was very common at the time. See Ian Grosvenor, 'A different reality: education and the racialization of the black child', *History of education*, 16:4 (1987), 299–308.

73 Castles and Kosack, *Immigrant Workers and Class Structure*, p. 49.

74 Brah, *Cartographies of Diaspora*, p. 34.

75 Binnie *et al.*, 'Editorial', p. 171.

76 Anderson, *Us and Them.*

77 Keith Halfacree and Paul Boyle, 'The challenge facing migration research: the case for a biographical approach', *Progress in human geography*, 17:3 (1993), 333–358.

78 Ibid., p. 342.

79 Rogaly and Taylor, *Moving Histories of Class and Community.*

80 See e.g. Kelly, 'Migration, transnationalism and the spaces of class identity'.

81 See e.g. McDowell, 'Thinking through work'.

82 Thomson, 'Moving stories'.

3

'If not you, they can get ten different workers in your place': racial capitalism and workplace resistance

Laura

> Actually, when I started to work among them, I found out that they are very frustrated, very angry, disappointed because just the amount of hard work that … So, basically people who joined Amazon many, many years ago, many years, I mean Amazon exist here in this city for like six, seven years perhaps. But who joined Amazon, let's say like four, five years ago, in their contract they had you have to kind of do best as you can, while now they have actually targets in the contract. So, whenever somebody didn't reach the target got a [warning], every week you would get a different [warning], so if you didn't meet target you could get every week one [warning] and after I think six [warnings], they just tell you, 'Sorry, you are not good enough, you have to go. There is not place for you.'

By the time I asked Laura Chłopeka, a former warehouse supervisor and agency manager, to reflect on her return to work at Amazon as a packer we had known each other for five years. She had first contacted me in 2012, having read on another Polish Peterborough resident's Facebook page about the biographical oral history work I was doing in the city. It was now July 2017, one year on from the EU referendum, and I was conducting a series of audio interviews as part of the research for a film, *Workers*, that I was co-producing about warehouse and food factory work.[1] Laura had been involved in discussions about the film project from its conception in 2014 and had attended a meeting in London the following year with the larger team that was putting together a funding application.

I knew from the first interviews with Laura that she had extensive and varied experience of agency work in Peterborough's food factories and warehouses. In 2005, aged nineteen and one year into a degree course in Poland, she had left to join her sister in Peterborough and, after a sleepless international coach journey, had been thrilled to find work within days:

> And then we called my parents because it was of course huge happiness that I got a job in a foreign country so quickly. You hear sometimes stories or at least we had so many stories that you could read on the internet and in newspapers that people are looking for weeks or months or they work in a field and they are really kind of exhausted because of work conditions and this looked quite good and I just got this work so quickly and we hoped that everything would be OK.

On her first morning, Laura turned up at the time and place appointed for her to be collected and driven to work. A car arrived exactly at the agreed time, and the man inside responded positively when she asked if he was from the agency. However, it turned out to be a kidnapping, and when Laura discovered that the driver was not taking her to the factory she dived out of the moving vehicle. When we spoke about this in 2012 she had still not told her parents. We recorded that interview sitting at a table in the apartment she was renting at the time with the South American man she had met in Peterborough and subsequently married. After the attempted kidnapping, and feeling badly shaken, Laura had returned to the agency with a friend of her sister's. She had been allocated a job packing cereals in a distribution centre. She laughed as she remembered what seemed to her an absurd and unjust division of labour.

> And this was quite funny because the first time in my life I saw that there is [laughs] something strange, like for example in factories, they don't look if you are a female or a male, if you are weak or if you are big and strong and they give you any job, even if it isn't suitable for you. So I went with four guys by car, by taxi, I was the only girl and what they got, they got little packs, a lot of packs of cereals on the side, they got little boxes of cereals, you know sometimes there are eight joined boxes, so they had to pick up like three or something and they were putting on machines. What I was doing I had different kinds of cereals it was like [pause] porridge and there were like 160 packs with porridge in one box and this was really heavy and it was on the floor and I had to take those packs and go somewhere with them. And after two hours I had really a backache for the first time ever I think [laughs ironically]. I just thought how unfair it is: four guys putting these little light things and I am with a box here and again I didn't speak English enough, I thought maybe I shouldn't say because I might lose my job.

Language ability has long been a key concern for Laura. She laughed again later in the same interview, recalling another occasion when she had been seeking work in Peterborough:

> and I didn't speak English much yet because in the factories also you have a lot of foreign people who make mistakes as well so you don't learn it properly but you learn more or less just to speak or you learn, 'You take, bring here', and you don't really say full sentences. So I remember there was a security guy, a black guy and I wanted to ask him (I was of course learning this by heart before I told him) and the sentence was, 'Hi, I'm looking for a job, can you help me?' And then I said, 'Hi, I'm looking for a job, can I help you?' And then he looked at me, he started to laugh and he said, 'Yes, first thing is go back home and learn English and then one day you can come back and you can get a job, we could give you an application.'

After the interview in 2012, Laura and I stayed in touch, and in 2017 I asked if I could interview her about warehouse and food factory work again as part of my research for the film. This time we sat in the kitchen in the house she and her husband had bought in the New Town area where Ron Singh, whom we met in Chapter 2, had gone to secondary school in the 1970s. The couple now had a three-year-old child. Laura had completed a BA and a BSc and was juggling her job as a senior National Health Service (NHS) administrator with home life. She spoke not only as a former line worker, supervisor and manager but also as a first-hand observer of what the intensifying workplace regimes in Peterborough's warehouses were doing to others.

> I don't know, it's not human really to treat people like that. They are not robots and they work, they try their best, they've got families, they want to have normal life. They work fast but they don't work fast enough, sometimes you might have stomach ache or worst day and because of this one day you have to work quicker, faster the next day because, for example on Thursday you do 80 per cent, then next day you have to make sure you do 120, so for the whole week you got 100 per cent. And people just said, 'OK, so I got [a warning]; I have to go upstairs and again they will be talking the same things and again I'm going to be talking and explaining myself that it's impossible, that I tried my best, that this and that', and they were coming back and discussing a lot about this actually.

Her mention of the discussions workers had about their treatment is notable because it suggests that in spite of the ever-faster pace and intensity of work that was being demanded of people, there remained spaces and opportunities to confer with others. Although she had worked in multiple companies in Peterborough, her first experience at Amazon was as a manager, sent to the warehouse by a temporary employment agency to supervise the staff it had deployed there. She enjoyed the international mix of people and listening to colleagues' stories and plans:

> Most of the people were around my age or younger. There were a lot of foreign people, a lot of Polish, Lithuanians and some Romanians, some Italian and you met a lot of different nationalities

> basically and, to tell the truth, I really liked the environment and maybe because of the age of these people or I don't know why but I actually met a lot of people who are ambitious there, who are doing some degrees or working just for a few months or had some plans, and I met so many lovely people there and sometimes some older people who would tell me their stories, like a Polish guy who said that he came here for a few years then his friend told him – after seven years – that there is a job he can get in Poland, really good job, he didn't know if he should go back. He went back, it didn't work, he's back here now trying to build everything from the beginning ... Basically, so many different stories, so many interesting stories.

The remainder of this chapter draws on multiple stories of people's experiences of temporary employment agencies in and around Peterborough, of working conditions in food factories and warehouses and their multi-ethnic and multi-national workforces, as well as of the spaces workers were able to carve out for themselves in spite of harsh supervision regimes. In the second section of the chapter I sketch out two concepts which I use to frame the ensuing discussion. The first, racial capitalism – capitalist employers putting racialised differences to use in the pursuit of profits – is key for understanding why businesses in the industrialised food supply chain and the broader warehouse distribution sector have, in historically and geographically specific ways, often sought out racialised minorities and/or migrants as workers. The second concept, workplace, involves returning to Doreen Massey's theory of place to develop a dynamic, historicised understanding of *work*places that also takes account of the relationship between the labour process at a particular site (e.g. field, food factory, warehouse) and the broader social, political and economic context. Along the way I also draw on authors who have extended the concept of the workplace spatially, going beyond the site of work to include spaces of recruitment, the cars, vans and buses used for journeys to work and workers' temporary accommodation.

The third section of the chapter uses workers' experiences in Peterborough as a lens to draw out wider insights regarding capitalist work in the twenty-first century. Extracts from oral history interviews reveal continuities over time in companies' approaches to recruitment, supervision and monitoring. An important strand of continuity is the use of employment agencies to source as well as manage labour, a practice that has roots in the region's history of recruiting seasonal agricultural labour through gangmasters. A second strand is the racialisation of people as 'migrants' by association with certain job roles. The most dramatic changes identified are the ways in which performance targets were introduced and then ratcheted up (confirming Laura's description above), and how these in turn were at times sources of division among workers. Such changes need to be understood in the context of wider national developments, including the deregulation of labour markets, the decimation of trade union power from the 1980s, the availability of workers from newly acceded members of the EU from 2004 onwards and the austerity that followed the 2008 bailout of the banks.

If the chapter as a whole draws attention to the grossly skewed distribution of power between logistics corporations and industrialised food sector businesses on the one hand and the people employed to work in low-paid, low-status roles in them on the other, the fourth section of the chapter explores how this also shapes possibilities for (and constraints on) non-elite cosmopolitan practices in the workplace, such as those hinted at above by Laura. In this section I will return to the oral history interviews, listening out for moments of conviviality emerging in spite, or perhaps because of, oppressive techniques of labour control in the increasingly harsh warehouse and industrialised food supply sector labour regimes.[2] The fifth and final section concludes the chapter.

Racial capitalism and the workplace

Just as the lives of three of the narrators in Chapter 2 – Sotindra, Pakzaad and Mam – were shaped in part by the structural racisms they came up against in British society, including racism at their places of work, so it has been shown more generally that 'techniques of racialised exclusion, division and differentiation have played – and continue to play – a central role in the practices of capitalist exploitation'.[3] The association of groups of workers racialised as inferior with certain work tasks can be seen as part of what Cedric Robinson and others have termed 'racial capitalism'.[4]

Moreover, the segregation of workforces 'along racial lines'[5] can serve individual businesses for which, as Elizabeth Esch and David Roediger have highlighted, 'in some jobs the daily grinding out of productivity is ... dependent on playing races against each other'. In such cases 'race management' is used as a tool in 'short-term efforts to quicken the pace of work'.[6] At the same time, it is important to avoid determinism: capitalism, as Gargi Bhattacharyya points out, is not 'inevitably racialised'.[7] Nevertheless, while difference is mobilised along a number of axes,

> [t]here remains something in the invocation of the 'racial' that lets us understand the arbitrary attribution of statuses that then become apparently unchanging and inescapable. The combination of rigid hierarchisation and boundaries between groups of people with a hailing of what is natural or given seems to go to the heart of what has been named 'raciality', however elastic and variable we admit that process to be. So, racial capitalism it remains.[8]

Indeed, businesses' role in the construction and use of human difference for the purpose of capital accumulation goes further than ideas about 'race'. As Lisa Lowe explains,

> [t]he term *racial capitalism* captures the sense that actually existing capitalism exploits through culturally and socially constructed differences such as race, gender, region, and nationality, and is lived through those.[9]

Importantly in the British context, as we saw in the previous chapter, inequalities rooted in colonialism continued to reverberate in the division of labour across several sectors after the formal ending of empire. According to Stuart Hall and his colleagues,

> [t]he differentiated structure of class interests between the British and the colonial working classes was then, in a complex

> manner, reproduced within the domestic economy by the use of imported immigrant labour, under conditions of full employment, often to fill jobs which the indigenous work force would no longer do.[10]

While the imported Caribbean labour that Hall and his colleagues refer to here was racialised as black, this is not of course the case for all those who cross international borders for work – even if in some contexts it may take light-skinned people generations to 'become white' as was the case for southern European immigrants to the USA in the first half of the twentieth century.[11] Indeed, in Berger and Mohr's account of southern European men migrating temporarily for industrial work in northern Europe in the early 1970s, the men involved were racialised as *migrants* once they had crossed the border en route to the place of employment. Through photography and text Berger and Mohr show how, '[o]n the far side of the frontier, when [a man] has crossed it, he becomes a migrant'.[12] These authors thus refer to 'migration' in a narrower sense than the one I am using in this book. By migration, they mean entering a national territory other than one's own to carry out a particular job and then returning. The association of the job with the status of being a 'migrant' is a form of racialisation that Berger and Mohr view as having historical provenance: 'the capitalist system claims that it has evolved and that the inhumanities of the past can never be repeated ... In the metropolitan centres the claim is generally believed. The most naked forms of exploitation are invisible ...'[13]

Work by these and other writers is therefore important in demonstrating the historical entanglement of unfree employment relations, including traces of colonialism and slavery, in capitalist work. Such entanglements have a long and sustained history in agriculture and associated sectors in multiple national contexts. The geographer Ruth Wilson Gilmore writes of racial capitalism that it is

> a mode of production developed in agriculture, improved by enclosure in the Old World, and captive land and labor in the Americas, perfected in slavery's time motion field-factory choreography ...[14]

The anthropologist Seth Holmes adds the category of citizenship, writing of an 'ethnicity-citizenship labour hierarchy' in the organisation of US agricultural labour and referring to his own ethnographic work in Californian berry farming and other studies carried out in the 1980s and 1990s.[15] As we shall see, racialised hierarchies and racialisation – including the racialisation of certain workers as 'migrants' – feature prominently in stories of employment in food supply chain businesses in England, for which Peterborough is an important hub.[16] Moreover, as this supply chain was industrialised and commercialised further from the 1990s onwards, its techniques of labour control were adopted and further transformed both by the retail distribution sector and by warehouse and logistics companies more generally.

The targets and punitive sanctions Laura Chłopeka described at the start of this chapter as being imposed on pickers and packers in Brexit-era Peterborough's giant warehouses resonate with accounts of similar workplaces elsewhere.[17] In the UK, where average real wages declined year on year in the decade following the bank bailout of 2008, workers in this and other sectors came under tighter, often digital, surveillance,[18] and at the same time experienced greater insecurity of employment and/or a diminution of workplace rights through quasi self-employment.[19]

However, the decline in the power of waged labour relative to capital in Britain and elsewhere in the Global North began much earlier, at the end of the 1970s. In his seminal book *Work-Place* published in the mid-1990s, Jamie Peck pulled no punches in attacking the effects of the deregulation occurring in the UK, the USA and elsewhere from the start of the neoliberal era. He observed that:

> Neoliberal attempts at deregulating the labor market have been associated with an unprecedented attack on the social and working conditions of labor ... Contrary to the nostrums of neoliberal ideology ... the imposition of market forces is associated with the degradation of labor.[20]

Yet while it expounded his critique of these broader trends, a key contribution of Peck's book was to draw attention to the differences in their effects across localities, highlighting in particular the uniqueness of 'local labor markets … each represent[ing] a *geographically specific institutionalization of labor market structures, conventions, and practices*'.[21] Peck's illustration of this demonstrates the importance of analysis that is attentive to historical and geographical contingency:

> While black workers may find themselves in the lower echelons of the labor market in both Birmingham, England, and Birmingham, Alabama, the nature and consequences of their marginalization in the labor market are quite different in each case. Why the 'same' general process has different effects in different places might lie in the distinctive ways the general process of ethnic segregation interacts with local industrial cultures and structures, localized patterns of immigration, and local forms of racism and racial exclusion.[22]

By the time Peck wrote these lines, the idea of studying the workings of capitalism in particular localities had already kicked up a storm of academic indignation.[23] However, Peck's argument that it is important to understand the ways in which 'distinct places are associated with sectoral and functional divisions of labour' is compelling.[24] Doreen Massey's 1984 book *Spatial Divisions of Labour* – a classic comparative study of localities – had been a key inspiration for Peck.[25] Massey's attention to localities signalled her subsequent development of the concept of place. Central to *Stories from a migrant city*, this way of thinking about place emphasises the different and unequal effects places have on one another at particular points in time. Both Massey and Peck also insisted on the importance of history. Massey's attempt to understand the *changes* in spatial divisions of labour demands a geographical approach to history that conceives of layers of 'social relations, networks of interconnections across space', each associated with a particular time period, earlier layers influencing later ones.[26]

Rather than viewing localities as fixed, therefore, Massey argued that their multiple and uneven connections with other places, together with the accompanying histories, gave them their particular character.

As Massey put it in advocating a non-parochial approach to 'locality studies',

> [t]his is the view of locality which stresses its linkages with the wider world. These links exist in many ways and at many levels and they are not just products of the modern era ... [tying] one locality to many others in a myriad different ways ... they are more than 'links', they are part of the constitution of the place, part of what gives it its own particular character.[27]

This relational way of thinking about place is also helpful for understanding *work*places. The institutions, practices and social relations that have built up over time in a specific locality, together with the multiple places elsewhere to which that locality is connected, shape the labour process at workplaces within it, and vice versa.[28] In their study of Glasgow call centres Thomas Hastings and Danny MacKinnon make this point skilfully through an analysis of the relations between the city of Glasgow as locality and the labour process in the call centres themselves.[29] They point out that the presence of a relatively large number of call centres in Glasgow in the early twenty-first century had been enabled by 'financial incentives' as well as 'the availability of low-cost accommodation'. The call centres are seen by the state as 'a means of absorbing segments of the local workless population'. While young men may have continued to aspire to 'blue collar' manual work, job-centre staff have actively 'sought to promote call centre work to job-seekers'.[30]

Classic studies of the labour process focus on workplaces as specific sites of paid labour, such as factories, and on the interplay in them between employers' attempts at labour control and domination on the one hand and workers' resistance on the other.[31] However, in *A Seventh Man* Berger and Mohr provide a visual as well as textual extension of what counts as the workplace, including, in addition to sites of paid work, workers' living spaces; dwellings in the places they moved from; and spaces of journeying and work-seeking.

Berger and Mohr differentiated the *back-and-forth* of migration from southern to northern Europe from the migration for settlement in Britain in the 1950s and 1960s by people arriving from its former colonies, who at that time, as we saw in Chapter 2, were legally categorised as citizens rather than migrants.[32] In their exploration of the racialised segmentation of Caribbean migrant workers in Britain in *Policing the Crisis*,[33] Stuart Hall and his colleagues too take a broader approach to understanding the workplace, for example through analysis of workers' housing:

> The residential concentration of the black immigrant population is one of the most significant features of their structural position ... [It was in the] inner-city areas where, alone, relatively cheap housing, tenable in a multi-occupancy fashion, was available in the early days as rented accommodation ... The decline and neglect of property by absentee owners, making a short, speculative profit on a deteriorated housing stock, and the strong-arm tactics of extortionate landlords – sometimes, themselves, immigrants, and, whether black or white, exploiting the vulnerable position of the black family – have been constant features of the housing condition of the majority black population.[34]

Inspired by Berger and Mohr and by Hall *et al.*, I conceive of workplaces in an expanded way. The concept of a workplace used in this sense avoids a false separation between life and labour.[35] I turn now to the agricultural antecedents of Peterborough's warehouse and food factory workplaces; to the temporary employment agencies that have at certain times and places integrated accommodation and transport provision into their businesses;[36] and to continuity and change in the local labour regime.

A local labour regime in Peterborough

From gang labour to temporary employment agencies

Gangs of temporary agricultural workers were vitally important in nineteenth-century England when cereal and root crops were hand-harvested. For example, a study of the period by historian Nicola Verdon found gangs to be involved in 'the cleaning of land by weeding and stonepicking, the planting and then the harvesting of root crops such as turnips, potatoes and mangolds'.[37] Gang labour was seen as advantageous to the employer, being hired when needed and 'easily dispensed with at the end of a task'.[38] The capitalist agriculture of the time exploited gendered and generational as well as racialised difference for profit. Tasks paid at a piece rate to men were, for gangs of women and children, instead remunerated at *daily* rates, creating more profits for the farmer, and removing any opportunities for workers to earn a bonus. 'The gangmaster profited from the system by being elevated to the position of overseer and received remuneration relative to this role.'[39]

The English system of gang labour first emerged in East Anglia, a region which includes Peterborough at its far west. Even in the early nineteenth century the system involved recruitment of foreign workers, in particular Irish people, who were racialised as inferior to the English. Indeed, Carl Griffin's book *The Rural War: Captain Swing and the Politics of Protest* describes racialised Irish migrant workers in England being attacked by ethnic-majority English workers in the hard times leading up to the Swing Riots of the early 1830s.[40] Beyond Irish workers, it was in the Fens – adjacent to Peterborough and straddling parts of the East Anglian and East Midlands regions – where, according to the agricultural historian E. J. T. Collins, 'the diversity was most apparent' and 'the tongues were once described as being as many as the "builders of Babel"'.[41]

Peterborough's long history as a destination for newcomers from other parts of the UK as well as from other countries is thus crucially important for an understanding of the dynamic connections of *both* the city as a whole *and* workplaces within it (and in its rural hinterland) to places elsewhere. These connections were intensely evident in the diversity of workers' origins and of their experiences of work and life in other places. Other kinds of connections were important too, including those associated with changes in the food supply chain. The packing and processing of imported fresh produce increased from the late twentieth century as supermarket retailers sought to make higher profits through a process known as valorisation.[42] Businesses supplying supermarkets relied for this on connections with places beyond the UK from which they could ensure their own supply of raw materials. Retailers' marketing strategies, and the shifting consumer expectations they helped to bring about, had created demand for the year-round availability of salads and fruit, for example, and an associated need for workers to prepare and pack them.[43] The Peterborough area became a global enclave for the production, packing and transformation of food.[44]

This was the context in which the long tradition of gang labour thus spawned larger and more commercial agencies that could match work-seekers with the changing array of temporary jobs.[45] These agencies were effectively the successors to agricultural gangs. Meanwhile, in agriculture itself, the ratio of agency-supplied workers to retained farmworkers continued to increase.[46]

The move to a greater reliance on temporary agency workers was not just a matter of the organisation of production that agricultural businesses – particularly horticultural units – sought, but was also to do with what a recent official report referred to as the 'international issue' of a 'lack of resident labour willing to engage in agricultural work, particularly seasonal work'.[47] Agencies that can arrange or provide transport are able to respond to businesses' short-term workforce shortages by delivering people – including international migrants – to work sites far from where they live. It is notable that in a landmark immigration policy White Paper in December 2018, the UK government highlighted agriculture as the one sector for which a quota of low-paid, so-called 'unskilled' international migrants would be permitted after the exit of the UK from the EU.[48]

Yet the idea that long-term residents were unwilling to do labour-intensive agricultural work was contested by Tom Smith, a white British Peterborough resident born in the Fens to agricultural labourers. Ironically, Tom also remembered desperately wanting to get out of having to work in an agricultural gang, even as he shared his memory of working with one in the potato harvest as a child in the 1960s. Tom spoke with me as we sat together at a quiet table in Peterborough's Bull Hotel one afternoon in May 2011.

Tom: I started doing that when I was ten in the holidays and that, and then at thirteen I was doing half a retch of potato picking and stuff in the summer,[49] fifteen I was doing a retch and doing ... well, fifteen, yes, I'd be doing a retch and I'd be doing really a man's job and stuff like that. Obviously the only way out was to try and get some sort of education, so I went to the Horticultural Institute, the only thing I could get a grant for.

Ben: But do you remember, were you in a gang then when you went out, or was it just like you were employed as an individual?

Tom: No, agricultural gang ... The van comes along, they collect you and you'd go to work, that's it ... They know where they're taking you, you really don't give a damn, you're just going there to work; you finish and you come home. Then my first job when I was sixteen, starting at quarter to seven in the morning, finishing in the summer at half ten at night and going from there.

Keely Mills, Peterborough's former poet laureate, remembered accompanying gangs of locally resident women employed by her father, a gangmaster, on long days of agricultural work when she was still a child in the 1980s. In contrast to Tom Smith, she expressed nostalgia for the gangs as we sat recording her oral history interview in the sunshine in the garden of her terraced home in the centre of Peterborough in 2011. She later channelled the emotion of her recollections into a new poem on the subject.[50] When larger, more commercial temporary work agencies specialising in international migrant workers became predominant from the 1990s, Keely had seen her family move out of the labour-supplying business because, she believed, it became impossible to both compete and be humane:

> And they were quite ... the gangmasters used to really drive a hard bargain with the bigger corporations or big farmers to get the best money they could for their workers, and for themselves, don't get me wrong; they're out for themselves. And I don't think that exists any more; I think it's just the hard bargain for themselves, I don't think it's for the worker.
>
> And pretty much within ten years, gangmastering as I know it just died, it died really. I know it sounds really awful, but with the onslaught of more [migrant] workers and with the big recruitment

> agencies they just couldn't compete, and also be humane, that's the best way I could put it, to the workers that are living here, for my uncle, he was just like, 'I can't do this any more.' And then he died in 2006, so he died the September that I moved back, and then his son took over the business. But now he's just doing big contractual work ... My uncle was saying already to my dad it's going to stop, we're going to have to stop, because he just couldn't compete and also pay the workers adequately.

By the time the gangmasters involved in recruitment of workers for horticulture and food packing and processing had been replaced by larger and more commercial temporary work agencies in the 1990s,[51] agencies' part in the logic of capitalist work in the UK and elsewhere had already extended well beyond the food sector.[52] It is notable that Peterborough became increasingly specialised in 'employment services' over the ten-year period from 2005 to 2014.[53] Arguably, the long history of agricultural gangs and their successor temporary work agencies in Peterborough facilitated the arrival of large retail distribution centres there (owned by supermarkets such as Tesco and Morrison), as well as Amazon, with which this chapter began.

The growth of employment in retail distribution and warehouses

The sociologist Huw Beynon indeed argues – albeit on a wider scale than any particular global enclave – that the labour process in Amazon and other giant logistics and distribution corporations followed on from developments in the industrialised food supply chain.[54] Beynon explains that Amazon's driving of the 'application of lean principles and digitalisation to the (once conventional) mail ordering business' emerged out of the retailing revolution that he refers to as 'Waltonism' whereby 'supermarket shopping is coordinated electronically through the bar code reader ... with a link to the central ordering department through a system known as EPOS (Electronic Point of Sale)'.[55] In her research in Ontario, Canada, the geographer Emily Reid-Musson has made similar connections. Reid-Musson refers to 'intimate and predatory forms of exploitation' that she calls 'management through algorithms', which are having 'profound effects on both consumers and producers

– in logistics and transportation in particular'.[56] Others have argued that 'changes in the modes of production and the development of global supply chains have put [storage and warehousing operations] at the heart of contemporary capitalism'.[57]

There had been fierce debate in Peterborough during the 2000s regarding the merits of allowing the development of large warehouses around the city's edge. According to the town planner Roger Johnson (not his real name) in a pair of interviews with me in 2011, the City Council's planners saw advantages, while the regeneration organisation Opportunity Peterborough expressed disdain. Roger summed this latter perspective up as 'Well, really I don't know why we've got IKEA here, it's just a horrible building.' In terms of the overall direction of the city's economy, he was upbeat:

> One of the interesting things about Peterborough is that although the battleground has tended to be over logistics, it actually has got a very balanced economy. It's got a mixture of agriculture, publishing, manufacturing, logistics and so on. I would certainly hope that that continues, because it gives a resilience as the economy changes.

Logistics and distribution have grown in their significance to the city's economy. A 2018 Cambridge University report on the changing economic structure of Peterborough noted that the city 'has some relative specialization in logistics, which appears to be increasing again after a period of relative decline'.[58] Both the report and Roger Johnson in his interview explained this with reference to the interconnected factors of, first, availability of land for development and, secondly, the economic dynamism evident over the two decades from the late 1960s, during which, as we saw in the last chapter, Peterborough expanded as one of England's New Towns. From 1968, when it was established, the designated New Town authority, the Peterborough Development Corporation, attracted 'manufacturing ... and increasingly distribution businesses' as well as other major new employers and tens of thousands of new residents.[59] It oversaw the construction of serviced sites, housing and other major new developments, including, as Ron Singh described vividly, the demolition of the city centre, the building of the Queensgate shopping centre in its place and the network of new dual carriageways (known locally as 'parkways') both across and around the city.[60]

The effect on Peterborough of being designated as a New Town, and the accompanying investments, should not be underestimated. They too are crucial to a relational understanding of Peterborough as a place: money, capital and people from a range of elsewheres, particularly London, transformed the city.[61] The overall growth in Peterborough's output and employment between 1971 and 2015 was much faster than in the Cambridge University study's other British cities, which 'were experiencing rapid deindustrialisation'.[62] Strikingly, 110,000 more people lived in Peterborough in 2015 than 1971 – representing population growth 25 per cent higher than the British average.[63] Yet the first part of this period contrasted sharply with the second: Peterborough flatlined after the closure of the Peterborough Development Corporation in 1988 according to Roger Johnson. The Cambridge University study confirmed this, showing that growth in output in Peterborough had slowed considerably from the late 1980s onwards and was below the national average from 2008 to 2015.[64]

This recent combination in Peterborough of low growth and productivity with high levels of employment is characteristic of the UK national economy in the Brexit era and consistent with ten years of stagnating real wages from the 2008 bank bailout until 2018. Yet a Latvian former warehouse worker, Armins Morozs, whom I interviewed in an office at the arts organisation Metal Peterborough in 2017, believed the effect of the 2008 crisis in Latvia had led to many job-seekers leaving there and heading for the UK:

> And I came back and I actually we started with the DHL. Most people went [there]. And it was, I think it was 2008 back then. And then I could feel there were more and more Latvians coming in because in 2008 the crisis hit, the recession, worldwide. That's when Latvians started coming in and the DHL warehouse had just opened, yeah, that's where we worked.

For many, including warehouse workers, employment conditions have worsened over time. Echoing the recollections of the former warehouse worker Laura Chłopeka, with which this chapter started,

Beynon observed in 2016 that there was a 'remorselessness' to workers' experiences in warehouses that was reminiscent of 'earlier times in manufacturing'.[65] Whether this was a picker having to walk fifteen miles in a single shift,[66] or what the journalist and author James Bloodworth has referred to as the 'needlessly capricious' ways in which 'the points-based disciplinary system' imposed sanctions on workers for 'days off with illness, not hitting pick rates or being late',[67] conditions were harsh – both physically and emotionally.

Just as the interconnected working conditions in the contemporary industrialised food supply chain and in warehouses can be seen more broadly as key features of capitalism in the Brexit era, there are, in addition to demand for temporary agency workers, other continuities with the past.

'Foreigners' work': the racialisation of migrants

One crucial element of continuity, evident in Peterborough and elsewhere in East Anglia, is the temporary employment of racialised minorities for particular low-paid, low-status roles. For example, some oral history narrators remembered how, in the decades following the Second World War, racialised groups, including temporary international migrants and Gypsies and Travellers, commonly formed part of the seasonal agricultural workforce alongside – at various different points – students, ex-miners and big-city-dwellers. Revealingly a Peterborough resident recalling her brothers' fruit farm in the 1970s told me in 2011 that Gypsies and Travellers were necessary because farmers 'didn't have the eastern European workforce then'.

This implication that there was a need for 'eastern European' workers because there were no longer Gypsies and Travellers available for agricultural work similarly reflects something akin to racial capitalism in the way agriculture has reproduced itself 'through logics and practices that create and marshal difference into its categories of value'.[68] By the Brexit era, working in the fields, packhouses, food-processing factories and warehouses in and around Peterborough had become firmly associated with international migrant workers. The same was true for warehouse work elsewhere in England. As one white British person interviewed in the Staffordshire town of Rugeley by James Bloodworth during his undercover study of low-paid work put it, '"[i]t was the first job I ever turned down ... It's *foreigners' work*, you know?"'[69] Bloodworth explores the extent to which this sentiment related to a sense of exclusion from a workforce made up of a majority of international migrants speaking languages other than English or the harshness of the working conditions. He goes with the latter: 'few English locals I spoke to were willing to put up with the conditions for any significant period of time'.[70] This notion of 'foreigners' work' is reminiscent of Elizabeth Esch and David Roediger's discussion of racialised hierarchies of work in the USA of the 1830s:

> The practice of race management linked race and work early and powerfully ... [T]he kinds of danger, filth, overwork, and subservience that could be particularly demanded of African-American workers, free and slave, had spawned a linguistic Americanism, with 'nigger work' enduringly entering the language. Similarly, to work hard came to be termed 'niggering it' alongside usages like 'slave like a nigger'. Still others derided whites working in cotton and sugar cultivation as those 'who make [N]egroes of themselves'. Specific jobs were connected to the race management practices directed against the vulnerable workers doing them. When poor, often immigrant, whites so needed those jobs that they displaced or joined black workers in doing them, they heard the terms 'white nigger' or increasingly 'Irish nigger'.[71]

Nationals of central and eastern European countries and Portugal made up the majority of the 'foreigners' hired in large numbers for work in Peterborough's food factories and warehouses. The local labour regime for low-paid, low-status roles, whether as warehouse operatives or line workers processing imported fruit, was contingent on national and international contexts. Importantly, unlike most other members of the EU, the UK waived transitional arrangements for nationals of the central and eastern European countries joining the EU in 2004. These people thus had immediate access to the UK labour market.[72] Trade unions had been targeted by the Thatcher regime of the 1980s and subsequent laws that constrained the right to organise workers, collective bargaining, and industrial action. By the 2000s, trade union membership had declined dramatically.[73]

These developments, together with those in digital technology already referred to, created the context for corporations in the industrialised food supply chain and in logistics to seek workers who could be paid little and driven hard. Companies sought certain kinds of workers racialised as migrants, who could be expected to work for a low wage yet whose output under intensive surveillance was higher than that of resident white British workers. Peterborough, with its long history of food-sector work and of inward migration, and its infrastructure of private temporary employment agencies, central location, excellent road and rail links and relatively cheap land available for the development of warehouses, was a key site for such employment.

Viewed from the perspective of Armins, who remembered badly wanting to leave his job in a magazine packing unit in Cambridge at the end of 2007, the number of jobs available in Peterborough had been striking:

> Every time we were browsing jobs or went into job centre, every job, I don't know why, but Peterborough came up. There was loads, abundancy of jobs in Peterborough ... And when we came here I got the job the same day ... I registered with the recruitment agency and I went into work the same evening.

Workplace experiences: the role of performance targets

Experiences of employment in Peterborough's evolving low-paid labour regime in the 2000s and 2010s can best be understood through listening to the stories of current and former workers such as Armins and Laura Chłopeka. They, like the other oral history narrators I interviewed in 2017 as part of my research for the film *Workers*, were unanimous on the main feature of change in the local low-paid labour regime during the first two decades of this century: the introduction of targets and their regular revision upwards, using digital technology to continuously monitor productivity. Yet, though it represented a change, the operation of this intensification of workplace demands relied on continuity with earlier practices of harsh, sometimes demeaning monitoring and enforcement of workers' performance by immediate supervisors and their managers, who were themselves placed under increasing pressure to deliver on targets.

Sabina, a former warehouse supervisor, described how management took advantage of workers who did not know how to play the system:

> And you had to be quite clever to reach the target because cheating and cherry-picking was on a daily basis,[74] and the knowledge of the system as well, how many labels you had to scan against how many units was actually school mathematics … how to work out your targets because some people, bless, were running to do their targets, they still couldn't achieve them. And that was quite brutal because you knew and as later on – I didn't know that from the beginning – but later, management, they knew very well that these people were working very hard and … whatever they have achieved was very low just because they had rubbish stuff. Let's say, six pairs of shoes instead of hundreds of ties, or something like that.

The packing and processing of food has in common with warehouse work the adding of value through either re-forming and re-packaging products or through convenience or speed of distribution. Corporate capitalists' determination to drive ever higher levels of added value from each worker was evident in the contradictory approach that companies took towards compulsory training and the implementation of health and safety regulations.

Agnieszka Kowalczyk-Wojcik, a graduate former teacher and customer relations officer, had been determined to get her husband out of his coal-mining job in Poland, and he eventually moved to the UK to work in a food factory near the Fen town of Spalding in 2014.[75] The following year she joined him, and within a few months Agnieszka had a long-term agency position at a warehouse and the couple felt able to bring over their primary-school aged daughter. But Agnieszka's initial experience at the warehouse was tough. She recalled returning to her role as a picker following a compulsory training session:

> When I go to picking, when I found scanner, log in, I think it passed eleven or twelve minutes. After few minutes came to me agency

> manager and asked me, 'Why you didn't pick twelve minutes?' I almost cried. It was the worst day in my life. I was so nervous that I couldn't breathe. It was the first time in my life when I felt like this. It was awful ... I felt so bad. They invigilate me. They check what I did twelve minutes. Maybe I had to go to toilet.

If Agnieszka felt demeaned by her experience of being rudely admonished for taking twelve minutes to return from compulsory training at her warehouse, Azwer Sabir, a Kurdish man, challenged the management's attitude to targets at another warehouse after they revealed a cavalier approach to his physical health. Azwer had moved to the UK from Iraqi Kurdistan in late 2001 and came to live in Peterborough the following summer after visiting a friend who was working for an agency and quickly finding a nearby job himself. He initially worked for three years preparing imported cut flowers. Although Azwer became a manager at this company he left after being blamed for a mistake over accounting for a delivery of flowers from Kenya, which he claimed was the fault of another employee. Azwer then worked as a forklift driver for a few months – a job he said he enjoyed more than any other in a food factory or warehouse. He got married during this period, and his wife Gilya – who had been based in Iraq – moved to Peterborough.

When Azwer wanted to find a job in a company where Gilya would also be able to find work, and which was nearer to their home, he applied for a position at a recently opened Peterborough warehouse. His confidence in applying directly to the company rather than through an agency is likely to have come from a combination of his fluency in English and his detailed knowledge of the local labour market. He accepted a job in the 'goods in' section of the warehouse, which meant that his key responsibility was to offload a target number of boxes when they were delivered. It was when two boxes fell on his back that he made the case to management that its health and safety policy for correct lifting was incompatible with the need to reach the target for offloading boxes.

> the supervisor[s] always put himself as the innocent ... What happened, once actually the box collapsed on my back. I was offloading and the box collapsed and two boxes hit my back.

> Then a week later the health safety manager, she was from the HR, called me to upstairs and we had a meeting and there were some boxes and trays, she say, 'Show me how to lift?' I say, 'OK', and I showed her how to lift. I say, 'OK, the reason the accident happened is not because I don't know how to lift ... You want me to lift the box in this way, guess how many boxes I can actually offload if I do it this way?' She said, 'not many', I said, 'OK then, the target used to be 250, now 350 for an hour, do you think we can do it?' Then she saying, 'Well, you know ...' I say, 'you have to think about the target.' But they never actually decreased, they always increased the number. I know when you have experience you can do more but still about the health safety people when they ... again, when they put the target like if you reach 150 per cent you will get bonus, people will ignore the health safety rules, another disadvantage ... That's natural, people want to have more money.'

Armins too emphasised his experience of warehouse supervisors' disregard of health and safety:

> they definitely didn't care about [health and safety] because they had orders from somebody above and the supervisors were there just to keep pushing us, like push, push, push. And the guy who was the supervisor, he was a football trainer, so his attitude, like standing in front in the middle of the warehouse and shouting ... It was really annoying and degrading, like talking you down, constantly shouting at you ...

Sabina had been an anti-globalisation activist in Poland. She told me that when she started work at a warehouse she felt as though she had 'sold her soul'. Yet she stayed for eight years.

> I felt like there was just jump, that I actually jumped from this street in Poland, where I was quite active against big corporations' policy and this kind of stuff, and on next day, I actually was working for one of them and I was a part of the big mechanism and that system. So, for actually ... all my years, I felt like I'm

> doing something against myself. Not just myself but generally, that I'm taking part [in a] system that I was fighting against before.

When I asked Sabina what had kept her doing the job for so long, she replied, 'Money. Money, only money.' She had been working in Poland as a teaching assistant and was completing a master's degree but had a number of caring responsibilities, and her prospective financial position after qualification looked as though it would not enable her to live independently. If Azwer had experienced a contradiction between health and safety policies and the companies' targets for his work at 'goods in', Sabina's memory of her induction suggested that this too was disingenuous:

> Oh my God. It was scary thing, you know, because you have to remember that I couldn't speak even a word in English, so the induction, that tests, that was everything quite ... Now I would say from this stance, I would say that was quite a good comedy, Monty Python, you know, because the people couldn't speak. We couldn't literally speak even a word in English and yeah, we had inductions, we had tests, so that says everything about the kind of company, how it works, the process is about just getting people in, cheap, I would say, cheap work resources, I don't know. You know what I mean ... [The tests] were real but as soon as we get into the room people, whoever was the supervisor, was actually leaving us and letting us know to actually ask each other to write down what the answer is. I know that is so different now because that possibly was found out but for a very, very long time it used to be the same.

Reflecting on the labour process more generally, Laura Chłopeka described how management also retained the power to decide when to ignore times when targets were not achieved. Workers would not know when those targets were being used in connection with a strict policy of sanctions that could lead to dismissal and when they were fictional – which was more likely when there was a seasonal shortage of workers. While managers *could* use failure to achieve a target to sanction people, and, as Laura explained from her experience at one warehouse, even to dismiss them if they received six stages or warnings, they did not *necessarily* do so. Nor did they always carry out the threat that anyone who was dismissed in this way could not be employed at any other of the same company's warehouses across the UK. This could be because there was a shortage of workers, or, as I go on to explore below, because workers were driving themselves to keep their levels of output moving upwards.

Competition and division among workers

Individual and small-group collective drive sometimes meant that not all performance had to be monitored in a draconian manner. Laura observed that some people worked incredibly hard to achieve much more than their targets, say 120 per cent or even 150 per cent, and management would take advantage:

> this is actually damaging because then managers sit and they say, 'OK, we have that many people who didn't reach the target but that many people managed to reach, and there are like twenty people on this department who reach 130 to 150. So, actually maybe target isn't that high. If they can do 150 we can increase it a little bit. These people who don't reach, OK, they will have to find maybe a different job, but we've got still quite a lot of good people.' So ... these workers who do very high targets, they try to show how good they are but also they do something bad for their colleagues who just have to do more quicker, more quicker.

In Peterborough's local labour regime some workers could also be relied on by management to compete with each other directly. A vivid example of this was related in 2017 by Agnieszka Sobieraj, who remembered her early months in Peterborough twelve years earlier as an agency worker processing imported fruit. Getting up at 3.30 a.m. to walk five kilometres to the agency office in the centre of town was a challenge, but not her biggest concern. Rather her main concern was that, although registered with the agency, she was not guaranteed work on any particular day. She was on a zero-hours arrangement and needed to show up in order to be considered, but could end up returning home with no work and no earnings. Agnieszka described a competition over speed in the fruit-processing factory that she remembered as being about proving one's value not just to the supervisor or manager but in relation to other workers as well. In her narrative, young, recently arrived international migrants with little or no English were likely to stick with others who spoke the same language. Yet Agnieszka also suggested that people arriving from central and eastern European countries as a whole were distinguishable in terms of work ethic from long-term resident white British workers:

Agnieszka: I think, I feel, we destroyed the system … I remember cutting the pineapple with Slovakian people, it was really competition, who is faster, and at some point, you think, 'What are we doing? Who are we doing this for? We are still getting the same money, no one will give us a medal or you know, you're not going to win anything. You're kind of settled at work so, what are we doing?' But it was something like 'maybe I will be better', I don't know, some personal issues you've got and a lot of us have got it so we wanted to prove something to ourselves.

Ben: Yes, so you're in that mode, trying to prove something to yourselves, in the competition. So, how did you destroy the system?

Agnieszka: By speeding things up and I think some of the English people couldn't follow us and this is what we've done wrong, we didn't cooperate with them so we could find some kind of background together how we supposed to do this, and then it was very noticeable, I was there for four months, I've noticed less and less English people were working there, only as the supervisors, because they couldn't follow us.

Ben: So, in a sense, what I'm getting from you is that actually, you were yourselves making the work more intense somehow?

Agnieszka: Yes.
Ben: But you weren't being paid more if you did it faster?
Agnieszka: No, but it was also the way, because we … This is the way how we work in our countries, so with this mentality because it was in Poland, you could work today and tomorrow you could be fired because of something and you didn't need to be given reason, good reason like here, you didn't have rights as a employee. So, everyone tried to do something just to be better than another person. And I think with this mentality we came to England and didn't help ourselves.

Referring to the newly built warehouse workplaces, several narrators also spoke about a system of group self-help that, in practice, divided workers. This was the 'cherry-picking' referred to by Sabina earlier in this section. It involved the delivery of batches of certain goods for packing that would enable the packers' target to be reached more quickly and easily than if they were to receive goods randomly. For example, Azwer witnessed forklift drivers deliberately delivering pallets with a large number of relatively small items to their friends:

> They knew this pallet have a lot of items and then they give it to their friend and their friend could easily reach the target, and if you reach 100 per cent of the target then you could get one pound extra for an hour.

Laura remembered cherry-picking as a mixture of individual initiative and collaboration among friends. She described how people knew that when they had a tray with a large number of small items they could achieve great progress in a relatively short time:

> if you have a … normal size of tray but with a lot of small items, let's say Sim cards or CDs, DVDs, so if you've got lots of things like that you can scan them very quickly and just put in envelopes and it's bang, bang, bang, you just throw them on line very quickly while when you have few trays where there are like six

> items and there is blender and there is book and there is huge calendar and you have to bring a box from a bit different, that slows you down …

Laura continued explaining how targets worked psychologically, so 'you just feel that your target is not that good, so you try to make this time up' – a situation that could make it particularly frustrating when others were seen to be benefiting from favourable treatment by the people in the role of 'water spiders' who 'basically bring the baskets to workers':

> Usually you have to take basket on your own from like big carts. But when they bring the baskets there is again another controversy that the water spiders who like particularly some people, they would bring them some cherries, the best basket …

As Sabina recalled from her time as a manager in a warehouse, management was quite happy to allow such divisive practices.

Summary

In a national context of deregulated labour markets and dramatically diminished trade union power since the 1980s, and with a huge amount of private capital concentrated in the largest food retailers and in giant logistics and distribution corporations, it is hardly surprising that workers in food factories and warehouses faced increasingly harsh workplace conditions, characterised by a punitive regime of targets enforced by sanctions. In Peterborough and its hinterland, companies backed by global capital were able to use this regime to build on established local practices of agricultural labour gangs, hiring the workers they needed through the labour gangs' successors: mostly larger, more commercialised temporary employment agencies. International migrants had been important for seasonal work in Fens agriculture for at least 200 years, and large numbers of Italians, New Commonwealth citizens and others had migrated to the city for work across the decades since the end of the Second World War. During the decade and a half leading up to the referendum on EU membership in 2016, and in spite of relatively low wages and low productivity across the UK, many more people were attracted to Peterborough by the knowledge that there was paid work available there. Relatively high levels of inward migration from the EU in this period thus built on a multiplicity of earlier moves to the city.

Certain kinds of role – particularly those involving zero-hours and/or limited-duration contracts and low-status, low-paid, fast-paced work – became associated with international migrants rather than British workers, having the effect of racialising the people employed in them *as migrants*. If this was seen as 'foreigners' work', the often multinational, multi-lingual workforces meant that workplaces were connected to, and influenced by, practices in other workplaces elsewhere, through people's previous experiences. For example, Agnieszka Sobieraj described how she and a group of young Polish women came to be noticed by the supervisors working on behalf of their employment agencies for working faster than other groups. She explained this high level of effort and pace with reference to a collective experience of insecure employment in Poland and elsewhere in central and eastern Europe.

Such practices could be divisive, unwittingly allowing management to put extra pressure on other workers. In certain circumstances, however, the tough demands of the workplace contributed to bringing about a 'common anger' among those who worked there.[76] In the next section of this chapter we will hear more from people employed in the Peterborough city region's industrialised food supply units and its warehouses, this time noting times and spaces of conviviality as well as the potential for solidarity and resistance. Narrating one's own biography can, in itself, be a form of resistance, especially when people refuse to be defined by any particular social category – including one derived from the way they currently earn their living – and insist instead on setting the terms by which their life and work should be seen and understood.

'There were so many communities'

Nicola Verdon ends her study of the 'English farmworker' with the argument that 'approaching the history of the farmworker *from their own perspective* is essential if we are to gain a better understanding of the rewards, constraints and meanings attached to that work'. She refers especially to 'the tens of thousands of casual workers'.[77] In this chapter I have drawn on biographical oral histories of people who have worked in agriculture and in other low-paid, low-status occupations in food factories and warehouses in and around Peterborough. So far, the emphasis has been on structural inequalities and the ways in which racialisation, and the production and maintenance of hierarchies of value, are used to enhance returns to capital. I have also drawn on instances where such hierarchies have been internalised by workers, and undergirded divisions between them.

Nevertheless, it is critically important for this book, in challenging the binary categories of 'local' and 'migrant' and the idea that cosmopolitanism is inevitably elite, also to listen out for where boundaries are being transgressed, where workers come to hear *each other*, and times and spaces through which common interests in a living wage and more humane terms and conditions of employment *may* be established. Trade unions attempt to challenge the worst conditions in contemporary food factories and warehouses but their presence is hardly felt.[78] On the other hand, as we learned from Laura Chłopeka in the opening section of the chapter, even in the intense working environment of an Amazon warehouse, people find spaces to exchange experiences of being sanctioned for undershooting a target. In the same interview Laura compared her experience of workers' interactions in warehouses favourably with the atmosphere among workers during her time as an office worker in the NHS:

> So, it could be one of the reasons why it was easier to build rapport [in warehouses], that [the workers] were younger, that they were also from foreign countries, so they had a bit of the same story. They came from somewhere, they started everything from the beginning, etc. But also, I've got a feeling that because they were working in warehouse or factory, they didn't have that much to lose if they spoke about something or someone, about a manager or someone, while in [NHS offices], [workers] tried to stay very professional because ... you know, there is just so many processes in place and you have to be very careful when

you work in place like that what you say. And in warehouse, who cares? If you work through agency and you say something and even you lose this job, you can get some different job in warehouse or factory because they are kind of ... People don't want to lose jobs but I feel that they are more open ... They would often show maybe quicker who they really are without pretending that everything is fine if it's not fine.

Laura's point about workers in Peterborough's warehouses tending to be 'from foreign countries' and therefore having 'a bit of the same story' was also highlighted by Agnieszka Kowalczyk-Wojcik, who had arrived in Peterborough in 2015 and, after a spell in a vegetable-processing unit in Spalding, had started working in the shipping department of a Peterborough warehouse. Agnieszka told me in July 2017, during her oral history interview in the upstairs room at the arts organisation Metal Peterborough, that she enjoyed speaking in English with others for whom English was not their first language.

Agnieszka: And on shipping I met people who didn't speak good English but I feel I can speak with them. I wasn't so embarrassed because they speak similar level like me so I start talking.

Ben: Were they Polish or were they different nationalities in shipping?

Agnieszka: Different nationalities. Polish, Romanian, Latvian, Lithuanian, Bulgarian.

Ben: How do you feel about that?

Agnieszka: Really good. When I start working at [the warehouse], I couldn't imagine that I can spend my off time during the break with people from Malaysia, we have one guy from New Zealand. It's amazing. I can sit with them and speak. I like it.

Ben: And what kinds of things happen? Do you sometimes talk about work with them and how it could be different or do you talk about other things?

Agnieszka: About other things. About food, about holidays. I have now really close friend from Portugal, we talk about our plans ... I like people. I like work with people ... I love work where you have to get relationship with people.

Although Agnieszka mentions Malaysia, much of the friendship she mentions is with white EU nationals, and it should not be assumed that the moments of conviviality they experience would extend frictionlessly to people who were not identified as white. Nevertheless, this had been the case for Azwer. He had formed close friendships with white women, central and eastern EU nationals, in the flower factory in Spalding where he worked from 2002 to 2005. Azwer's job there had been to trim the stem and leaves from rose plants imported from Kenya and Holland. Sometimes he was involved on the line making bouquets. Azwer was one of a number of young Iraqi Kurdish men.

> We were all single and it was a good opportunity for us to meet the different people with different culture, different language and we didn't hesitate to speak English because we were on the same stage ... Sometimes because our English wasn't good enough and we used to translate our joke into the English language. I don't know, sometime we laughed at each other but we didn't get much of the jokes <laughs>.

Azwer's propensity for workplace conviviality continued after his wife Gilya joined him in the UK, when they worked together at a warehouse. Their shifts from 6 a.m. to 2 p.m. were the same, though, as an agency worker, his wife sometimes had to work compulsory overtime. Having their own car, they gave lifts to and from work to Polish and Lithuanian women colleagues.

Azwer: During the breaks mostly my wife and I we sit together, we have break at the same time and sometimes actually we joined other people on the same table to talk.

Ben: And this was other people speaking which language?

Azwer: I would say majority were Polish. The large number of this warehouse were Polish, but then all other communities actually working there, depends, Bulgarian, Romanian,

> Lithuanian, Latvian ... Kurd – actually then my friend left, we stayed only my wife and I, we stayed there. There were so many different communities ... Sometimes we sit with English people as well; honestly, it does all depend on individuals. Some of the English people I still have friendships with them.

Workplace connections made across differences of nationality in some cases enabled workers to come together informally to protest against abuse by managers or supervisors. Judita Grubliene moved to Peterborough from Lithuania in 2009 to join her brother and sister-in-law. The financial crisis of 2007–08 had badly affected her husband's business in the car trade. Despite making and selling jewellery and working as a private tutor she had been finding it very difficult to make ends meet. In Peterborough she worked for an agency and had been pleased to move from a meat factory to work in a warehouse, where she stayed for five years. When faced with the need to challenge a manager, she found that workers of multiple nationalities were willing to join her. Judita objected to the way this manager tightly policed toilet breaks:

> he is waiting for you near the toilet and when you're coming back he is showing you to the clock and he's saying, 'you spend more than five minutes, you can't spend so long time in the toilet'.

More than this, he also discriminated against people from certain national backgrounds, not allowing them to talk to each other during a shift:

> If, for example, Englishes or Polishes are talking between each other or with each other during the work, it's OK, it doesn't matter for him. But if others east Europeans, Lithuanians, Latvians, Bulgarians, Romanians want to speak something or to say something between each other, he's coming to you and he's shouting to you, 'you can't talk here you just have to work'.

At first Judita challenged the manager herself, pointing out the inconsistency in the way he treated workers of different nationalities. When she received an angry and threatening response, and found her approach questioned by the temporary agency she was employed by, she was met with solidarity from her fellow workers.

> they were with me on that case and because he was doing not just with me that but with others, so I found all each person whom he was, how to say, doing like this and we sign, I prepared at home a form, claim form for him about discrimination and I wrote everything, all things he was doing with us in discrimination way and I asked people to sign and they signed this paper and I then gave one paper for our shift manager, another one for our agency bosses and yes, I understood what I am doing and that my work in this warehousing is finished with that thing, with that claim to him, and he …

She remembered that between five and seven colleagues joined in with her. They varied in background, including people with Turkish, Lithuanian and Latvian nationality. She knew these colleagues as friends and would meet up with them after work. Although she and the rest of the group lost their jobs as a result, the experience left Judita with positive memories of interactions among the warehouse workforce in contrast to the less than convivial relations she had experienced in her earlier job in the meat factory.

> But in warehouse, it was a little bit different people, different kind of people so they were more communicating and they were more welcome to each other because in warehouse sometimes you have to work with groups and sometimes you have to work alone, but alone doesn't mean just alone, anyway others are around you and you have to communicate. So, it was very kind people.

Conclusion

Judita's favourable comparison here of her experience of warehouse work with her earlier spell in a meat factory resonates with Laura Chłopeka's observation elsewhere in the chapter that she found Peterborough's multi-national warehouse workforces more open with each other than the colleagues she had met in her office job. Yet neither Judita nor Laura leave any doubt about the toughness of the local labour regime for food-supply and warehouse distribution workers. Laura's opening reflection on the use of performance targets at Amazon has been elaborated on in the remainder of the chapter by drawing on the stories of other workers. Taken together, these reveal harsh supervision regimes and a sense that workers are often made to feel, and indeed from the point of view of capitalists often *are*, disposable.

In continuity with the history of Peterborough and its hinterland going back to at least the nineteenth century, the local labour regime in recent decades has relied heavily on international migrant workers. In this way and in others, Peterborough and its workplaces are made and continually remade through their connections with places elsewhere. According to two of the people I have quoted, both of them international migrants, the effect of the 2007–08 financial crisis in their countries caused many people to move to the UK to seek work. Peterborough was known to have jobs available. Another narrator described how the insecurity of employment at home in Poland, and in her view other central and eastern European countries, led young adults who were newly arrived in the UK in the late 2000s to work extra hard in an effort to to prove their value and secure regular daily work.

The labour regime described in this chapter relies centrally on temporary employment agencies that are involved to varying degrees in the accommodation and transport of people to their places of work as well as recruitment and supervision. In and around Peterborough this builds on a history of agricultural gangmastering. With this established practice, the region was well placed to respond to the industrialisation of food supply in the last decades of the twentieth century and first two decades of the twenty-first. More commercial agencies now provide workers not only to horticulture but also to jobs in food processing and packing, as well as to work in the growing number of logistics and distribution companies that took advantage of the availability of land and the infrastructure that was put in place with the construction of the city's New Towns. I have argued that the regime is a form of racial capitalism, always changing, but keeping constant the creation of difference within workforces in the interests of capital and, in particular ways at specific points in time, the association of racialised and gendered others with the lowest-status and most intensive work.

Peterborough's food factories and warehouses can teach us much about changes in capitalist work in the Global North. And, alongside shifts in the ways capital seeks to organise production, those who work or have worked there also have meaningful stories to tell about conviviality, solidarity and non-elite cosmopolitan practices and dispositions, even though all of these retain elements of racialised friction. It is to further evidence of such friction in a Peterborough neighbourhood, its coexistence with non-elite cosmopolitanism and the challenges and possibilities for urban citizenship to which this contradiction gives rise that I will now turn.

Notes

1 *Workers* was directed by Jay Gearing and is available online at: https://creativeinterruptions.com/workers (accessed January 2019). The process of making the film is discussed further in Chapter 5.

2 This builds on others' research on aspects of the labour process in warehouses and food factories in the Global North, including Kirsty Newsome, 'Value in motion: labour and logistics in the contemporary political economy', in Kirsty Newsome *et al.* (eds), *Putting Labour in its Place: Labour Process Analysis and Global Value Chains* (London: Palgrave, 2015), pp. 29–44; Amanda Wise, 'Convivial labour and the "joking relationship": humour and everyday multiculturalism at work', *Journal of intercultural studies*, 37:5 (2016), 481–500; and Peter Lugosi, Hania Janta and Barbara Wilczek, 'Work(ing) dynamics of migrant networking among Poles employed in hospitality and food production', *The sociological review*, 64:4 (2016), 894–911.

3 Gargi Bhattacharyya, *Rethinking Racial Capitalism: Questions of Reproduction and Survival* (London: Rowman & Littlefield International, 2018), p. 102.

4 Cedric J. Robinson, *Black Marxism: The Making of the Black Radical Tradition* (London: Zed, 1983); Lisa Lowe, *The Intimacies of Four Continents* (Durham, NC: Duke University Press, 2015); Bhattacharyya, *Rethinking Racial Capitalism.*

5 Stuart Hall *et al.*, *Policing the Crisis: Mugging, the State and Law and Order* (second edition, Basingstoke: Palgrave Macmillan, 2013), p. 339.

6 Elizabeth Esch and David Roediger, '"One symptom of originality": race and the management of labor in US history', in David Roediger, *Class, Race and Marxism* (London: Verso, 2017), p. 122.
7 Bhattacharyya, *Rethinking Racial Capitalism*, p. 101.
8 Ibid., p. 104.
9 Lowe, *The Intimacies of Four Continents*, p. 149.
10 Hall *et al.*, *Policing the Crisis*, p. 339.
11 Alastair Bonnett, *White Identities: Historical and International Perspectives* (London: Routledge, 2000); R. D. Kelley, 'Foreword', in Cedric J. Robinson, *Black Marxism: The Making of the Black Radical Tradition* (1983; revised edition, Chapel Hill: University of North Carolina Press, 2000), pp. xi–xxvi.
12 John Berger and Jean Mohr, *A Seventh Man: A Book of Images and Words about the Experiences of Migrant Workers in Europe* (1975; second edition, London: Verso, 2010), pp. 47–48.
13 Ibid., pp. 100 and 103.
14 Ruth Wilson Gilmore, 'Abolition geography and the problem of innocence', in Gaye Theresa Johnson and Alex Lubin (eds), *Futures of Black Radicalism* (London and New York: Verso, 2017), pp. 225–226.
15 Seth M. Holmes, '"Oaxacans like to work bent over": the naturalization of social suffering among berry farm workers', *International migration*, 45:3 (2007), 48.
16 Ben Rogaly and Kaveri Qureshi, '"That's where my perception of it all was shattered": oral histories and moral geographies of food sector workers in an English city region', *Geoforum*, 78 (2017), 189–198.
17 James Bloodworth, *Hired: Six Months Undercover in Low-Wage Britain* (London: Atlantic Books, 2018); Carlotta Benvegnù, Bettina Haidinger and Devi Sacchetto, 'Restructuring labour relations and employment in the European logistics sector: unions' responses to a segmented workforce', in Virginia Doellgast, Nathan Lillie and Valeria Pulignano (eds), *Reconstructing Solidarity: Labour Unions, Precarious Work and the Politics of Institutional Change in Europe* (Oxford: Oxford University Press, 2018); Huw Beynon, 'Beyond Fordism', in Stephen Edgell, Heidi Gottfried and Edward Granter (eds), *The SAGE Handbook of the Sociology of Work and Employment* (London: Sage, 2015), pp. 306–328.
18 Phoebe Moore, 'On work and machines: a labour process of agility', *Soundings*, 69:69 (2018), 15–31.
19 Bloodworth, *Hired*, p. 2.
20 Jamie Peck, *Work-Place: The Social Regulation of Labor Markets* (New York: Guilford Press, 1996), p. 2.
21 Ibid., p. 266, emphasis in original.
22 Ibid., p. 267.

23 David Harvey, 'Three myths in search of a reality in urban studies', *Environment and planning D: Society and space*, 5:4 (1987), 367–376; and Neil Smith, 'Dangers of the empirical turn: some comments on the CURS initiative', *Antipode*, 19:1 (1987), 59–68.
24 Peck, *Work-Place*, p. 14.
25 Doreen Massey, *Spatial Divisions of Labour: Social Structures and the Geography of Production* (second edition, New York: Routledge, 1995).
26 Ibid., p. 321.
27 Doreen Massey, 'Questions of locality', *Geography*, 78:2 (1993), 144.
28 Adrian Smith *et al.*, 'Labor regimes, global production networks and European trade union policy: labor standards and export production in the Moldovan clothing industry', *Economic geography*, 94:5 (2018), 550–574. On the concept of local labour control regimes see Andrew Jonas, 'Local labour control regimes: uneven development and the social regulation of production', *Journal of regional studies*, 30:4 (1996), 323–338.
29 Thomas Hastings and Danny MacKinnon, 'Re-embedding agency at the workplace scale: workers and labour control in Glasgow call centres', *Environment and planning A*, 49:1 (2016), 104–120.
30 Ibid., p. 108.
31 See, for example, Harry Braverman, *Labor and Monopoly Capital: The Degradation of Work in the Twentieth Century* (New York: Monthly Review Press, 1974); Michael Burawoy, *Manufacturing Consent: Changes in the Labor Process under Monopoly Capitalism* (Chicago: University of Chicago Press, 1979). For some excellent contemporary labour process studies, see Kirsty Newsome *et al.* (eds), *Putting Labour in its Place: Labour Process Analysis and Global Value Chains* (London: Palgrave, 2015).
32 Through changes to citizenship law, many were automatically reclassified as immigrants in the 1960s and 1970s (see Gurminder Bhambra, 'Viewpoint: Brexit, class and British 'national' identity', *Discover Society*, 5 July 2016, available online at: https://discoversociety.org/2016/07/05/viewpoint-brexit-class-and-british-national-identity/ (accessed February 2019). This latter migration usually involved *settlement*, although as we saw in in the cases of Mam, Sotindra and Pakzaad in Chapter 2, it could also be associated with a range of mobilities and fixities. Indeed, some of those who arrived from the Caribbean in the 1950s were wrongfully deported back there several decades later in what became known as the Windrush scandal.
33 Hall *et al.*, *Policing the Crisis*.
34 Ibid., p. 338.

35 The same strategy was advocated, for example, by Devi Sacchetto and Domenico Perrotta in their call for as much attention to be paid to workers' housing as to their experiences of carrying out paid work, 'Migrant farmworkers in southern Italy: ghettoes, caporalato and collective action', *Workers of the world: international journal on strikes and social conflicts*, 1:5 (2014), 58–74.

36 Bridget Anderson and Ben Rogaly, 'Forced labour and migration to the UK', study prepared by Centre on Migration, Policy and Society in collaboration with the Trades Union Congress, 2005, available online at: www.compas.ox.ac.uk/wp-content/uploads/PR-2007-Forced_Labour_TUC.pdf (accessed February 2019).

37 Nicola Verdon, 'The employment of women and children in agriculture: a reassessment of agricultural gangs in nineteenth-century Norfolk', *Agricultural history review*, 49:1 (2001), 44.

38 Ibid.

39 Ibid.

40 Carl Griffin, *The Rural War: Captain Swing and the Politics of Protest* (Manchester: Manchester University Press, 2012).

41 E. J. T. Collins, 'Migrant labour in British agriculture in the nineteenth century', *Economic history review*, 29:1 (1976), 43.

42 Julie Guthman, *Agrarian Dreams: The Paradox of Organic Farming in California* (second edition, Berkeley: University of California Press, 2014).

43 Nicola Verdon, *Working the Land: A History of the Farmworker in England from 1850 to the Present Day* (London: Palgrave Macmillan, 2017).

44 Lydia Medland, 'Working for social sustainability: insights from a Spanish organic production enclave', *Agroecology and sustainable food systems*, 40:10 (2016), 1133–1156. An enclave in a different sense from that used by Medland in that the Peterborough city region was importing, processing and packing food (rather than exporting), though like the enclave she wrote about it relied heavily on international migrant workers from the 1990s.

45 Ben Rogaly, 'Intensification of workplace regimes in British horticulture: the role of migrant workers', *Population, space and place*, 14:6 (2008), 497–510.

46 Verdon, *Working the Land*, Chapter 9.

47 Migration Advisory Committee, *Migrant Seasonal Workers: The Impact on the Horticulture and Food Processing Sectors of Closing the Seasonal Agricultural Workers Scheme and the Sectors Based Scheme* (London: Home Office, 2013), p. 13.

48 See www.gov.uk/government/publications/the-uks-future-skills-based-immigration-system (accessed January 2019).

49 A retch is a unit of length in a row of potatoes. See www.greatfen.org.uk/sites/default/files/Farming%20Life%20in%20the%20Fens%201.62Mb.pdf (accessed September 2018).

50 Part of a performance of the poem by Keely can be viewed from 2′30″ in the film *A Place for All* made by Zain Awan in 2012 at the culmination of the 'Places for All?' research project. Available online at www.youtube.com/watch?v=8I-21FRcqhY (accessed January 2019). For more details about the project, see Chapter 1.

51 Rogaly, 'Intensification of workplace regimes'.

52 Migration Advisory Committee, *Migrant Seasonal Workers*; Trades Union Congress, 'Insecure work and ethnicity' (London, 2017), available online at: www.tuc.org.uk/research-analysis/reports/insecure-work-and-ethnicity (accessed January 2019).

53 Peter Tyler, Emil Evenhuis and Ron Martin, 'Case study report: Peterborough', Structural Transformation, Adaptability and City Economic Evolutions, Working Paper 10 (UK Economic and Social Research Council Urban Transformations Initiative, 2018), p. 18, available online at: www.cityevolutions.org.uk/working-paper-peterborough-case-study/ (accessed January 2019).

54 Beynon, 'Beyond Fordism'.

55 Ibid., p. 311.

56 Emily Reid-Musson, 'Intersectional rhythmanalysis: power, rhythm, and everyday life', *Progress in human geography*, 42:6 (2018), p. 894.

57 Benvegnù, Haidinger and Sacchetto, 'Restructuring labour relations', p. 95.

58 Tyler, Evenhuis and Martin, 'Case study report: Peterborough', p. 16.

59 Ibid., p. 8.

60 The 2013 play *Parkway Dreams* written by Kenneth Emson and produced by Eastern Angles was based on archival and oral history evidence collected as part of the 'Forty Years On' project, a collaboration between Eastern Angles and Vivacity (Peterborough City Council's arts and leisure arm) that focused on the Peterborough Development Corporation.

61 Mark Roberts has lucidly shown how one legacy of this for local politics in Peterborough is a faction on the City Council that remains critical of intervention by anyone 'up from London'. Mark Roberts, 'Communication breakdown: understanding the role of policy narratives in conflict and consensus', *Critical policy studies*, 12:1 (2016), 82–102.

62 Tyler, Evenhuis and Martin, 'Case study report: Peterborough', p. 10.

63 Ibid., p. 10.

64 Ibid., p. 3.

65 Beynon, 'Beyond Fordism', p. 312.

66 Ibid.

67 Bloodworth, *Hired*, p. 39.
68 Werner *et al.*, 'Feminist political economy in geography: why now, what is different, and what for?', *Geoforum*, 79:1 (2017), 2.
69 Bloodworth, *Hired*, pp. 33–34, emphasis added. A similar division of labour was portrayed by the 2008 BBC documentary set in and around Peterborough, *The Poles are Coming*.
70 Bloodworth, *Hired*, p. 35.
71 Esch and Roediger, '"One symptom of originality"', p. 129. In her biographical oral history narrative, Maria, a Peterborough-based white Polish woman, explicitly resisted any association of the harsh conditions she experienced with those of 'African' people or 'slaves'. See Rogaly and Qureshi, 'That's where my perception of it all was shattered', pp. 192–193.
72 Bridget Anderson *et al.*, *Fair Enough? Central and Eastern European Migrants in the Low Wage Employment in the UK*, Centre on Migration, Policy and Society Research Report (London: Joseph Rowntree Foundation, 2006), available online at: www.compas.ox.ac.uk/2006/pr-2006-changing_status_fair_enough/ (accessed January 2019).
73 Sundari Anitha and Ruth Pearson, *Striking Women: Struggles and Strategies of South Asian Women Workers from Grunwick to Gate Gourmet* (London: Lawrence and Wishart, 2018).
74 Discussed further below, 'cherry-picking' refers to the selection of items of a certain size and convenience to pack that enable a higher level of output than could be obtained with items that take longer or are more awkward to pack.
75 Spalding is 33 miles (53 kilometres) to the north-east of Peterborough.
76 As I elaborated in Chapter 1, this concept is inspired by Doreen Massey's use of it in *Landscape/Space/Politics: An Essay* (2011), available online at: http://thefutureoflandscape.wordpress.com/landscapespacepolitics-an-essay/ (accessed January 2019).
77 Verdon, *Working the Land*, p. 262, emphasis added.
78 For example, the General and Municipal Boilermakers Union (GMB) has been campaigning against Amazon's worst excesses. See Marcus Bennet, 'Organising Amazon', *Tribune Magazine*, November 2018, available online at: https://tribunemag.co.uk/2018/11/organising-amazon (accessed January 2019).

4

'We're not just guardians of the area but of the whole city': urban citizenship struggles and the racialised outsider

Introduction

Charles Wood, a sixty-something businessman, remembered working as a teenager in the potato harvest in fields on the eastern edge of Peterborough. His family were Travelling Showmen who had spent large parts of each summer on the road running fairground entertainments. When Charles was six they moved their winter base to Peterborough. He recalled the potato-picking work as being:

> 'very, very cold'. He didn't want to be doing the picking work, 'hard work', he preferred to be a catcher, catching the bags of potatoes as they were thrown up by the pickers onto the trailer, emptying the bag and throwing it back. Though he then added this was 'just as hard'. He was paid by his Mum he remembered, who was paid by the ganger they worked with and who was not from a Travelling Showman background.[1] You do what you learn to do. [Directing himself to me he continued] 'I couldn't stand up in a room of a thousand people; you couldn't do that potato work'. When I later said I'd done strawberry picking, he immediately retorted 'but you weren't cold then' – the strawberry harvest being in the summer.[2] (Author's fieldnotes, 23 November 2011)

Following my interview with him, Charles invited me and the photographer Liz Hingley to visit his house at Haddon, a rural area at the southern edge of Peterborough that had been earmarked for future housing development.[3]

> Charles was dressed up in suit trousers, white shirt and smart tie. His house was pristine and there was no one else there. A white fur drape ran along the back of the super-comfortable settee in the living room. The white oval artificial fire was glowing in the grate. It was warm finally – though I still felt a bit unwell, found it took quite a bit of energy keeping up the conversation with Charles while Liz photographed him. He'd dressed up in stiff clothes – he later said he didn't want to be portrayed as a 'poor Fair boy',[4] but as a 'successful businessman' ... He showed us the power-point of the fairground rides and other offerings he shows to corporate clients. He organizes many things in the city, including the Christmas lights and what was the Bridge Fair. (Author's fieldnotes, 23 November 2011)

As we learned earlier in this book, Charles remembered being treated as an outsider when he started primary school in Peterborough not only because of his peripatetic lifestyle but also because of his stigmatised identity as a 'Fair boy'. His biographical oral history recorded sixty years later contains both a sense of anger at having been spoken down to at various points in his life because of his Travelling Showman heritage, and the 'homely privilege of automatic belonging', to use Les Back's words,[5] as a 'local' in the city, a British national, a former Conservative candidate for the council and the erstwhile owner of a detached house in Thorpe Road. Charles had had his eye on owning a property in this part of Peterborough, considered by many to be the most desirable, when, in the 1970s, as the owner of an oil haulage company, he would regularly drive his oil tanker past a house that had his second initial on it:

> [I] used to come in Peterborough on Thorpe Road, 'cause you used to go through Castor and all that if you remember it? And then you come into the top of Thorpe Road and all as you come

> in there, there was this big old house in the corner, and it was Wheatley's Trailers who had it built, and it had a big W on the front, holding like a porch. 'I want that house, that's got my initial there!' ... It was just an ego, wasn't it? I was driving a tanker at that fucking time, I can't afford two bob, but you know ... the thought was there. Anyroad, like I say ... probably four, five years later, [my wife's] seen this house two doors from that, and that's the one we bought. Beautiful it was, sat in its own grounds, had three-tier garden that went down on steps, looked over to the river, little roundabout in the front and all that. Lovely house. Had that for a few years and then that's when I went into the estate agents. Which kicked me right up the loops.

Charles ran his estate agency business on Lincoln Road in the heart of the Millfield area in the 1990s. As Chapters 2 and 3 attested, new arrivals to the city often found accommodation in Millfield (or the Gladstone area immediately to its south), especially people seeking work through employment agencies in low-paid manufacturing, food-processing or warehouse operative roles. Since at least as far back as the 1960s, the area has had a relatively large number of homes of multiple occupancy. Later in this chapter I will elaborate on how resistance grew in the 2000s from mainly white British people, nominally Christians,[6] who saw themselves as guardians of the neighbourhood and indeed the city (whether or not they had been born and brought up in Peterborough) and believed that it was being taken over by 'Asians', 'Muslims' and foreign nationals, particularly 'eastern Europeans'. I will argue that this culminated in the early 2010s in a local tremor that prefigured the much larger, national agenda encapsulated by the slogan 'take back control' adopted by the Leave campaign in the 2016 referendum on EU membership.

Charles himself became part of the fabric of Peterborough, for example through the organisation of Christmas lights and a major annual fair. He has been the owner of a range of businesses in the city and beyond. Between his oil haulage company in the 1970s and his estate agency in the 1990s, he invested in several amusement arcades with ventures in Peterborough and as far afield as Clacton-upon-Sea in Essex and Dawlish in Devon. At the time of the interview he owned thirty-five catering vans that had the contract for the Peterborough United Football Club home games, and was in charge of the Sunday morning car boot sale at the same site.[7] This meant that he had contacts in the police force that could be useful if and when there was any trouble. Yet Charles's position was not simple. On the one hand, he knew what it was to be discriminated against and therefore felt an affinity with others experiencing racialisation and discrimination

> I suppose as a 'Fair boy' I feel that I'm underestimated shall we say ... Like the Italians, they felt they was hard-done-by and I suppose the blacks go that way now.

On the other hand, his narration of the purchase of properties by people with South Asian heritage in Millfield and beyond in the early 1990s used terminology that conveyed his position as an *insider*, an estate agent and someone implicitly passing as a white British person who was native to Peterborough:

> The English were selling ... well they was moving out.[8] What it was, Cromwell Road is really the Asian area, or Gladstone Street, and what happened in them nineties ... they started buying behind Lincoln Road, Park Road, that sort of area, if you get my drift.
>
> So yeah, really when I think of it, I mean there was English buying but the majority was the Asians when I think about that. There was one man that worked at the bloody bus company. He must have bought five or six houses off us. Which he must have been renting out at the time. I bought two or three ... but the interest rates went from 7 to 14 per cent within six months. People were just throwing the keys back in the letter box.[9]

His reference here to 'the bloody bus company' implies that there was something unusual in an 'Asian' bus driver being able to buy several properties; moreover, his mention of the 'Asian community' in the list of 'foreigners' below suggests he saw them as such regardless of whether they were British nationals. However, in spite of not having been born in the city himself, Charles's own sense of belonging was also intensely *local*. He referred to the Londoners who moved to Peterborough at the time of the construction of the New Towns in the same language he used for 'Asians', that is, as 'foreigners', along with the thousands of non-British EU nationals who arrived in the 2000s. Charles spoke of an

> influxion of foreigners and different people ... there's probably 25,000 Polish, Czech, blah, blah, blah, which is in Peterborough. So that's 25,000 and that's without the Asian community. So it ain't Peterborough ...

As Daniel James showed in *Doña Maria's Story*, there is a relationship in biographical oral history between the narrative that aims to 'creat[e] coherence and continuity and other elements that clarify, obscure, make more complex, or simply leave in the tension-laden coexistence of contradictory themes and ambivalent meanings in an account of a life'.[10] Charles's telling of his own story also allowed him, as he put it, to 'talk on the other side of the fence' when it came to the claims of Gypsies and Travellers to authorised sites in the city.

> Charles: It's only the latter part of years where the government are giving Fair people sites. We've got one in Stanground where Fair people stay, for the winter and that. They should do; there's so many foreigners getting away with everything ... and our industry, we're prepared to buy the places and develop them ourselves, so there shouldn't be an issue in it, for fairground people to have locations, which is ... I think it should be. I mean I'm all right because we've got houses, but the people that still travel, which is my auntie, my cousins, my sister-in-law, they have to go and say, 'Can I come in your yard?' Which is wrong really ...
>
> Ben: What about other people who call themselves Gypsies or Travellers?
>
> Charles: But you see Traveller is a long word or covers a lot of people. Because [my relatives] live in a caravan, so they get tarred ... like I did. I used to be called an 'old Gypsy', [by people who] didn't realise the difference between

a 'Fair boy' and a 'Gypsy boy' shall we say … There's good and bad [among Gypsies and Travellers]. They should have locations, but implement them properly. My boy had a car pinched … and it ended up down Oxney Road which is a Gypsy site. So I seen it down there, been robbed, nothing on it, it was thrown on the floor with no wheels on it, nothing, everything had been robbed out but it had my private number on, old Charlie Wood, so I rang the police, I said, 'Look my car's down here. I need you to come down to clarify that it's here because it's got a private number on. I don't want to lose the private number.' 'All right then Charlie,' 'cos I knew them from the football, 'all right Charlie, we'll be down there.' This van comes down there, gets out the van, the policemen, two of them, puts bullet-proof vests on [laughs]. I said, 'What you doing?' Goes to the front, lowers this thing over the windscreen. I said, 'Whatever are you doing?' He says, 'Charlie, they're fucking lunatics here!' I said, 'What do you mean?' So any-road, put that down, walk round there, there's the motor. So I said, 'Look there it is' blah blah … so all of them start coming out, don't they? All the Gypsies come out the site [and] get hold of the policeman, 'What's this jacket on for mate? What you doing?' I said, 'Woah' 'cause I obviously know a bit, and I talked to them in their language. I said, 'One of you lot's pinched my motor. I don't care what you mumble and bullshit, leave him alone because he's here to do a job to make sure this motor's here and no one of you lot's fucking thieved it. Fuck off and leave him alone.' A little bit loud, you know? 'Oh all right mush, all right mush, all right …' So they went. I said [to the policemen], 'What was all that?' They said the [Gypsies and Travellers at the site] used to have ball-bearings and fucking throw them. I said, 'You know what I would do with these? I'd throw a petrol bomb in there and say, "Right now, if you want problems, we'll sort it out."' But they're frightened of

> them. But ... that's what Gypsies do, they're all bounce and try and frighten you into it. But I suppose we're all as bad one way or the other.

Charles's narrative of this incident illustrates the confident way in which he was able to move between worlds, using his status as both insider and outsider. Charles had a voice in city affairs, albeit one that was limited in power because of his being a racialised outsider. This tension came across in Chapter 1 when we heard him speak about being on the Conservative Party committee in Peterborough – part of the city establishment – yet at the same time feeling that his ethnic, class and geographical heritage meant that new arrivals from London who were on the same committee could speak down to him and appropriate his ideas. Charles had had to restrain himself from saying 'you Cockney boy, you know it all don't you?' and learn instead to *suggest* approaches that later became adopted in others' names.

*

These extracts from Charles's biographical oral history offer glimpses into struggles over the city of Peterborough and over certain spaces within it at particular points in time, struggles that, as I will shortly argue, can also be usefully understood in terms of *citizenship*. In the rest of this chapter I continue to draw on Peterborough as a lens for understanding such urban citizenship struggles, moving the focus forward to the 2000s and 2010s.[11] In the 2000s Peterborough developed a reputation among local authority policy makers across England as a city where large numbers of work-seeking EU nationals headed following the enlargement of the EU in 2004.[12] Situated on the main London–Edinburgh train line and just forty-five minutes from London on the fastest trains, Peterborough was visited regularly by national-level politicians and journalists wanting to investigate the impact of immigration in the UK as a whole or to make announcements about national immigration policy initiatives.[13] Analysis of the most recent Census in 2011 appears to bear out the city's reputation regarding the increased number of non-UK EU nationals: the proportion of Peterborough's population self-identifying in the 'Other White' category rose from 3 per cent in 2001 to 10.6 per cent at the time of census,[14] while over half of the 20.6 per cent of the population born outside the UK had arrived since 2004. In the lead-up to the 2015 general election, the then leader of the anti-EU United Kingdom Independence Party, Nigel Farage, referred to Peterborough on national radio:

> Well, go to Peterborough, you know ... go and see the fact that we don't have integration ... And what's happened, unsurprisingly, in some ways, what's happened with very large numbers of people coming, is you get quarters and districts of towns and cities that get taken over by one particular group ...[15]

However, as Charles Wood's story suggested, the picture of migration, citizenship and rights in the city of Peterborough and its surrounding rural areas is, unsurprisingly, more complex than its reputation as a major reception city for international migrant workers, or Nigel Farage's portrayal of the consequences of this, might imply.

In this chapter I argue that a focus on urban citizenship struggles can provide grounds for hope in contemporary England, in spite of highly divisive national-level debates before, during and after the 2016 referendum. At the same time, it is important not to romanticise the potential of city-wide or neighbourhood-level citizenship as inherently offering greater inclusivity and equality in terms of rights and representation, as opposed to when citizenship is understood entirely as defining a person's relationship to a nation-state.[16] Moreover, struggles at the scale of the city or the neighbourhood take place in a national and international context. Since the 2016 referendum, EU nationals in the UK have experienced continuing uncertainty over their future rights. This period overlaps with ongoing, plural, shifting forms of racism, including a post-9/11 growth in anti-Muslim racism,[17] and a 'xeno-racism ... that is meted out to impoverished strangers even if they are white'.[18] In seeking to explore this apparent contradiction in a *provincial* city I am inspired by Les Back's concept of the 'metropolitan paradox' developed in the global city context of London, where, in an ethnographic study conducted in the 1990s, he argued that racisms coexisted side by side with spaces and moments of urban conviviality and everyday multiculture.[19]

At the national level, the Leave campaign in the referendum repeatedly used the slogan 'take back control', emphasising the importance the campaign attached to the UK's sovereignty, including sovereignty over immigration policy. The referendum thus also, in part, like Nigel Farage's approach to the general election the year before, contributed to an ongoing struggle over citizenship. This struggle was most notable regarding whether it would be the free-movement requirements of the EU or the national policy of the government of the UK that determined which EU citizens could enter the country and on what, if any, conditions. This chapter provides a rare glimpse into continuity and change in citizenship struggles at the scale of a provincial city and of certain neighbourhoods within it, while attending to the relationships between these and more generalised national and international struggles. Like that of Anne Visser and Sheryl-Ann Simpson,[20] my approach highlights relations between scales across time.

The next two sections of the chapter explain, in turn, what I mean by citizenship struggle and by a relational approach to scale. I go on in two subsequent sections to explore an earlier citizenship struggle in Peterborough that foreshadowed the outcome of the 2016 referendum, and then to exemplify hopeful acts of sub-national citizenship. The final section briefly concludes the chapter.

Citizenship and struggle

Citizenship is an amorphous concept. Some have even suggested that it 'risks losing its meaning ... [through a] combination of overuse and confusion'.[21] Yet I choose to consider multiple dimensions of citizenship together,[22] rather than attempting to slice it up into different 'types'. *Struggles* over citizenship are thus treated here as plural. They include struggles over labelling and categories – how people are spoken about and referred to in prevalent discourses in online and print media, as well as in physical locations such as workplaces, schools and public outdoor space. Equally, they incorporate struggles over the distribution of resources, and over representation and meaningful involvement in decision-making processes.[23]

Noting the renewed anti-migrant moral panic that followed the UK granting nationals of newly acceded EU states access to its labour market in 2004, and that then surged following the 2007–08 financial crisis, Ian Fitzgerald and Rafal Smoczynski argue that this situation led not only to the stigmatisation of nationals of central and eastern EU states, but also to a fight back.[24] Focusing on the experience of Polish migrants in particular, Fitzgerald and Smoczynski extend their argument to other EU nationalities, stating that the notion of the 'Polish migrant' operated as a 'floating signifier' that related to 'a broader Eastern European migrant community'.[25] The fight back, as a form of citizenship struggle, consisted of 'resist[ing] social exclusion' including through:

> the proliferation of ethnic on-line media that provide[d] comprehensive information on the rights of EU citizens ... Respondents that were equipped with greater cultural capital resources (language skills, education) were significantly less likely to be interpellated as a 'deviant migrant' ... *Polish migrants' strategy of fighting back ... clearly calls for further research*.[26]

Etienne Balibar proposes more generally that 'struggles [over citizenship] are always necessary ...', whether over 'an exclusion from recognition (or dignity, or rights, or property, or security, or speech, or decision-making)' because 'the subproletariat or underclass of the insecure, immigrants, and especially youth ... are *pushed* or *left outside* representation ...'.[27] The kind of dialectic referred to by Balibar is echoed in the review by Lynn Staeheli and her colleagues of the ways in which citizenship struggles have emerged in 'ordinary' life, with 'ordinary' used in its double meaning as *both* 'standard and routine' *and* 'invok[ing] order and authority'.[28]

Citizenship struggles are thus waged both from above, through the 'governmental reproduction of normative distinctions of citizen and non-citizen',[29] and from below. Actors in contemporary contestations over citizenship in the UK include relatively recently arrived international migrants and longer-term residents of all ethnicities. Citizenship struggles are very often racialised, and, as in the USA, understanding them requires analysis of how 'race', faith identities and immigration intersect.[30] However, this is not a dialectical battle between two clearly defined opposing forces. Acts of citizenship emerging 'from below' have varying degrees of instrumentality, strength and duration.[31] They may include resources deployed in everyday life and 'claims rooted in family, in community, and in an expanded range of moral universes ... [among them] values of care, mutuality, love, respect and other-regardingness'.[32]

Importantly, however, claims relating to 'family and community' may be deployed in reactionary ways, for example, in efforts by long-term residents and/or majority white populations to 'take back control'. Thus as well as hitherto marginalised people and groups seeking greater enfranchisement and representation, the actors may include people and organisations seeking to exclude certain others from various aspects of citizenship, with 'acts and interventions... that are actively *destructive* of other ways of being ... [e.g.] the affective politics of hate, the saliency of desires to retain and protect privilege, and the rejection of forms of solidarity that seek to extend concern to others'.[33] Such positions reflect ongoing contests over the nation in the UK and elsewhere, as part of which 'claims about "proper" conventions may articulate exclusionary national identities, or inclusively seek to broaden the range of practices conceived as national *along with the people who practise them*'.[34]

The location of this book in a specific historical time period – from the financial crisis of 2007–08 until 2017, the year after the referendum – avoids the 'empirical presentism' that Luis Guarnizo found characteristic of many contemporary studies of citizenship.[35] Earlier periods are relevant to the analysis here too, with citizenship struggles in the UK often characterised in ways that carry echoes of the UK's relatively recent past as a coloniser.[36] Temporality is also important in ways not confined to historical time: not only may citizenship acts from below be fleeting,[37] but some of the actors themselves may see their presence in national, city, or neighbourhood space as transient. Moreover, people's intentions to stay in a particular place or national territory, degrees of citizenship and connection to places elsewhere are unlikely to be fixed.[38] The modes of governance of recently arrived people, the degree to which their presence is constructed by themselves or others as transient and the implications of the latter for whether and to what extent they are regarded as citizens are all subject to struggle.[39]

Scale, urban citizenship and a relational understanding of place

Regarding the scales at which citizenship struggles occur, I am persuaded by Guarnizo's argument that the analysis of citizenship needs to move away from an either-or stance (e.g. either city or nation-state), towards a more relational understanding that *both* recognises the importance of scalar particularity *and* rejects the idea of a nested hierarchy of discrete scales.[40] Guarnizo proposed that scales are always interwoven and inter-related. So citizenship struggles are not simply analytically re-scaled from the nation-state back to the city,[41] but occur *simultaneously* and in *related* ways at *multiple* scales.[42] For EU nationals in the UK the process of negotiating Brexit has brought a heightened degree of uncertainty over the terms of their formal political citizenship, including their rights to reside, work and invite family members to join them in the UK. The tension was heightened by the UK government's deliberate creation of a 'hostile environment' for low-income migrants from outside the EU, as well as the deportation of Caribbean-heritage and other Commonwealth citizens who moved to the UK in the 1950s but did not formally acquire the correct papers when changes to immigration law turned them into immigrants.[43]

The debate over EU nationals revealed major differences between the UK's constituent nations and cities, with arguments made at various points by the Scottish government and the Greater London Assembly for more comprehensive citizenship rights for EU nationals (both current residents and future arrivals) than would be the case in the rest of the UK if some of the more restrictionist national positions were to be adopted. At the time of writing, the status of EU nationals in the UK is subject to ongoing negotiations between the UK government and the twenty-seven other national governments that form the EU.

A relational, multi-scalar approach to examining citizenship struggles resonates, as Stijn Oosterlynck and his colleagues echoing Doreen Massey (see Chapter 1) argue, with a relational understanding of place, and with an emphasis on citizenship *practices*:

> Places themselves are open and fluid, and issues of recognition, redistribution and representation can be made visible and negotiated through the enactment of citizenship relating to that place. Places then become sites for the everyday agonistic negotiation of claims of diverse subjects.[44]

The call of Oosterlynck and his colleague for attention to citizen practices in place allows for the possibility of situated solidarity between recent arrivals and longer-term residents, and between racialised minorities and majority populations.[45] In an environment characterised by neoliberal urbanism and austerity, this implicitly turns local citizenship struggles back to the question of class, resonating with Massey's suggestion that differently displaced people – including people who have *had* to move residence and people who have had no choice but to stay put – might come together in 'common anger'.[46]

For Oosterlynck and his colleagues,

> relationality as a starting point ... opens up perspectives for solidarity among heterogeneous populations who do not have anything in common apart from the place they share. In schools, parks, factories, offices, sports fields or neighbourhood centres, innovative forms of solidarity develop around the joint appropriation and the envisaged common future of a particular place ...[47]

So any attempt to 'reinvent' urban citizenship[48] needs to avoid 'methodological cityism'[49] by considering the relation between more localised, site-specific and neighbourhood practices on the one hand and the scale of the city on the other. At the same time, such efforts should retain an analytical alertness to the connections between both of these and struggles over differential citizenship and the nation-state and supra-national institutions beyond. Such an approach recognises the uneven social geography of the city, and its causes,[50] while also potentially providing a pathway to claiming a 'right to the city' from the ground up for all *residents*.

Residence in the city is at the same time the basis for Harald Bauder's exploration of the possibility of a *legal* urban citizenship, *jus domicilii*,[51] in contrast to the more commonly used grounds for citizenship based on parentage or place of birth. Both Bauder and Oosterlynck and his colleagues – albeit in very different ways – thus offer urban counterweights to the uncontested transplanting of hierarchical forms of citizenship based on differentiated rights of residence, work and access to social benefits that otherwise flow from unequal legal statuses produced by the nation-state. However, Myrte Hoekstra's comparative study of Amsterdam and The Hague shows that the implementation of a residence-based urban citizenship approach by city authorities is not necessarily equally inclusive of all residents. As she points out, for example, recent arrivals in The Hague are required to make an active choice to be citizens while 'native majority members are exempted from such demonstrations of loyalty'.[52]

Returning to Peterborough, the next section explores an example of a local struggle for long-term residents' rights over place that could be seen as a small-scale precursor of the national campaign to 'take back control' in 2016. Noting the marked lack of representation for non-British EU citizens at both the local and national scales, the subsequent section then discusses examples of convivial, everyday citizenship acts in Peterborough, that, while not created as part of an instrumental struggle, nevertheless can be seen as part of a larger set of claims being made from below for a more inclusive place-based citizenship.

Researching citizenship struggles in Peterborough

Citizenship was a central theme of the research I conducted in Peterborough from 2011 to 2017. I was curious to understand concurrent overlapping citizenship struggles, including those over the right to determine the pace and nature of change in the physical environment of central neighbourhoods with long histories of initial settlement by international migrants;[53] over the broader right to co-determine to whom the city belongs both in the present and in the future;[54] and, as elaborated in Chapter 3, over workplace justice in the intensive food and logistics sectors. All these were in turn inter-related with ongoing struggles at other scales.

Although citizenship was not the *sole* focus of the research drawn on in this book, the research grant that first took me to Peterborough *was* part of what might be understood – from its name Citizen Power Peterborough (CPP) – as a would-be urban citizenship promotion scheme.[55] Emanating out of an alliance between the Director of the London-based think-tank the Royal Society of Arts (RSA) and the then leader of Peterborough City Council, the legacy of CPP is disputed. For example, Jill Rutter suggests that during its three-year duration it was the 'largest' initiative 'involved in activities to build better relations between different ethnic groups and between new migrants and longer-settled residents' and that it thereby gave rise to 'social links and friendships ... that ... acted to resolve tensions in the centre of the city'.[56] On the other hand, Joanna Rajkowska and Maggie Humm point to a more discordant aspect of the CPP's record, appearing to hold local actors responsible for the withdrawal of permission for an art installation commissioned by the Royal Society of Arts from Rajkowska, an artist based in London and Nowogród, Poland. Rajkowska faced extremely challenging personal circumstances at the time she was staying in Peterborough. Her experience caused her to conclude that 'there was no point in staying' in the city, 'having started to feel extremely ill-at-ease [there]'.[57] Like her, I am an outsider to the city, but my relationship with Peterborough has been different. I have continued to be pulled back there, inspired by organisations and individuals already engaged in struggles for equality and against racism in an era of economic austerity.[58] This is in spite of my ambivalent relation to the CPP scheme itself.[59]

While I was living part-time in Peterborough for the first nine months of the research, and continuing to be a regular overnight visitor there up to the time of writing, a key question remaining at the forefront of my mind concerned exclusions from urban citizenship. The question was expressed in slightly different terms in the title of the original project: 'Places for All?'[60] The question mark deliberately evoked a pluralistic vision for a right to this city based on residence – not formal political citizenship necessarily, but nevertheless in the spirit of Bauder's *jus domicilii*. The plural 'Places' opened up questions of difference between neighbourhoods in the city, as well as struggles over citizenship at the neighbourhood level.

As this book has already highlighted, Peterborough is a multi-ethnic, multi-faith city. For example, a relatively high proportion of residents self-identified as Muslim in the 2011 Census – 9.4 per cent against a figure for England and Wales of 4.8 per cent. Moreover, the city has long been a destination for people moving there in response to job openings or to seek work unsolicited, whether from abroad or from elsewhere in the UK. Tens of thousands of international migrants moved to Peterborough from the 1950s, including people arriving from Italy, South Asia and the Caribbean.[61] Peterborough City Council welcomed east African Asian and Vietnamese refugees in the 1970s and early 1980s respectively; the city was also designated as a dispersal area for asylum-seekers at the turn of the millennium.[62] Nevertheless, the largest single flow of migrants to the city was made up of mainly white British Londoners and Scots at the time of the building of the city's satellite New Town areas in the 1970s and 1980s.

In 2011 and 2012, as a national programme of austerity was being rolled out and swingeing cuts were made to the budget of Peterborough City Council,[63] we were interested in exploring commonalities between long-term residents and recently arrived people of all ethnic and national backgrounds. At the same time we wanted to understand the nature of everyday citizenship in the city for EU nationals, many of whom had come – from Portugal and from central and eastern European countries – to work in local food factories and warehouses, without necessarily knowing whether they would seek to reside in the UK long-term.

Understanding citizenship struggles in Peterborough in the twenty-first century must include an examination of the claims made by temporary migrant workers, including EU nationals, to rights and representation in the city. As the last chapter showed, it also requires engagement with the changing dynamics of food-sector capitalism. From the UK's vote to leave the EU in June 2016 through the subsequent years of uncertainty during Brexit negotiations, EU citizens did not seek work in these sectors to the same degree. Meanwhile, national business organisations clamoured for the UK government to pay attention to emerging labour shortages.[64]

Pre-Brexit tremors in a Peterborough neighbourhood

'Brexit' was a term yet to be invented in 2011 but my fieldnotes from that year contain an early hint, a murmur, of what its effects might be for EU nationals living and working in Peterborough. On 9 December, the then UK Prime Minister David Cameron had deployed the British veto against EU treaty change to support the ailing Euro and, in the process, had, according to the *Guardian* newspaper, 'appear[ed] to query whether being in the EU would remain in Britain's interests'.[65] I had been discussing the anti-Muslim English Defence League's attempted recruitment of Polish workers at a retail distribution centre in Peterborough with a Polish worker there and her partner. I wrote in my notebook that

> This all came up in the context of a discussion about the Cameron announcement on Europe and the niggling anxiety that they talked about this creating in the minds of accession country nationals who were settling/considering settling. (14 December 2011)

The question of what kind of citizenship nationals of EU member countries other than the UK had in Peterborough persisted in the research from its inception. This anticipated the wider national and EU-level debates following the referendum over the future status of EU citizens living in countries of the EU other than their own.[66]

Yet the most striking element of the city-level citizenship struggles engaged in by non-British EU nationals in Brexit-era Peterborough remained the absence of institutionalised representation. A community organisation worker interviewed for an earlier research project reported a similar absence for recently arrived Kurdish people in the mid-2000s, and the consequences of this for narratives about Kurdish residents and thus for citizenship struggles with which they were engaged.[67]

The importance of representation and its absence is further illustrated by the emergence and demise of a dedicated reception and signposting organisation for newly arrived international migrants in the city: New Link. New Link began operating in 2004, sited on Lincoln Road in the Millfield area, in which much private rental accommodation used by recently arrived migrant workers was located. An oral history interview with a former New Link worker suggested that the original bid, which had won funding of £2.2 million from the Home Office, arose out of long-term residents' reactions both to the arrival of asylum-seekers – following Peterborough's designation as a dispersal area in 1999 – and to the large numbers of non-British EU citizens who came to the city to seek work following EU enlargement in 2004. In 2001–02

> tensions [had been] rising among settled residents and all the people coming in, because nobody knew who they were, so they thought everybody was a 'bogus' asylum seeker ... Then when the migrant workers started to come, it exacerbated it. So what then happened was we ... put in a bid, which went into the Home Office with the Police, Health and City Council.

Yet according to the same narrator the funding

> caused this massive problem with the politicians and the residents, because all this money was being used to help foreign people, and

> that was really the beginning of what became more interesting about it, because it was dealing with that that we learned so much.

Another oral history narrator provided fragments of the story of the citizenship struggle that led first to New Link being relocated in 2010, with a smaller team, to the main council offices at Bayard House in the city centre, and then to lose all its council funding the following year.[68] The narrator was a white British long-term resident of the city who had been part of a campaign to shut down New Link. With hindsight, this local campaign can be seen to have been akin to elements of the national 'take back control' campaign in the 2016 referendum. In spite of the ethno-national diversity of the area, the campaign was led by a residents' association made up mainly of white British people, who portrayed themselves as asserting the rights of so-called 'indigenous' people in this particular area of the city, regardless of their own migration histories. The main message of the campaign was that newly arrived international migrants should not receive dedicated services. The rhetoric used suggested an entitlement associated with both whiteness and British nationality.

> What they did was they brought in, let's just say Romanians, or they brought in Lithuanians or Albanians or whatever, Polish, and they taught them the basics of what to expect *but* rather than integrate with the community, they kept them in their little cubbyholes and all of a sudden … we had a festival of something to do with Lithuania or something to do with Latvia or something of which the indigenous population was invited to come and see how they do things … The indigenous population had to go out of their way to see what these people did and not the other way round. And that, I think, understandably, went up the noses of quite a few people.

Although the board of the residents' association was elected, the franchise extended to people living outside the area who had a connection to it, people who felt entitled to lobby both on issues of direct concern in the area and on the heritage of the city as a whole:

> You have to have a connection with the area to be able to vote but it's fairly loose. And it's done deliberately because that way

> we can actually get people who are really interested in promoting the area involved.
>
> We also voice our opinions on things that are completely out of our area but we feel will have an impact one way or another … Such as [names building] which we believed was going to affect the heritage of the city because they were going to demolish it … we actually put our objections into it because although we didn't live in the area, it was part of our heritage of the city, the same as we would comment on anything to do with heritage in the city. And purely and simply from the fact that we live here, we need to know that we're not just guardians of this area, we're guardians of the whole thing.

Moreover, the campaign was supported by sympathetic councillors, its language resonating with a police officer who had told Kaveri Qureshi and me in an interview that:

> We always consider 'cohesion' … But not the white English majority, who increasingly feel that they're not getting a voice or resources, and are starting to feel like a minority themselves.[69]

Prefiguring the surprise that Leave campaign leaders expressed at the Leave victory in the national referendum five years later, the same campaign member told me of his disbelief at the speed of its success:

> Well things moved rapidly. With the council if it happens in six months that's lightning speed, but we've had real … even quicker than lightning in relation to how we've dealt with that.

Following an earlier interview in the City Council offices I had noted:

> [A council officer] said [the council] were considering the use of compulsory purchase orders, [because] the 'indigenous' population were saying they've lost what there was and would like 'heritage and history reclaimed'. (27 July 2011)

Umut Erel has argued that the relatively high number of new arrivals from other EU countries in the 2000s had the effect of re-intensifying the racialisation of long-settled British Muslims with South Asian heritage in Peterborough.[70] For those advocating for the rights of so-called 'indigenous' ethnic majority white British people in this part of Peterborough, the number of new arrivals, including non-British EU nationals in the city, was *both* a genuine matter of concern *and* a surface issue obscuring a deeper unease with ethnic diversity and particularly the number of residents with Pakistani Muslim heritage, their allegedly disproportionate role in the provision of homes of multiple occupation to the new arrivals, and the effect of this on the property market. Another sign of this was the letter sent in January 2010 from two councillors representing Peterborough's North Ward to the leaders of the three main national political parties. The letter expressed the councillors' concerns both with many years of spending cuts leading to a reduction in services the council was able to provide, and with what they referred to as the 'dramatic' impact on those services of the growing number of non-British EU citizens in Peterborough. Yet, tellingly, and in spite of the fact that one of the councillors, a former leader of the council, had a long record of anti-racist work, having energetically welcomed Ugandan Asian and Vietnamese refugees to the city in the 1970s and 1980s and having been instrumental in adding Urdu to the curriculum of the city's secondary schools, the passage about the impact on a school in North Ward pointed to the low number of primary school reception class pupils who were 'white British'.[71]

This dynamic too prefigured national developments during and after the 2016 referendum campaign when the highlighting of the case for ending the free movement of workers from the EU seemed to be read by some as legitimating a wider antagonism towards people who looked or sounded other than white British, in some cases leading to racist hate crimes against black and minority-ethnic people, especially those visibly appearing as Muslim, regardless of how they had voted in the referendum.[72] As Angharad Closs Stephens put it, '[a]ll sorts of divisions have come into view between those who believe "we have always been here" and those whose right to citizenship is now questioned.'[73] In this vein, the politically motivated elision between the argument against the free movement of (mostly white, Christian-heritage) non-British EU citizens and the play on popular racialised and anti-Muslim tropes became explicit in the language of some Leave campaign leaders.[74] Such messages left no room for ambiguity. Two important examples were first the notorious 'Breaking Point' poster that pictured large numbers of dark-skinned people, mainly male and implicitly Muslim, heading across Europe and, secondly, the campaign's regular reference to the likelihood that Turkey would soon join the EU and that Turkish nationals would have the automatic right to live and work in the UK.

Everyday citizenship acts in a provincial city

The UK-wide exclusion of non-British EU citizens from having a vote in the 2016 referendum compounded the ongoing lack of representation in the city for recently arrived international migrants.[75] In 2015, Peterborough City Council had attempted to increase its engagement with Lithuanian, Latvian, Slovakian and Czech communities, advertising four 'Community Connector' posts. However, these were restructured in 2017 and no longer provided a formal bridge between the council and specific national or linguistic communities. Yet, running alongside, and against, local and national agendas of 'tak[ing] back control' and multiple forms of racism, recent arrivals to the city, their long-term resident allies and anti-racist and pro-migrant organisations have made individual and sometimes collective transformations in the experience of urban citizenship in Peterborough. These have involved acts of citizenship that vary, echoing Jonathan Darling, in terms of the degree to which they are instrumental, as well as in strength and duration.[76]

Some such acts have been based on language or country of origin and include the popular and well-attended Lithuanian and Polish weekend language schools and national or linguistic community-based websites, such as Polonia Peterborough and Nasze Strony. Others have involved everyday acts of convivial citizenship across boundaries of ethno-national identification, practices of non-elite cosmopolitanism that, this book argues, reveal the potential for a more hopeful national politics. These should not be exaggerated or over-celebrated. As shown by Paul Gilroy,[77] conviviality does not operate outside racisms but is, rather, interwoven with them in specific space-time configurations.[78]

Agnieszka Sobieraj ran a film club in Peterborough that met monthly for a free screening and, initially envisaged for bringing Polish people together, attracted people of multiple nationalities. A lone parent, Agnieszka had found that as her daughter entered her teens their taste in films diverged:

> my daughter didn't want to watch movies any more with me because she started to watch these really cheesy romantic ones and I couldn't. Then another thing, I felt that I was involved in Polish community and we had a lot of people who didn't speak English or didn't make any effort to expose themselves to the English community, so I thought film club could be the place where we watch movies with English subtitles, they can learn, maybe some English people or other nationalities will come and slowly we could build that confidence in these people.

Finding suitable venues first in a local pub and then in a community hall, owned by a local general practitioner in Millfield, Agnieszka initially used networks among Polish residents of Peterborough:

> Everything was around Polish school and I was there so I had a lot of connections in Polish school and you know, here is the photographer, here is this person, this person, this person, so everyone came and it was like advertisement by itself. And it worked well … we started to put sofas up there, make it like a proper cinema.

The film club started to develop audiences among multiple nationalities when it moved to the city centre location run by the arts organisation Metal Peterborough. Agnieszka had decided she did not want to compromise on showing films in English, including arthouse films:

> If I will rely on Polish society to have a bigger audience, I will have to change the type of movies I want to show, and I didn't want to compromise. And they didn't follow my thinking, so they didn't come to learn English. Whoever wanted to speak English, they already started to do something about this and I thought, 'I'm not going to influence or force anyone', so I just will do it in English language here.

When I had attended the film club the previous year, the film that was screened was a documentary on supermarkets and food waste based on the story of a couple in Canada who lived entirely on goods that supermarkets were disposing of. I noted that it had been

> brilliantly organized and hosted by Agnieszka Sobieraj [and attracted] an age, gender, and, from people's accents, nationally diverse crowd of twenty-five. The discussion afterwards stuck to the issues, the work of a weekly voluntary lunch put on by another organisation in the city ... There were many expressions of anger at food waste and sharing of practical ideas. People referred to living alone and there was a noticeable presence of childless people in their 20s. One white man, who sounded English, talked of how years working in the meat industry and getting older had made him vegetarian. Agnieszka Sobieraj was helped by French woman Claudette. I was struck by the version of everyday multiculture this event seemed to represent. Unremarkable and unremarked mix of EU nationalities in the post-referendum era. (27 July 2016)

If the mix of nationalities and the preponderance of young adults were striking, so was the general whiteness of the club. At that time Metal Peterborough, where I was Writer-in-Residence, was still evolving networks across the city's racialised and faith-based minorities. Agnieszka told me on another occasion that she had observed more generally that the people at arts events in the city belonged to a 'certain network'.[79] One woman with South Asian heritage, who wore a hijab and identified as Muslim, had remarked on this at a talk I gave at Metal Peterborough earlier the same month. Yet in a city where white EU nationals had arrived in large numbers in the 2000s,[80] the club represented an act of resistance to an excluding and xenophobic public sphere. In an earlier conversation with Agnieszka Sobieraj just weeks after the referendum she told me she had cried a lot when the result was announced. It felt like a personal rejection. Moreover, since the referendum, her daughter, who worked in a customer-facing role in the city-centre branch of a fast-food chain, had experienced drunk customers telling her to go back to her 'own country' just on the basis of her name. The film club was clearly a source of satisfaction to Agnieszka, including the social life it had engendered for others.

> Agnieszka had started a multinational film club – about thirty people and growing. 24 went on a trip to Poland. She felt like a 'Mum' towards them. She said there are Latvians, Lithuanians, English and other people. Some have become couples. Some work in factories. They go to a local bar afterwards. She likes its artiness. (Author's fieldnotes, 27 July 2016)

Agnieszka later told me more about the social side of the film club and the work she put into organising the trips, although she played down the effort this entailed.

> it's not only film and discussion but after the film, going for a pint of beer. And whoever is shy or don't want to talk, then is able to talk, and we've met the group I think it was, sometimes it was like 30 people or one time we went 24 of us for hiking trip, usually we go for hiking trips, so it's nice because you just do one click on Facebook, who is going where, here and there, and they say, 'Yes' ... We go usually bank holiday weekends so it's a bit longer. Or sometimes just one day, Peak District. Saturday in the morning, who is going, few cars, and off we go and we come back in the evening ... I don't know if people think, 'OK, she's organising something so she's good at it and it's easier all the time instead of finding accommodation, collecting money and, you know, finding cars, organising everything so everything gets done', but I think I like it, I like to organise things.

Acts of citizenship that involved non-elite cosmopolitan practices also included *workplace* actions by multi-ethnic, multi-national workforces, as I argued in the last chapter. We heard there how Azwer Sabir and other current and former food factory and warehouse workers I interviewed in 2017 found work in these sectors to have become increasingly intense over time with raised targets, fines and even dismissals for underperformance. Yet, alongside racialised hierarchies in such workplaces, the organisation of work could lead workers to develop connections across ethno-national difference, providing increased potential for collective refusal to comply with a particular supervisor or target.

Such events, and the narration of them, can be seen as acts of citizenship, as demands to have a narrative, to build a life and to be heard. They resonated with the earliest interviews Kaveri Qureshi and I carried out in Peterborough in 2011, during which other workers criticised supervisory regimes that prevented more than minimal interaction at work. One placed explicit value on the ethno-national diversity of food factory and warehouse workforces around Peterborough.[81] Randy, who moved to England from Bangladesh as a child in 1982, worked in a chocolate factory in Corby before moving to Peterborough. His face 'lit up with pleasure' when he told Kaveri about the experience of working among a mix of nationalities and ethnicities there,[82] contrasting it with his earlier work in a restaurant:

> Polish people, Bengali people, English people, Jamaicans, different people. And you get to make a conversation with them, 'How's life back home?' Different countries; different languages; different religion and things ... because as you're working, you can talk whereas in the restaurant, you are taking orders, 'Yes, sir, yes sir ...' and you take it in the kitchen, come back in, you're not talking to no one.[83]

Towards the end of the same year, I had been invited to a party in the community centre on the ground floor of a block of social housing. The party itself can be understood as an act of convivial urban citizenship. I wrote about it in my fieldnotes the next day:

> I had been invited some weeks ago by Maria [a Polish research participant]. It was a party for St Andrews Day – that precedes [the Christian season of] Advent [and was held in the community room at her block of flats].
>
> There were about twenty people there in all – we were greeted on arrival by young Polish women in their twenties with three- and four-year-old children. Two were married to Egyptian husbands – neither of whom were there. There was a fair amount of chaos – we were not offered drinks – people were helping

themselves. The Buddhist son of Patrycja, another Polish research participant, was working his way through blue WKD vodka. Sarah's daughter Jo was there with her partner Enrique who is Argentinian. Jo has a job as a teaching assistant. She has travelled round India and Latin America – met Enrique in Argentina. Jo's sister also turned up later.

I pledged to interview Sarah again and also Sean [both of whom are white British]. Sean is a sixty year-old lorry driver who has lived in Peterborough all his life. He's married to Deirdre, from Sunderland. He's travelled a lot on his lorry and has no romance about Peterborough but lots to tell about his younger days – remembered delivering telegrams in the city beginning 1966 – in fact to the area where the flats we were partying in were built when it was just streets – a rough area then according to both Sarah and Sean. Deirdre, Sean's partner, is a care worker.

We were sat down for the meal around a large table. I had already been given a sweet pastry, and now it was time for borscht (beetroot) soup with meat dumplings, accompanied by empañadas made by Jo with Quorn and herbs. There was chicken stew to follow with spices and tomatoes – I think Patrycja had cooked that. Then there was delicious Polish salad – lots of mayonnaise and pickle in it. A chocolate cake cut into squares in front of us and lovely Polish bread. Patrycja and Maria served the food. Really nice atmosphere – there was an elderly couple there too, at least one of whom was English.

I spoke with a Polish woman, Beata who was married to an Egyptian, with whom she'd had a son, now 27 months old. Beata, who is very tall with long blond hair; has become Muslim. She said she believes women who are Muslim should wear hijab but that her family are not ready for it. She's been to visit his family in Egypt and had a good time. She said she's learned Arabic cooking and that she likes cooking. She works in the same factory as Maria. Her husband is working through an agency – tonight he was driving a fork-lift truck in a warehouse. Beata's mother is currently living with them and looking after their son. Beata speaks to her son in Polish and to her husband in Arabic. They are waiting for English until he goes to school.

> It was a lovely evening – I also had a conversation with Patrycja's son. He told me about the macho boys' culture on the line at the Japanese tie-up with Perkins Engineering where he works … The workers survey each other for mistakes that they can report on each other – the machismo is over turning out the perfect product. He claims to have found efficiencies in every part of the manufacturing process – to handle him, he claims, the company has given him a training role across all the parts of the process. He spent 3–4 weeks in Thailand in the summer including 2 weeks in his girlfriend's village.

My notes following the party concur with the argument of Oosterlynck and his colleagues for the potential for solidarity rooted in common experiences of class and place across differences in ethnicity, national identity, immigration status and length of residence.[84] As I wrote at the time, 'This was bottom up integration in practice. Ordinary everyday working class conviviality across generations. Very gendered, with Patrycja shouldering much of the cooking and Maria having to clear up quite a bit.'

Conclusion

Taken together, these examples illustrate the inter-relation between citizenship practices and struggles at a variety of sites and scales, including workplaces, neighbourhoods and the city as a whole. They also suggest that some localised citizenship acts can be seen as an everyday cosmopolitan 'politics of presence',[85] which is inclusive of people whose presence is temporary and may be formally resident elsewhere. Most can be seen as 'alternative accounts, feelings and lived complexities of place' that 'can remain unrecognized, not valued or simply erased by more powerful interests'.[86] However, the chapter has also drawn on stories of people who saw themselves as 'guardians of the city' and thus illustrated how, in historically and geographically situated ways, convivial acts are located alongside and in relation to practices and discourses that promote division and a lack of mutual regard at multiple scales.

I want to emphasise that revisiting the first years of my research in Peterborough in 2011 and 2012 serves as a reminder that the push-back against both international migrants and ethnic minorities, particularly Muslims, that formed part of the Leave campaign in the 2016 referendum, did not come out of the blue. On the contrary, it was prefigured at different scales especially throughout the whole period of austerity, declining wages and deteriorating job quality that followed the 2007–08 financial crisis. Yet the referendum campaign and its result *did* significantly change the context for citizenship struggles by EU nationals in the UK.

Such struggles have been researched in detail in Scotland,[87] and are also borne out by my more recent period of fieldwork in Peterborough in 2016 and 2017. Individual post-referendum experiences are neither uniform nor constant, but, while in the Brexit era much national attention has been paid to the ethnicised notion of working-class life that prioritises the experience of white British nationals within that class, it is important to pay attention to the widespread evidence of hurt, of having been kicked in the solar plexus, that the Leave vote represented for many EU nationals. In Peterborough, where many non-British EU citizens work and have made their home and yet have no formal or informal representation in city decision-making, struggles over urban citizenship continued up to the time of writing. The more uncertain and hostile the national environment felt, the more people who had lived and worked in the city for many years considered a return to their country of origin. Yet many remained and continued to be a numerically significant part of the city's multi-ethnic, multi-nationality, multi-lingual workforce. In the next chapter I turn to non-elite cultural production and what it reveals about the relation of a place to its multiple elsewheres. For my lens, I draw on the example of four very different books published in 2016 – the year of the referendum – and written by (or about) Peterborough residents.

Notes

1 'Ganger' is another word for 'gangmaster'. See Chapter 3.
2 In all our encounters Charles would pull my leg about my occupation as a university lecturer and the secure income he associated with it.
3 Liz Hingley was part of the 'Places for All?' team. Her work with the project, including her photograph of Charles Wood, can be found at www.placesforall.co.uk/photos/. Liz's wider work can be viewed at www.lizhingley.com (both accessed February 2019).

4 'Fair boy' was a demeaning, pejorative term when used to refer to someone with Travelling Showman heritage by someone who did not share that heritage. However, Charles regularly appropriated it and the related term 'Fair people' for his own narrative.

5 Les Back, 'Researching community and its moral projects', *Twenty-first century society*, 4:2 (2009), 207.

6 Abby Day, *Believing in Belonging: Belief and Social Identity in the Modern World* (Oxford: Oxford University Press, 2011).

7 Ben Rogaly and Kaveri Qureshi, 'Diversity, urban space and the right to the provincial city', *Identities: global studies in culture and power*, 20:4 (2013), 423–437.

8 It is possible that this category of 'English' is used here by Charles to refer to long-settled 'white' people with multiple national, ethnic and religious heritage, including people with Italian heritage. I did not seek clarification on this.

9 Interest rates in the UK fluctuated between a low of 7 per cent and a high of 15 per cent per year between 1988 and 1992. See 'Fact check: how high were interest rates in the eighties?', *Channel 4 News*, 22 September 2008, available online at: www.channel4.com/news/articles/politics/domestic_politics/factcheck+how+high+were+interest+rates+in+the+eighties/2470357.html (accessed March 2019).

10 Daniel James, *Doña Maria's Story: Life History, Memory and Political Identity* (Durham, NC: Duke University Press, 2000), pp. 165–166.

11 The rest of the chapter is a revised version of Ben Rogaly, 'Rescaling citizenship struggles in provincial urban England', in Jonathan Darling and Harald Bauder (eds), *Sanctuary Cities and Urban Struggles: Rescaling Migration, Citizenship and Rights* (Manchester: Manchester University Press, 2019), pp. 217–241.

12 Hannah Jones, *Negotiating Cohesion, Inequality and Change: Uncomfortable Positions in Local Government* (Bristol: Policy Press, 2013).

13 Jon Burnett, *The New Geographies of Racism: Peterborough* (London: Institute of Race Relations, 2012), p. 4; Ben Rogaly, '"Don't show the play at the football ground, nobody will come": the micro-sociality of co-produced research in an English provincial city', *Sociological review*, 64:4 (2016), 663.

14 'Other White' was the second largest self-identification category in the 2011 Census (after 'White British'), and largely made up of non-UK EU nationals. See Office for National Statistics, *2011 Census Analysis: Ethnicity and the Labour Market, England and Wales* (13 November 2014), available online at: www.ons.gov.uk/peoplepopulationandcommunity/culturalidentity/ethnicity/articles/ethnicityandthelabourmarket2011censusenglandandwales/2014-11-13 (accessed March 2018).

15 BBC Radio 4, *Today* programme, 2 April 2015. Nigel Farage returned to Peterborough in May and June 2019 spearheading the unsuccessful campaign of his newly formed Brexit Party in a closely fought parliamentary byelection in which bookmakers had made the Brexit Party odds-on favourites to win.

16 Marco Antonsich and Tatiana Matejskova, 'Conclusion: nation and diversity – a false conundrum', in Tatiana Matejskova and Marco Antonsich (eds), *Governing through Diversity: Migration Societies in Post-Multiculturalist Times* (Basingstoke: Palgrave Macmillan, 2015), pp. 201–209; Jonathan Darling, 'Acts, ambiguities and the labour of contesting citizenship', *Citizenship studies*, 21:6 (2017), 727–736; Myrte Hoekstra, 'Diverse cities and good citizenship: how local governments in the Netherlands recast national integration discourses', *Ethnic and racial studies*, 38:10 (2015), 1798–1814; Graham Hudson, 'City of hope, city of fear: sanctuary and security in Toronto, Canada', in Jonathan Darling and Harald Bauder (eds), *Sanctuary Cities and Urban Struggles: Rescaling Migration, Citizenship and Rights* (Manchester: Manchester University Press, 2019), pp. 77–104; Anne Visser and Sheryl-Ann Simpson, 'Understanding local government's engagement in immigrant policy making in the US', in Jonathan Darling and Harald Bauder (eds), *Sanctuary Cities and Urban Struggles: Rescaling Migration, Citizenship and Rights* (Manchester: Manchester University Press, 2019), pp. 165–190.

17 Satnam Virdee and Brendan McGeever, 'Racism, crisis, Brexit', *Ethnic and racial studies*, 41:10 (2017), 1802–1819. The effect of anti-Muslim racism on the educational prospects of young people is incisively discussed by Alison Davies in 'Tradition and transformation: Pakistani-heritage young people explore the influences upon their educational progress', *Race Ethnicity and Education*, available online (early view), DOI: 10.1080/13613324.2017.1395320 (accessed June 2019).

18 Ambalavaner Sivanandan, 'Poverty is the new black', *Race and class*, 43:2 (2001), 2; Ben Gidley, 'Sivanandan's pessimistic hope in a degraded age', *The Sociological Review Blog*, 10 February 2018, available online at: www.thesociologicalreview.com/blog/sivanandan-s-pessimistic-hope-in-a-degraded-age.html (accessed April 2019).

19 Les Back, *New Ethnicities and Urban Culture: Racisms and Multiculture in Young Lives* (London: University College London Press, 1996). In a study conducted in 2005–06 in Peterborough, Umut Erel similarly identified 'both convivial and more conflictual modes of everyday life' and connected these to 'new migrations' ('Complex belongings: racialization and migration in a small English city', *Ethnic and racial studies*, 34:12 (2011), 2053). For definitions of conviviality and everyday multiculture see, respectively, Amanda Wise and Greg

Noble, 'Convivialities: an orientation', *Journal of intercultural studies*, 37:5 (2016), 423–431; and Ben Gidley, 'Landscapes of belonging, portraits of life: researching everyday multiculture in an inner city estate', *Identities: global studies in culture and power*, 20:4 (2013), 361–376.

20 Visser and Simpson, 'Understanding local government's engagement'.

21 Bridget Anderson and Vanessa Hughes, 'Introduction', in Bridget Anderson and Vanessa Hughes (eds), *Citizenship and its Others* (Basingstoke: Palgrave Macmillan, 2015), p. 1; Irene Bloemraad and Alicia Sheares, 'Understanding membership in a world of global migration: (how) does citizenship matter?', *International migration review*, 51:4 (2017) 854.

22 These dimensions include both formalised political status, and informal practices that are part of everyday 'social interactions and identity negotiations that become a micro-politics of daily life' (Bloemraad and Sheares, 'Understanding membership in a world of global migration', p. 854).

23 Danielle Allen, 'Foreword', in Iris Young, *Justice and the Politics of Difference* (second edition, Princeton: Princeton University Press, 2011), p. ix; Janika Kuge, 'Uncovering sanctuary cities: between policy, practice and politics', in Jonathan Darling and Harald Bauder (eds), *Sanctuary Cities and Urban Struggles: Rescaling Migration, Citizenship and Rights* (Manchester: Manchester University Press, 2019), pp. 50–76.

24 Ian Fitzgerald and Rafal Smoczynski, 'Anti-Polish migrant moral panic in the UK: rethinking employment insecurities and moral regulation', *Czech sociological review*, 51:3 (2015), 339–361.

25 Ibid., pp. 340–341.

26 Ibid., p. 355, emphasis added.

27 Etienne Balibar, 'The "impossible" community of the citizens: past and present problems', *Environment and planning D: Society and space*, 30 (2012), pp. 438 and 441, author's emphasis.

28 Lynn Staeheli *et al.*, 'Dreaming the ordinary: daily life and the complex geographies of citizenship', *Progress in human geography*, 36:5 (2012), 628.

29 Darling, 'Acts, ambiguities and the labour of contesting citizenship', p. 728.

30 Patricia Ehrkamp, 'Geographies of migration II: the racial-spatial politics of immigration', *Progress in human geography*, 43:2 (2019), 363–375.

31 Darling, 'Acts, ambiguities and the labour of contesting citizenship', pp. 730–731; see also Jen Bagelman, 'Sanctuary artivism: expanding geopolitical imaginations', in Jonathan Darling and Harald Bauder (eds), *Sanctuary Cities and Urban Struggles: Rescaling Migration, Citizenship and Rights* (Manchester: Manchester University Press, 2019), pp. 131–164.

32 Staeheli *et al.*, 'Dreaming the ordinary', p. 640.
33 Darling, 'Acts, ambiguities and the labour of contesting citizenship', p. 734, author's emphasis.
34 Tim Edensor, 'Reconsidering national temporalities: institutional times, everyday routines, serial spaces and synchronicities', *European journal of social theory*, 9:4 (2006), p. 533, emphasis added; see also Visser and Simpson, 'Understanding local government's engagement'.
35 Luis Guarnizo, 'The fluid, multi-scalar, and contradictory construction of citizenship', in Michael Smith and Michael McQuarrie (eds), *Remaking Urban Citizenship: Organizations, Institutions and the Right to the City* (New Brunswick and London: Transaction, 2012), p. 17.
36 See Ann Stoler, 'On degrees of imperial sovereignty', *Public culture*, 18:1 (2006), 125–146; Ben Rogaly and Becky Taylor, '"They called them communists then ... what d'you call 'em now? Insurgents?" Narratives of British military expatriates in the context of the new imperialism', *Journal of ethnic and migration studies*, 36:8 (2010), 1335–1351; Ash Amin, *Land of Strangers* (Cambridge: Polity Press, 2012), p. 92; Kathryne Mitchell, 'Difference', in Roger Lee *et al.* (eds), *The SAGE Handbook of Human Geography* (London: Sage, 2014), pp. 69–93. See Benedict Anderson, *Imagined Communities: Reflections on the Origins and Spread of Nationalism* (1983; revised edition, London: Verso, 2016), chapter 10 for an explanation of the role of censuses, maps and museums in producing categories for Dutch colonial rule in south-east Asia as well as for its undoing.
37 Darling, 'Acts, ambiguities and the labour of contesting citizenship', p. 731.
38 Max Andrucki and Jen Dickinson, 'Rethinking centers and margins in geography: bodies, life course, and the performance of transnational space', *Annals of the Association of American Geographers*, 105:1 (2015), 203–218.
39 Eleonora Canepari and Elisabetta Rosa, 'A quiet claim to citizenship: mobility, urban spaces and city practices over time', *Citizenship studies*, 21:6 (2017), 658.
40 Guarnizo, 'The fluid, multi-scalar, and contradictory construction of citizenship'.
41 Luis Guarnizo insisted on taking the citizenship concept back to its roots in cities of the ancient world.
42 See also Rhys Jones and Carwyn Fowler, 'Placing and scaling the nation', *Environment and planning D: Society and space*, 25 (2007), 332–354; Visser and Simpson, 'Understanding local government's engagement'.
43 See Gurminder Bhambra, 'Viewpoint: Brexit, class and British "national" identity', *Discover Society*, 5 July 2016, available online at: https://

discoversociety.org/2016/07/05/viewpoint-brexit-class-and-british-national-identity/ (accessed February 2019).

44 Stijn Oosterlynck *et al.*, 'Putting flesh on the bone: looking for solidarity in diversity, here and now', *Ethnic and racial studies*, 39:5 (2016), 775.

45 See also Kye Askins, 'Emotional citizenry: everyday geographies of befriending, belonging and intercultural encounter', *Transactions of the Institute of British Geographers*, 41:4 (2016), 515–527; Les Back and Shamser Sinha *et al.*, *Migrant City* (London: Routledge, 2018).

46 Doreen Massey, *Landscape/Space/Politics: An Essay* (2011) available online at: http://thefutureoflandscape.wordpress.com/landscapespace-politics-an-essay/ (accessed January 2019).

47 Oosterlynck *et al.*, 'Putting flesh on the bone', p. 775.

48 Rainer Bauböck, 'Reinventing urban citizenship', *Citizenship studies*, 7:2 (2003), 139–160.

49 Ferrucio Pastore and Irene Ponzo (eds), *Inter-Group Relations and Migrant Integration in European Cities: Changing Neighbourhoods* (London: Springer Open, 2016).

50 David Harvey, *Social Justice and the City* (1973; revised edition, Atlanta: University of Georgia Press, 2009).

51 Harald Bauder, 'Domicile citizenship, human mobility and territoriality', *Progress in human geography*, 38:1 (2014), 91–106.

52 Hoekstra, 'Diverse cities and good citizenship', p. 1811.

53 Including many who arrived in the UK as Commonwealth Citizens and only later became 'migrants'. See Gurminder Bhambra, 'Brexit, the Commonwealth, and exclusionary citizenship', *Open Democracy*, 8 December 2016, available online at: www.opendemocracy.net/gurminder-k-bhambra/brexit-commonwealth-and-exclusionary-citizenship (accessed April 2019).

54 Massey, *Landscape/Space/Politics*; Rogaly and Qureshi, 'Diversity, urban space and the right to the provincial city'.

55 The 'Places for All?' project is described in Chapter 1. See www.placesforall.co.uk (accessed March 2019).

56 Jill Rutter, *Moving Up and Getting On: Migration, Integration and Social Cohesion in the UK* (Bristol: Policy Press, 2015), p. 236.

57 Joanna Rajkowska and Maggie Humm, '*The Peterborough Child* and Joanna Rajkowska: themes, influences, art', in Debra Shaw and Maggie Humm (eds), *Radical Space: Exploring Politics and Practice* (London: Rowman and Littlefield, 2016), pp. 12–13.

58 Rogaly, '"Don't show the play at the football ground, nobody will come"', pp. 668–669.

59 Ibid., pp. 664–666.

60 See Chapter 1.

61 Julie Cameron, 'Postwar economic integration: how did a brick shortage change Peterborough?' (MA dissertation, Birbeck College, University of London, 2012).
62 Burnett, *The New Geographies of Racism*, p. 7. The policy of dispersal was implemented as part of the UK's Immigration and Asylum Act, 1999.
63 Rutter, *Moving Up and Getting On.*
64 See Lisa O'Carroll, 'Farmers tell Gove: lack of migrant workers now "mission critical"', *The Guardian*, 20 February 2018, available online at: www.theguardian.com/politics/2018/feb/20/farmers-tell-gove-lack-of-migrant-workers-now-mission-critical (accessed February 2018), and Alan Travis, 'Number of eastern EU nationals in UK workforce falls by 5%', *The Guardian*, 21 February 2018, available online at: www.theguardian.com/uk-news/2018/feb/21/number-of-western-eu-nationals-in-uk-workforce-falls-by-5-percent (accessed February 2018).
65 Ian Traynor *et al.*, 'David Cameron blocks EU treaty with veto, casting Britain adrift in Europe', *The Guardian*, available online at: https://www.theguardian.com/world/2011/dec/09/david-cameron-blocks-eu-treaty (accessed June 2019).
66 Alexandra Bulat, 'The rights of non-UK EU citizens living here are not a "done deal". This is why', *LSE Brexit Blog*, 27 February 2018, available online at: https://blogs.lse.ac.uk/brexit/2018/02/27/the-rights-of-non-uk-eu-citizens-living-here-are-not-a-done-deal-this-is-why/ (accessed April 2019).
67 Hannah Jones, 'Uncomfortable positions: how policy practitioners negotiate difficult subjects' (PhD dissertation, Goldsmiths, University of London, 2011), pp. 227–228.
68 The interview was recorded across a number of separate meetings in the summer of 2011.
69 Quoted in Rogaly and Qureshi, 'Diversity, urban space and the right to the provincial city', p. 427.
70 Erel, 'Complex belongings'.
71 Letter published by the *Daily Mail*, 10 April 2010, available online at: www.dailymail.co.uk/news/article-1264930/Peterborough-struggling-immigration-toll.html (accessed 1 March 2018). Cited by Burnett, *The New Geographies of Racism.*
72 Jon Burnett, *Racial Violence and the Brexit State* (London: Institute of Race Relations, 2016).
73 Angharad Closs Stephens, 'National atmospheres and the "Brexit" revolt', *Society and Space Blog*, 23 August 2016, available online at: https://societyandspace.org/2016/08/23/national-atmospheres-and-the-brexit-revolt-angharad-closs-stephens/ (accessed March 2019).
74 Virdee and McGeever, 'Racism, crisis, Brexit'.

75 Who has the right to vote in UK referenda is legislated for separately before each referendum. Non-UK EU citizens have the right to vote in local government elections in the UK but not in parliamentary elections.
76 Darling, 'Acts, ambiguities and the labour of contesting citizenship'.
77 Paul Gilroy, *After Empire: Multiculture or Postcolonial Melancholia* (London: Routledge, 2004).
78 See also Anoop Nayak, 'Purging the nation: race, conviviality and embodied encounters in the lives of British Bangladeshi Muslim young women', *Transactions of the Institute of British Geographers*, 42:2 (2017), 289–302.
79 See Rogaly, '"Don't show the play at the football ground, nobody will come"'.
80 New arrivals also included Portuguese nationals racialised as black and Czech and Slovakian nationals with Roma heritage.
81 Ben Rogaly and Kaveri Qureshi, '"That's where my perception of it all was shattered": oral histories and moral geographies of food sector workers in an English city region', *Geoforum*, 78 (2017), 189–198.
82 Ibid., p. 195.
83 Quoted in ibid.
84 Oosterlynck *et al.*, 'Putting flesh on the bone'.
85 Jonathan Darling, 'Sanctuary, presence and the politics of urbanism', in Jonathan Darling and Harald Bauder (eds), *Sanctuary Cities and Urban Struggles: Rescaling Migration, Citizenship and Rights* (Manchester: Manchester University Press, 2019), pp. 242–264.
86 Emma Jackson and Hannah Jones, 'Conclusion: creeping familiarity and cosmopolitan futures', in Hannah Jones and Emma Jackson (eds), *Stories of Cosmopolitan Belonging: Emotion and Location* (London: Earthscan, 2014), p. 198.
87 See Kate Botterill, 'Rethinking communities relationally: Polish communities in Scotland before and after Brexit', *Transactions of the Institute of British Geographers*, 43:4 (2018), 540–554.

5

'And then we just let our creativity take over': cultural production in a provincial city

Introduction

> it's funny because it was writing to [my old friend] that I realised the experience that changed my mindset about multiculturalism. I went to Cuba when I was twenty-two and I'd not felt relaxed with black, brown people, whatever ... Because they always seemed to have a chip on their shoulder, and it became my chip on my shoulder I suppose. But I went there and I was with people who were just totally relaxed, whoever they were, whatever colour they were and when I came back I've never been any different.

By then in her mid-fifties, Caroline Nightingale, a white British woman, lived in Millfield (immediately to the north of the Gladstone area where Ron Singh grew up), where other white British Peterborough residents were struggling to 'take back control' – as described in the last chapter. She was talking to me in May 2011, in the comfort of her book-lined home of over a quarter of a century. Having briefly rented in the area when she moved to Peterborough from the north of England in her early twenties, Caroline linked her choice to move back to Millfield to buy a house a few years later to her positive views about its friendliness and its multiculture:

> I wanted to move back to this area, so I was looking at properties, just walked in here and just knew it was the place ... I've always

> found it a very, very friendly area where neighbours are neighbours and look out for each other ... It's always been changing and changing and changing. I mean it's changed vastly in the last few years and yet again. But I can imagine that as an ongoing process, because these are small houses, and they tend to be where people come when they first come to the city and then they move out. But I like staying here ... I don't have to travel any more because [the whole world] comes here. [chuckles]

Caroline and the old friend she had recently got back in touch with were at school together in Kent in the 1970s.[1] As Caroline put it herself, partly out of necessity 'after thirty-five years of not knowing', she had been 'putting down, obviously editing it vastly ... a lot of [her] life story'. She was thus already engaged in framing a narrative of her own life, and, along the way, of her part in local and national processes of change. As we shall hear in the version of her story summarised here, Caroline had in common with many other oral history narrators experience of employment in a food factory. Yet, as was also the case with others, she did not want this experience alone to define who she was, and I begin this chapter with her story in part because it illustrates 'humanity's ability to make its own world, to become the subject and not merely the victim of history'.[2] Just as importantly, Caroline's story evokes the meanings to her of places within Peterborough and beyond at different points in time, and illustrates the importance of Peterborough's multiple elsewheres – particularly its residents' connections to other places through their own residential moves – for an understanding of ongoing processes of change in the city.

Writings such as Caroline's have been called 'vernacular creativities' to distinguish them from professionally produced creative outputs. The cultural geographer Harriet Hawkins writes that

> [a]s a process that is carried out by someone, sometimes alone, sometimes as part of a collective, creativity plays a key role in shaping individual and collective lives and identities ... shaping our subjectivities.[3]

Attention to vernacular creativities can also push back against the disdain for working-class cultures and provincial places emanating from the commercialised worlds of art and literature.[4] It is because of such disdain that there has been little attention in metropolitan circles to the everyday cultural production in (and of) a multi-ethnic, working-class city like Peterborough.

This chapter, in contrast, focuses directly on cultural production in Peterborough through a discussion of four mainly non-fiction books based on the stories of residents of the city, all of which were published in 2016, the year of the referendum on the UK's continuing membership of the EU. While others have correctly emphasised the disproportionate influence of global cities and other urban centres of power on the cultural (as well as economic and political) worlds of smaller, more provincial places,[5] in this chapter I add to that story by illustrating the possibility of simultaneous flows in both directions, however unequal such flows may be.

The books, themselves evocative of – in some ways produced out of – Peterborough residents' connections to multiple places elsewhere, can also be seen as among the city's offerings to the cultural and political life of other places. Before introducing the four Peterborough books, let's return to Caroline herself. Another medium for Caroline's story-telling – a story of her own life interwoven with stories about the places and times she was living through – was her involvement in a one-off organised attempt to engage a larger group of people, who lived and/or worked in Peterborough, with deeply felt stories of place.[6] As a leader for one session of the 'Take Me To' project in the winter of 2010–11, Caroline had chosen to take participants to her local laundrette, where, over the years, she had 'spent many, many hours ...':

> When people come into an area, they don't have washing machines, so they go to the laundrette ... And it was there I became aware of different people coming in and I didn't know where they were from, and I couldn't place them and actually had two living next [door to me] ... They're from Kosovo. And I told a story about ... I had two lads living next to me and they were lovely and they were always chirpy and happy and that. And then one day I heard one of them go out and the other one just put on some Kosovan music, just put it on ever so loud and he just sobbed his heart out. And it's so devastating because I did nothing except bear witness to his pain and then of course he has to put his

front on. But it brought to me what people go through leaving their home countries.

In communicating another individual's painful expression of loss and absence to a wider group of 'Take Me To' participants, Caroline was contributing to building a sense of common humanity across ethnicity, nationality and class. The anecdote also suggests a way in which certain spaces in Peterborough, perhaps sometimes the city as a whole, could reflect, or even produce, a cosmopolitan disposition. While narrating her life story to me, Caroline also spoke about her work at a potato-processing factory in the Fens throughout the 1980s. Towards the end of 2012 this became evident again when she attended a tea party that a group of us had organised for oral history narrators and – to their mutual surprise – met a Pakistani-heritage man who was a former colleague of hers from that time. I invited both of them to narrate their stories on film as part of the film *Workers* (mentioned at the start of Chapter 3). Both, along with fifteen others, came to a dinner that the arts organisation Metal Peterborough put on for potential film narrators in May 2017. All, including Caroline, were curious to explore how we might work together to interrogate certain myths about people who were employed in working-class occupations, and in particular to highlight the false disjuncture made in much public commentary between working-class life and the places associated with it on the one hand, and art and creativity on the other.

As the feminist oral historians Karen Olson and Linda Stopes put it:

> as a person narrates a life story, and the account wends its way through the accumulated details of a life, social categories are exploded: the subject becomes an actor in simultaneous, multiple roles that do not conform to easy generalizations ...[7]

Caroline's narration of her own story in those interviews with me in 2011 had planted a seed which is likely to have contributed to the emergence of the idea to look behind easy generalisations regarding factory workers (something I touched on, albeit obliquely, in Chapter 2). The ten years during which she ended up working at the potato-processing factory had caused Caroline to reach the conclusion that people doing factory work did not conform to a social category:

> it made me realise, people who do factory work are not a certain sort of people, they're a mixture of people who've come … I'm still friends with one person that I worked with there who trained as an architect but he ended up being there, and going down a different route since then. And as I say, a lot of them were Ugandan Asians who'd been turfed out of Uganda and they were making their own, building up their lives again. Work-wise I was lucky because I was good at my job and I was conscientious, but I was quick. And in between doing my samples vigorously, not cheating or anything like that, because that's not the sort of person I am, I read my way through an incredible amount of English Literature that I would never have time to read again. [chuckles]

Just as Caroline drew attention to the way she had devoted a considerable amount of time to reading fiction while at work – something she admitted she was enabled to do by her particular role and which would have been impossible in the more intensive and often harsh working conditions of more recent times (on which see Chapter 3) – she was equally determined to share the story of her political activism from the same years.

When I left her house after my interview with her in 2011, Caroline had confirmed that she 'certainly' wanted there to be a follow-up, and on my return four weeks later she had prepared a list of topics she wanted to be sure to cover. In this way she was taking at least partial control of the narrative of her life. She told me she had thought a lot about the earlier interview and in particular how focusing on the time she worked at the potato-processing factory had caused her to think more about her part in the broader political struggles of the 1980s. Caroline's desire to connect her activism of that time with the story of her working life and the national historic context of the period reflects another strength of oral history according to Alessandro Portelli:

> Oral sources, especially from nonhegemonic groups … become unique and necessary because of their *plot* – the way in which

> the story materials are arranged by narrators in order to tell their story. The organisation of the narrative reveals a great deal of the speaker's relationship to their history.[8]

Caroline framed her working life in terms of decades, which made sense to her as these corresponded to periods of continuity in terms of her occupation.

> I was at the chip factory for ten years, but I thought actually *that* ten years was full of other things as well … and I actually went and looked through small photographs …

She regarded the 1980s as a time when 'it was all very political'. It was a period that coincided with her being on the Executive Committee of Peterborough Trades Union Council. In addition to going on workers' low-cost tours to Russia, Cuba and Algeria, Caroline also took part in the Anti-Apartheid Movement and in protests against the widely detested poll tax of the then British Prime Minister, Margaret Thatcher..[9] She was particularly keen to tell me about the creative forms of protest she had been involved in.

> I think one of the best [anti-apartheid] demonstrations we did locally was a friend of mine took his steel pan, because we were picketing the Shell garages, and it was about three of us, and he was playing his steel pan. So it's not aggressive, but you're making a point and you've got leaflets to give people if you … Because I don't like aggressive protests, I think there's cleverer ways of doing it, which is the one thing … There was one amazing thing I was involved in [chuckles] in a very small way which came through the Trades Council. Because there was a very … this being the eighties, because it's related to the poll tax. And there was a wonderful guy came on the Trades Council … and he was very active, he was a brilliant song-writer … And he had the idea … [addressing herself to me as a newcomer to Peterborough] Have you seen the Conservative Club? You know where the library is, you carry on down that road and it's at the end, but it's right next to a very, very busy junction at the traffic

> lights. Opposite the Job Centre. And he made a sign that just said 'beep your horn if you're against the poll tax', and about three of us went there, tied it to the railings and just stood there. Well, we were only there for about two hours and people just came and … [laughter] But it was such a small thing that he thought oh … but it was just so effective, because you were giving the information direct to the people that needed to know.

Caroline's recollections of her involvement in 'small' political acts stretched forward from the 1980s to her re-encountering of Peterborough Trades Union Council at a protest it had organised against an English Defence League rally in the city in 2010.[10] There once again was the 'wonderful old banner, well it was a new banner and it had all the modern industries on it'.

As much as the film I made with Jay Gearing, *Workers*, was intended to engage with, and value, the creativity of people who worked in food factories and warehouses, I was equally hopeful that, as part of this, it would portray creative acts of resistance, whether at the workplace or beyond. Caroline's chosen emphasis on her activism in the narration of her life story six years earlier is likely to have contributed to these ideas. Moreover, in speaking out against apartheid, the poll tax and, later, the anti-Muslim politics of the English Defence League Caroline contributed directly to what the city she lived in stood for in relation to important national and international issues. The presence of the banner reinforced the point that her individual acts formed part of collective ones. The cloth of the banner and its images told certain stories of their own.

In his extended review of Max Raphael's *The Demands of Art*, John Berger sums up Raphael's view of 'the function of the work of art' as being 'to lead us from the work to the process of creation which it contains'.[11] This attention to the process of creation and what it tells the spectator (or in the case of books the reader) about values is also important as a way of appreciating vernacular creativity, such as the making of the union banner nostalgically remembered by Caroline.

> In comparison to other studies of creativity where the focus is resolutely on the thing produced – the model railway built, the

> amateur play created – here [in studies of vernacular creativities] the concern is with *what happens in the process of doing* and being part of these activities ...[12]

In the process of making *Workers* in 2017 and 2018 Jay and I regularly discussed what kind of images, words, and overall message we were looking for.[13] Work on the film began just one year after the 2016 referendum, a time of anxiety for many, especially people of colour and non-British EU nationals.[14] The series of audio interviews I recorded as part of this process brought potential narrators into the conversation and helped shape our ideas. These then fed through into the film – a cultural production in and of Peterborough that, through screenings, being made available online and publicised via social media, was viewed and responded to by people beyond that city as well as within it.

The four books discussed in turn in the remainder of the chapter are also, in one sense, offerings from Peterborough to the world. Although they were all produced towards the end of the same highly significant year (for the UK) during which the Brexit referendum was held, none, unlike our film, address Brexit debates directly. Peterborough had voted to Leave and had done so by a considerably wider margin (61 per cent Leave to 39 per cent Remain) than the average for the rest of England (53 per cent Leave to 47 per cent Remain). One of the main arguments of this book is that the binary often presented between 'locals' and 'migrants' needs to be looked at critically and unpacked. This is especially important in the context of the anti-migration, xenophobic and anti-Muslim messaging of significant parts of the Leave campaign in the referendum during which, as discussed in Chapter 1, migration in general, and the free movement of EU nationals in particular, were portrayed as endangering wages and jobs, and English national identity was promoted as white and nominally Christian.[15] Significantly, one year after the city voted in favour of leaving the EU, it elected a black Labour MP, Fiona Onasanya, who was loyal to the Labour Party leadership's much softer and anti-racist approach to Brexit.

> in attending to the mundane spaces and ordinary practices of vernacular creativities we need to appreciate how these creativities,

> as much as professional arts practices are both produced by, and productive of the sites, spaces and cultures in which they are produced and consumed.[16]

Reading the four books discussed below as products of Peterborough makes the turnaround between the referendum and the general election less surprising and contradictory than it may otherwise seem.[17] Taken together, the books are illustrative of the importance of migration and the connections emanating from it to the everyday cultural life of the city.

Four Peterborough books, 2016

The four books are *Being Krystyna* by Carol Browne; *Parveen the Spice Queen* by Parveen Ashraf; *Re: Development* edited by Jessie Brennan; and *Reunions* by Chris Porsz. Each book offers stories of place, and of people's connections between places and across time. Each is a story in itself, yet contains many other stories within it. This has the combined effect of pushing back against any attempt at a single representation of Peterborough as a place. Indeed, as we shall see, while place speaks through them all, they are not *about* Peterborough but rather, like this book, see the world through the lens of that city.

> Those who read or listen to our stories see everything as through a lens. This lens is the secret of narration, and it is ground anew in every story, ground between the temporal and the timeless. If we storytellers are Death's Secretaries, we are so because, in our brief mortal lives, we are grinders of these lenses ...[18]

Read together, the four books offer a migrant cacophony – multiple voices that suggest a place changing over time in relation to its multiple elsewheres. They are all produced by professionals, or to a professional standard by 'professional amateurs' (pro-ams),[19] but each of them contains elements of vernacular creativity. While each evokes the cosmopolitan dispositions that, as we have seen, sit alongside and are entangled with racism and xenophobia in the city, none is elite.

Bringing them together in this chapter adds published stories to the directly recorded biographical oral histories of previous chapters, bolstering and consolidating three of the four main arguments of this book: challenging the false binary of 'migrant' and 'local', highlighting non-elite cosmopolitanism and building a provincial illustration and extension of Doreen Massey's theory of places as porous, extroverted and produced in dynamic relationships with other places.[20] Along the way this chapter rebuts the cultural snobbery that often centres white middle-class metropolitan taste and relegates provincial, working-class and non-white creativity to low status, the margins or both.

My experience of attending Peterborough's Gladstone Community Association's annual general meetings and certificate presentation ceremonies for its English for speakers of other languages (ESOL) students in 2017 and 2018 provided further evidence of how important a provincial place's non-elite cosmopolitanism might be at a time of deepening divisiveness between and within countries. Each of the annual general meetings brought together approximately two hundred people with multiple ethnic, national and faith heritages, many of them relatively recent arrivals earning a living through low-paid work. Written the day after the 2017 annual general meeting, my fieldnotes noted the power of this, though not uncritically as they also hinted at the hierarchical curation of the evening. I recalled a conversation with the guest speaker,

> Adrian Chapman, who I knew as a senior figure in the council responsible for overseeing [the Citizen Power Peterborough (CPP) project – on which see Chapter 4]. I recorded his speech, which began with him throwing away his notes and enthusing about the international presence and ethnic diversity of Peterborough, as someone who was born in the city. Food was provided afterwards for [ESOL] students and for guests (in separate rooms) – large plates of lamb biryani in the guests' room with home made samosas. I caught up with Adrian and said to him that I thought Peterborough was an example to other places. He energetically built on this to argue that it was an example to the nation and the world at a time of divisive discourse. Exactly the message of my proposed book. He said he remembered me from

> CPP but he also sounded like he would rather not remember CPP. He said something to the effect of why do you need a bunch of people to come from London to tell you how to do things when you have events like this that are community based? I had a similar conversation about the grass roots-ness of this gathering with [a former East Timorese liberation fighter and current warehouse worker whom I had interviewed in 2011 and whom Jay and I had been trying to contact again to make a section of the *Workers* film with] and two other Timorese people he introduced me to. It was a wonderful moment when I saw him there as I thought I recognised him and then as he came up to collect a certificate a huge roar went out from [several people including the founder of the erstwhile New Link service for new arrivals, the demise of which in the face of a local 'take back control' campaign was detailed in Chapter 4] – I had been trying to contact him for weeks to set up a meeting and there he was. He was apologetic, said he was busy and agreed to meet on Wednesday. I took his address down wrong and it remains to be seen whether it will happen. (31 October 2017)[21]

As discussed in Chapter 1, Massey provides a helpful framing for this book's discussion of place via the questions 'what does this place stand for?' and 'to whom does this place belong?'[22] The power of these two 'place questions' lies not only in their political provocation but also in Massey's more fundamental contributions to the theorisation of place. Places, as well as being contested, are, very importantly, multi-scalar and relational. Cities are places of sorts, as well as containing a multitude of places within them. Massey critiques the hierarchy of value that makes for greater attention to megacities, and within that category, global cities. For Massey the question of 'what does this place stand for?' 'should be asked of any place' [and] 'is a question that makes each and every place a potential arena for political contest about its answer'.[23] With this question Massey thus insists on simultaneously examining the internal contestations within cities as places, and the relations that those places have with other places elsewhere.

Asking how places are related to other places, and to their pasts, and attending to contestations over place militates against reducing any place to a single image or soundbite. However, this is not the approach taken by some journalists and politicians. Peterborough is often dismissed or ignored by monied people and national movers and shakers in the worlds of academia or so-called 'high culture' passing through it on the London–Edinburgh east coast main line or living and working in the city of Cambridge, just 62 kilometres to the south, with which Peterborough shares an elected mayor. The *Guardian* journalist John Harris gets his teeth into questions about Peterborough as a place in a video story on EU nationals working in East Anglia when he stands in the centre of Peterborough and states that 'a large part of the British economy ticks over here'.[24] Focusing on migrant workers based in Peterborough who, as we saw in Chapter 3, are bussed out of the city by employment agencies for picking and packing work, Harris's film makes an important point about low pay, hard working conditions and the role of agencies as suppliers and allocators of just-in-time labour. He rightly links this to the workings of contemporary capitalism and the concentrated power of supermarkets, themselves engaged in price wars, as well as to the importance of low food prices to consumers. I share Harris's concern with structures of power at work here, and, as I have argued so far in this book, going beyond the connections he makes with the deterioration in working conditions emerging from capital's search for accumulation in the food sector, it is important to see the dynamics that Harris's film portrays in the context of England's history of racisms, its recent decades of neoliberalist policies and deindustrialisation and, in particular, the austerity that followed the 2007–08 financial crisis.

However, I do not believe that what Peterborough, the place, stands for is fairly summed up in this piece by John Harris, or in others by the many national and international journalists that descended on the city in the lead-up to the June 2019 byelection there.[25] Nor am I about to offer a succinct alternative. On the contrary, I am reminded of Michele Lobo's work in the small city of Darwin in Australia, which she tells readers has variously been portrayed as 'a tropical multi-cultural paradise with Asian style open air markets, a creative city with arts practitioners, a remote northern city with redneck racism, a carceral city with prisons/detention centres and a multicultural city with a transient "fly-in/fly-out population"'.[26] Lobo too sidesteps any single representation and engages instead with 'a shared passion for creativity among people and places on the margins' in a specific suburb of Darwin, and in particular with vernacular creativity '[that] is central to the emergence of fragile friendships among residents whose affective engagements with places "underground" escape attention'.[27]

Friendship is a major theme of Chris Porsz's remarkable book *Reunions*, which uses photography almost entirely located in Peterborough to capture emotional, visual and visceral experiences of time passing. Porsz, now in his sixties, has a day job as a paramedic and describes himself as an amateur photographer, but through his regular 'Paramedic Paparazzi' column in the *Peterborough Telegraph*, coupled with his multiple encounters with city residents in urgent medical need and his open, friendly and engaged on-street presence with trademark rucksack and camera equipment, he has become a unique and well-known contributor to the life of the city. Porsz's *Reunions* involved bringing together friends, relatives and strangers, whom he originally shot in the city in the early 1980s, to be photographed again mostly in the same locations and poses some thirty-five years later. Some of the reunion photographs are reunions not of two or more photographic subjects but reunions between a single subject and Porsz himself.

The process of making *Reunions* was intense, in particular Porsz's efforts to trace the subjects of the earlier photographs to try to arrange the reunion shots. He and I had become friends over years of conversations about our respective work and family lives.[28] Notes I made after bumping into him in Peterborough in 2016 on my way to meet with Joanna Szczepaniak about her possible involvement in what would become the *Workers* film project show how the two projects-in-progress were in close communication:[29]

> Joanna appeared in the cold sunshine by the Guildhall in Cathedral Square pretty much on time. It was great to see her again. She remembered Chris P and they had a good chat generally – he practised his Polish and said he hoped that Nasze Strony [the regional Polish newspaper that Joanna wrote for and co-edited] would cover his new work on reunions among the Polish community. He feels emotional about not being able to speak Polish. Jo remembered his work on Ferry Meadows.[30] (16 January 2016)

My notes following another meeting nine months later indicate how in the final stages of his book Porsz was totally focused:

> [Chris Porsz's] book *Reunions* which he's recently worked on for as long as 14 hours a day is almost ready. He needs to decide the order but the number of [reunion shots] goes above the 135 [his limit]. He told me about the huge emotional labour that he'd put into the project. (2 October 2016)

The earlier photographs in *Reunions* extend the theme of Porsz's *New England*, a photographic social history of the 1970s and 1980s.[31] Many – though not all – of these original photographs in *Reunions* are in black and white, and most were taken in the era of Margaret Thatcher's premiership referred to already in the discussion of Caroline Nightingale's life story – a period of intensified neoliberal economic and fiscal policies, deindustrialisation and a concerted government effort to crush trade union power. Two of the photographs capture demonstrations against the effects of Thatcher's policies, including cuts to education and social services budgets and low pay for nurses, while a third pictures a picket line during a strike at a water sewage works.[32] The 1980s photographs in *Reunions* also include a boarded shopfront, a rubble strewn terraced front garden and Papa Luigi's first international pizza-eating competition.

Throughout his work on *Reunions* Porsz regularly visited his nonagenarian mother, Krystyna, who suffered from dementia, in Lavender Nursing Home in Peterborough, where she lived. In the early 1980s Krystyna worked at Peterborough's Embassy cinema, once the Embassy Theatre. A photograph of young people and children queuing at the cinema in 1982 is included in the book with a reference to this being Porsz's mother's place of employment at the time.[33] I shall return to Porsz's mother later in the chapter as she is the subject of another of the four books.

The move from black and white to colour between time periods is striking, as are people's changed physical appearances. Along the way they reveal part of the history of international migration to Peterborough over the period – it is nothing new after all, contrary to the implication of John Harris's video – with textual and/or visual references to an

Italian grocery shop, butcher's shop and stovetop coffee maker, and a Sikh temple in a terraced house.[34] There is an unstated working-class pride in the photographs. If this is part of what Peterborough stands for, written between the lines is spatial mobility that gives the lie to the post-liberal David Goodhart's division of the UK into Anywhere people and Somewhere people (summarised in Chapter 1), according to which schema people who are white and working class do not move around at all.

The evidence of spatial mobility emerges from the words that run alongside the photographs, put together by the journalist Jo Riley via interviews with the subjects. These convey a to-ing and fro-ing as well as longer-term residential moves around the UK and internationally to places such as Halifax (Yorkshire), Hong Kong, Bristol, Aberdeen, Australia, Essex, Spalding, Colorado, Kings Lynn, London and Aotearoa/New Zealand. In spite of the presence of the University Centre Peterborough, Peterborough is not a university town, and it is true that many of the photographic subjects retain jobs that do not require university degrees. But, contrary to Goodhart, Porsz portrays a working-class culture that is both multi-ethnic and non-metropolitan, giving the lie to the conceptual dichotomy of contemporary debates that pit a beleaguered white working class against a cosmopolitan liberal elite. Part of his achievement is that this is communicated beyond any particular bubble. Self-taught and often self-deprecatingly describing himself as amateur, Porsz is a prolific photographer and social commentator. Yet one metropolitan art publisher's assessment of *Reunions* as 'a bit parochial'[35] was not shared by the print and broadcast media, which covered *Reunions* on its publication in late 2016 on national and international television stations, as well as through double-page spreads in the *Daily Mirror*, the *Guardian* and the *Daily Mail*.

In *The Art of Listening*, Les Back describes the 'About the Streets' project on which he worked with Paul Halliday in Brick Lane in east London. The photographers in the project were Halliday's students at Croydon College. The project, like much of Chris Porsz's work, had the effect of, as Back puts it, 'offering recognition to those who are usually not recognized'.[36] Back goes on to argue that 'The photographs are like epitaphs to the living – unlike the flesh of the subject they depict, they will not age.'[37]

In Porsz's *Reunions* the use of the same pose and site for each pair of photographs, with a gap in time that is in most cases over three decades, means that some of the original subjects are missing. If one of the original subjects died between the photographs Jo Riley's text gives the name of the deceased person, and in some of the reunion photographs a friend or family member replaces them in tribute, especially if the person died young. This all adds to the emotionality of the book and its evocation of human frailty and mortality, as well as the joy of reunion and the playfulness of trying to restage an old photograph.

In spite of Porsz's increasing renown (since *Reunions* Porsz has published three further books, *Streets of Europe*, *Streets of Britain* and *Barking*), there is an element of vernacular creativity in *Reunions*. This was evident in the snooty dismissal of the book by the London publisher Porsz approached and is also signalled by the book's emphasis on the joy of convivial relations where they exist among family and friends. As Harriet Hawkins put it in her discussion of Tim Edensor and Gareth Millington's writing about the groups of people who visit the Blackpool illuminations,[38]

> amongst visitors what was important was less the look of the lights – aesthetic qualities or an exercise in discernment – rather emphasis is placed on consolidating bonds with family and friends. These bonds evolved around nostalgia and shared conviviality and the experience of a good atmosphere beyond one's immediate group ...[39]

Family conviviality around food was a key inspiration for the second book, *Parveen the Spice Queen* by Parveen Ashraf. The book was also a tribute to Ashraf's Bradford-based mother, who died in April 2016. Her mother had taught her cooking, and the book was a labour of love for Ashraf, who writes in her introduction that

> [g]rowing up, the focal point of family life was meal times, in the evenings mum would make fabulous tasting food and we would all sit around the dinner table, eat and chat, we were like the Asian Waltons.[40]

On the face of it, *Parveen the Spice Queen* is simply a cookbook. Beautifully produced with photographs of every dish and detailed explanations of the spices required for the kind of South Asian cookery that Ashraf relates, it would make any reader hungry. Ashraf is a resident of Peterborough who moved there from London with her civil engineer husband when he took a job with a developer involved in building one of Peterborough's more recent New Towns, at Hampton. She was born and brought up in Bradford and wears her Yorkshire identity on her sleeve. In explaining her preference for tea over wine, simultaneously hinting at her Muslim identity at the same time, Ashraf adds to her recommendation that readers drink a glass of wine while they cook.

> I suggest that you open a bottle of wine, put on the radio and enjoy the process (If like me you don't drink wine, stick the kettle on and have a cup of tea – you can take the girl out of Yorkshire but you can't take Yorkshire out of the girl!)[41]

I first met Ashraf at a meeting at the Ramada Hotel in Peterborough in June 2011 entitled 'Black and Multicultural Youth Work – Managing Funding Cuts'. These were the early years of UK finance minister George Osborne's austerity programme, and voluntary organisations as well as the City Council had begun to face savage spending cuts. Somewhat bizarrely given the national as well as local spending cuts, I was in the first year of my two-year research fellowship focusing on Peterborough, 'Places for All?'[42] Towards the end of the project, in November 2012, Ashraf, along with Peterborough-based Jabeen Maqbool, organised and devised the catering for the project's final community event: a tea party designed to attract both ethnic-minority and ethnic-majority residents – the party at which Caroline Nightingale, with whose story this chapter started, met her former colleague from the potato-processing factory …

When I started to visit Peterborough regularly again, from 2016 onwards,[43] I renewed my acquaintance with Ashraf, who talked excitedly about the book and its connection to her various other culinary businesses (including the manufacture and sale of spice mixes sold with recipes; catering; and teaching cookery). After *Parveen the Spice Queen* was published, she, like Chris Porsz, was offered a weekly column in the *Peterborough Telegraph*. I sent her an early version of this chapter that I was preparing for a workshop at Goldsmiths, University of London, in May 2017.[44] My notes from conversations with her later that year convey the entrepreneurial energy she put into her different business activities. We had become friends, and I also made a note of the advice she gave me for my children – similar ages to her own – as they entered the world of work.

> I drove to Parveen's house. Parveen talked excitedly about her work – her new range, the incredible app that allows you to focus the phone on a picture of one of her dishes in the newspaper or in her book and get taken to a video of how to make it. She is thrilled by how many people she is now working with – often paid in kind – e.g. brand manager, social media person, others. We also exchanged family news and walked around her local park, via two charity shops (she likes to look out for potential crockery from the 1980s for her catering gigs). We ended up at a café in Werrington Village with both a St George's Cross and union jacks on the tables. She said to me it's not right that these flags are automatically seen as symbols of racism and nativism. I agreed and said I felt they needed to be reclaimed ... Parveen loaded me up with spices and a naan mix from her new range and gave me advice to help [my children's] job applications: covering letter vital; cv top details to bottom and to start just with the punchy paragraph to grab attention; attach generic references to say how good [they are] to work with. (5 July 2017)
>
> Parveen ... had invited me for a light lunch. Parveen talked at length about her business, her clients who are purchasing dinners and cookery lessons, and her spice kits, their new branding etc. It was a delicious lunch of keema, Greek salad, beans and sweet potato and she also gave me a homemade sugarless granola bar. She is trying to give up wheat and sugar entirely. (30 October 2017)

This last point is ironic given that the very first food picture is a gorgeous close-up of Gajar-ka-halwa with a quote in large font stating not only that this was Ashraf's mother's 'signature dessert', but that it was based on one of her 'signature shawls'. Ashraf's text throughout the book, whether she is talking of her family, including her late parents, or about the food, is chatty, as if she is speaking directly to the reader. In discussing her recipe for okra she makes an explicit connection with her memory of her mother.

> I first made this under my mother's instructions when I was 15. She wanted me to learn to cook the summer before my 'O' levels (yes, I am that old, now called GCSE's). Mum had told me when cooking vegetables to soak them after cutting, so that they didn't discolour. I had taken this on board. I cut the okra and dutifully soaked it. When it was time to take the okra pieces out of the water, I realised I had created an almighty messy gloop! It was a disaster. Even now when I cook okra, I can see the look of disdain on my mother's face. I may have come a long way from the underconfident, gangly teenager with a mono brow; but every time I make okra, I think of my mum and smile to myself.[45]

Ashraf sees her book as speaking to a widespread desire among people in Britain without South Asian heritage to cook South Asian food, and also sees a potential market in twenty-something British South Asians who did not learn to cook South Asian food while growing up and would like to do so in adult life. She describes the recipes as 'Kashmiri/northern Pakistani style'. It is Peterborough that she sees as having given her the opportunity to develop her cooking through her catering business. She recently told me: 'It wouldn't have happened in Bradford, too many really good restaurant and eateries' (although she did turn to Bradford networks for a printer that would deliver at a reasonable price, having once been burned elsewhere). Now being a Peterborough resident was essential (for other reasons). 'Everything I needed was on my doorstep. People helped me because I was a local Peterborough girl.' The text evokes Ashraf's excitement at the whole project, for example her joy in working with the Peterborough-based photographer Dana Al-Gharabally:

> I cooked everything in my kitchen, used my own crockery (well mostly, although I did borrow some from friends) and then we

just let our creativity take over. Dana and I had a blast, we were in our creative groove; styling the food, getting excited over every shot and best of all, eating the food.[46]

Ashraf's tone is never preachy. Yet in a very unforced way, often through the references to her family, her text pushes against the 'othering' that many British South Asian Muslims have experienced, especially since 9/11. There is an ordinariness, for example, in her story of the day trips that Ashraf, her parents and siblings would make to Blackpool, the sight of the aforementioned illuminations, in the 1970s:

> I remember when I was a child, mum would make a huge stack of aloo parathas and a flask of sweet chai when we were going on a family day trip to Blackpool. We would stop off for a picnic en route and eat our parathas and drink our chai out of plastic cups. It may sound very basic but it was a happy time. Even now when I make aloo paratha, I think of those happy day trips travelling up to Blackpool Pleasure Beach, in the back of dad's van listening to his old Indian classic songs.[47]

Very gently, in reference to her daughter's tastes, Ashraf suggests that multiculture in the form of syncretic taste is the current norm in the UK:

> This is one of my daughter's favourite dishes. In her teenage years, she went through a vegetarian phase ... which was just after her goth phase ... Her favourite way of eating it is on top of spaghetti with a little cheese, not very Asian I know – more Indo-Italian, well we are a multicultural society after all.[48]

It's only in the dessert section towards the end that Ashraf moves to reference Muslim culture in particular, and even here, when she introduces the first dessert, the reference is distanced and involves translation, with a continuing focus on how much she loves tea:

> [On Dry Sweet Vermicelli:] This is one of my husband's favourite Asian desserts. This dish is usually served on special occasions like 'Eid' (Muslim festival, similar to Christmas) and often a popular dessert when I have guests for dinner ... I usually serve

> my sevia in small glass dessert bowls, alongside chai lattes or just English breakfast tea ... well I do love a cup of tea.[49]

As one reads on, however, the connection to Eid becomes more immediate and sensuous, Ashraf allowing the emotions of a childhood memory to come to the fore and momentarily leaving aside her more usual practices of bridging, of translating for her readers:

> [On Milky Sweet Vermicelli:] I can remember as a child waking up on Eid mornings to the smell of gently simmering cardamom milk wafting through the house. Even now I associate that sweet smell with happy times on Eid with my brothers and sisters.[50]

Home and family play a major part in the book through references to Ashraf's three children. Her family make their presence felt not only in the text but also in the collage of family photographs – both black and white and colour on the page facing the introduction. These offer an epitaph, in Les Back's words,[51] to Ashraf's late mother and father, and a celebration of key moments in her life with her husband and children, including foreign holidays and her daughter's graduation, as well as her own career as a teacher of cookery.

In sociological terms, the book is gendered with references like: 'as a general rule, like most Asian mums, I make chapattis as a staple for my family ... Perhaps I am being a little stereotypical but you get the general idea.'[52] While it makes reference to a middle-class present, it is also proudly working class and British:

> I was born in Bradford, West Yorkshire, the curry capital of the North in my opinion ... For some people, the 70s may have been a dark and depressing time in the North but we had mum's onion bhajis to come home to, which we ate by candlelight. For me, it was a magical time and when my love affair with food began.[53]
>
> All my three children love their Bhaji Butties.[54]

Throughout the time I have been visiting Peterborough I have occasionally stopped at Café Asia just next to the library. I have come to think of it as a workers' café – with food that is cheap and plentiful, served fast, with television on in the background and a lively and convivial atmosphere. It is run by Kurdish-heritage men, who greet anyone sitting down at one of the brown Formica tables with a small complimentary soup before taking their order. In autumn 2017 I had arranged to catch up over a meal there with Sophie Antonelli, the co-founder of The Green Backyard (GBY), a 2.3-acre community-growing project in the middle of Peterborough that had successfully fought for the right to continue to exist in the face of intense efforts to sell the land by its owner, Peterborough City Council. GBY – the subject of the third book, *Re: Development: Voices, Cyanotypes and Writings from The Green Backyard* – is an activist project that directly contested both the questions of to whom the place that it was situated in belonged, and what that place and the wider city it was part of stood for. I wrote at the time that

> The TV being on didn't help my enjoyment but it is always good meeting Sophie and I caught up on The Green Backyard which now at last has a lease – though she hates it because of the terms – like the piece of land on Oundle Road is going to be a car park for the council though the GBY will have an access road through it. (30 October 2017)

It was entirely due to Sophie that the London-based artist Jessie Brennan, who devised, edited and made *Re: Development*, contacted me early in 2016 to ask if I would write a contribution to the book as Kaveri Qureshi and I had written briefly about the GBY a few years earlier in a section of an article for the academic journal *Identities*.[55] I readily agreed, not realising how significant Brennan's work would become in the struggle over the future of the GBY. In retrospect, Brennan's professional creative practice in Peterborough fits well with what Harriet Hawkins refers to as

> a set of practices and spaces wherein artistic practices, creativity and political activism are interwoven to create overlappings and reconfigurations of the political, artistic and creative, [and] in doing so opening up spaces in which we might be able to live differently.[56]

The section on the GBY in the article I wrote with Kaveri was built around quotes from oral history interviews with Sophie and her father and fellow GBY founder, Renny Antonelli. Kaveri and I traced some of the impetus and vision behind the GBY to the pair's Italian heritage. In *Re: Development*, Jessie Brennan brings to bear a vastly wider world of involvement by Peterborough residents in the GBY than we had attempted, revealing multiple connections across space and time between the GBY and the people who value it, and new politics and political vision that successfully fought back against the council's notification (in 2011) that the land would be sold.

According to Brennan the GBY 'is not only a haven of green and peace but also a site for people's political agitations … [It] intermingles the anti-capitalism of allotments with the strong utopian pragmatism of the Garden City movement and the eco-activism of community gardens with [something like] guerrilla gardening through "claiming" and "politicising" of land.' Brennan's aim was to create a 'visual and audio archive – for the current social use and value of the land' that, if the GBY's campaign to get its lease renewed did not succeed, could be a 'potent trace' of 'social aspirations' and 'political failure', or, if it did, would become a 'celebrated symbol of the hard-won fight for citizens' democratic rights to nature'.[57]

The process entailed in the making of Brennan's art thus became, for a period, inseparable from the GBY itself. Involving a year's residency based in a repurposed garden shed at the GBY site, more than one hundred self-recorded interviews with Peterborough residents and the same number of cyanotypes (cameraless photographs) of GBY objects, Brennan's project of art, writing, activism and curation across a range of media is suffused both with the vernacular creativity of people who come to the GBY – one volunteer, Chris Erskine, notes that 'there is a deep commitment to what I would call DiY culture, a real innovation and creativity' – and with the multiple elsewheres to which people quoted in *Re: Development* related. Moreover, the book itself formed just one of several ways in which Brennan's work enabled people, ideas and events in Peterborough to contribute to places beyond it.

One of the other ways in which her work reached beyond the city was through Brennan's nineteen-metre-long giant yellow-lettered installation 'If this were to be lost' that for twelve months from June

2016 was visible to passengers on the east coast main line between London and Edinburgh as they slowed down approaching Peterborough, or pulled away from it. More specifically, this was also one of several ways in which the GBY and Brennan together took the central challenge they were making to the corporate developers' vision for the city centre to a much wider audience. As Luke Payn, a GBY trustee and one of more than a hundred voices in the project, put it:

> There are hundreds of people that travel from London to Edinburgh up and down the adjacent train tracks; we're feet away from something that is pulsing through the backbone of this country, so The Green Backyard is very connected.[58]

As far as I know, neither Ashraf nor Porsz had an academic readership in mind for their book. In contrast, by including pieces by academic contributors (including myself) in *Re: Development*, the London-based artist Jessie Brennan would have known that she would be subject to academic review, and indeed the book has been reviewed very enthusiastically in a long piece available online in *Antipode*. In inviting Sophie Antonelli, myself and eight other authors to write about the GBY in her book, Brennan also explicitly charted a further route to move the work's influence beyond Peterborough. One of the contributors, Dougald Hine, captured part of Brennan's skill in enabling the GBY as a project of urban citizenship both to reflect a multiplicity of Peterborough-based lived experiences and to communicate it outwards:

> Here the artist takes the role of listener, making time to go beyond the first answers that people might give to a survey or a journalistic vox pop, getting closer to the heart of why a project matters to the people who come into contact with it, then drawing out the words that sing to her and giving them new forms … [There is also a] web of lives and skills woven together into the project … The work of weaving together such unexpected combinations into a human fabric is a kind of gentle magic.[59]

Re-reading this reminded me of writer Rebecca Solnit's praise for *Portraits* by the legendary Marxist art critic John Berger. Solnit wrote that John Berger encouraged people to believe that

> you can be passionately, radically political and also concerned with the precise details of artistic production and everyday life, that the beautiful and the revolutionary belong together ... that you can make words on the page sing and liberate minds that way.[60]

Re: Development has been produced as an object of art in itself and, at the same time, it conveys an exchange of ideas across space into and out of Peterborough that build on, inform and inspire actions such as those of the GBY, which Sophie Antonelli refers to in her chapter title as 'Digging for Our Lives'.[61] It connects with wider national and international challenges to what Anna Minton calls the 'financialisation of space, land and property', which, she adds, in one of the book's many tributes to Doreen Massey, risks the 'obliteration of ... ongoing histories and stories'.[62] (Indeed Brennan had met Massey at a conference when she was devising the book; they had stayed in touch, and Massey had been looking forward to contributing a chapter but sadly died before this became possible.)[63]

The voices of Peterborough residents quoted from in the book, put online by Brennan and played on a loop at some of her exhibitions of the work, speak of multiple mobilities that make this particular place and collectively, as Brennan explains in her introduction, question the notion of 'redevelopment'. The recordings were made by people on their own, without any interviewer present. Brennan gave them the recording device and asked them to go to find a private space and speak into it. Each person was asked to choose and speak about an object at the GBY that was particularly meaningful to them. One visitor, Caroline Cumberpatch, whose chosen GBY object was the pond, speaks of an equality in gardening that links diverse communities. Agnese Lazzari, a volunteer, who chose the sun shining on a piece of wood at the site, concurs:

> that's what The Green Backyard can do: it gathers together people – all sorts of people – from different backgrounds, from all different cultures, with thousands of different skills (and also fears and problems and issues), we're not perfect at all – we're all vulnerable to a certain degree.

This multiplicity is also emphasised by Rose Croft, who chose the willow arch. Rose Croft was visiting with a group of Year 1 children from a local school on the day she recorded her interview for Brennan's collection.

> Walking around [The Green Backyard] definitely involves a huge sense of pride in the space. And not pride because it's tidy or a lot of money has been spent but pride because I know – I can see – the marks from so many different people that have worked here and put energy into this place.

Rich Hill chose a toothbrush that had been donated during collections made for Syrian refugees in the camp at Calais, for which the GBY was a delivery point. He said that '[t]here was nowhere else in the local area that was taking a collection for the refugees who are waiting at Calais to try to find a safe refuge in Europe somewhere'. Samantha Hope, a volunteer, chose a marker pen. She explained that on the day of the recording she had been 'sorting and distributing all the clothes and donations for the people who are seeking refuge at camps in Calais'.

The final book discussed in this chapter, *Being Krystyna: A Story of Survival in WWII* by the novelist Carol Browne, who lives just outside Peterborough, speaks of an earlier displacement in Europe during and after the Second World War. The book, Browne's first (mostly) non-fiction publication, is the only one of the four that a reader would be likely to choose to read from cover to cover in one sitting. It is based on the partly fictionalised life story of the Holocaust survivor Krystyna Porsz, mother of the *Reunions* author Chris Porsz, who died in 2017 after the book had been published. Browne met Krystyna Porsz once in Lavender Nursing Home. However, in addition to internet research, Browne also draws on extensive notes kept about his mother by Chris Porsz based on conversations he had with her over a much longer period, as well as his own and other family members' memories. And importantly, she brings in her friend Agnieszka Coutinho in the figure of the narrator. While it is clearly stated that Coutinho is not responsible for any views attributed to her namesake in the book, it was her chance meeting with Chris Porsz in his role as a paramedic after she fainted one day at the gym that led him, happy to chat to her in his limited Polish and intrigued that she had grown up in his father's home town of Torun in Poland, to first invite her to meet his mother. Coutinho then introduced Carol Browne to the Porszes.

I had known Agnieszka for over four years by the time *Being Krystyna* was published, and we stayed regularly in touch via WhatsApp and email. Visiting her and her husband in Peterborough and hosting them when they came to Brighton, I became aware that Agnieszka too is a writer with many published articles and more than one book on the go, including one about her life,[64] and that both she and her husband continued to attempt business start-ups beyond their paid work. The couple regularly invited me to stay with them when I was in Peterborough, and on one occasion when I did so I noted that:

> they were tired as was I and we talked generally with [their daughter] playing and chatting too. I went to bed early at about 9.15. It was a nice comfortable night. [Agnieszka's husband] has been quite down because he lost his job due to a mess up over his papers and it had been a good position at Amazon. He has been making skits/vlogs while unemployed and studying his access courses in computing and business. He has not exercised for a long time he said. I slept in his 'studio' where he had the equipment for his filming and I thought in the morning there is potential for him to be involved in the filming for our project. (2 April 2016)

A year later I was at their house again, and Agnieszka told me that to increase their income

> they are considering starting two businesses, his a food catering business for night shift workers at Amazon, hers a t-shirt business with positive life-enhancing logos on the front like 'me time'. (2 July 2017)

Coutinho and her husband's pro-am creative entrepreneurialism and her life as a writer give her much in common with Caroline Nightingale, with whom this chapter started. In an article about her life for the November 2018 issue of Peterborough's *Moment Magazine*, Coutinho writes about the satisfaction she gained from becoming a teacher of English for speakers of other languages to relatively recently arrived international migrants in Peterborough,[65] something she mentions in her chapter of the film I made with Jay Gearing, *Workers*, in which she also speaks about the conditions she experienced working in food factories and warehouses.[66] In the magazine article, Coutinho writes of feelings about her role in *Being Krystyna*:

> I'm also honoured that I became one of the main characters in a book written by local author Carol Browne. *Being Krystyna: A Story of Survival in WWII* is a moving account of one woman's experiences in the Holocaust based on authentic events. I met Krystyna on several occasions in her care home in Peterborough and our conversations, as well as those with her son (Peterborough paramedic and photographer Chris Porsz) formed the basis for the book.[67]

Krystyna Porsz, Agnieszka Coutinho and Carol Browne all migrated to Peterborough. Browne grew up in Crewe and studied English at the University of Nottingham. Coutinho did multiple jobs when she first came to the UK aged twenty, and at the time when the book was written was a receptionist in a busy general practitioners' surgery in the heart of the Millfield area, Caroline Nightingale's neighbourhood. The book reflects on the transformation that happened in Warsaw with the Nazi occupation in the 1940s, and the consequences that flowed from this for Krystyna and her two sisters, whose ages then were similar to that of Coutinho when she came to England.

While Browne states that 'Krystyna's descriptions of her own experiences are entirely true and accurate and based upon her original account of what happened to her',[68] she also added material from 'other sources in the public domain'. As part of my own research in Peterborough I had recorded a version of Krystyna Porsz's story in her nursing home room at the invitation of Chris Porsz and in his presence.[69] Krystyna Porsz was already suffering from dementia, and Chris used much sensitivity to inform her of its purpose and to gain her consent for me to record it. Chris was active throughout the interview, using old family photographs to prompt her memory. He himself had heard her speak about her life history in multiple conversations and had written it up into an illustrated booklet he entitled *The Three Beauties*.[70] In the preface to *Being Krystyna*, Browne clarifies the contributions of Chris Porsz and Agnieszka Coutinho to her text:

> The following fact-based narrative is a creatively expanded version of [Krystyna Porsz's] life story recorded several years ago by her son, Chris Porsz ... Further conversations between my friend Agnieszka Coutinho and Krystyna and, on one occasion, between Krystyna and myself, added extra information to what was already known. However, as Krystyna's dementia has grown steadily worse over the years, uncovering all the details of the full story has been impossible. To compensate for this, I have filled in the gaps with my own research ... Agnieszka Coutinho ... did not volunteer to be Krystyna's biographer, believing that I would be better suited to the task. I have used Agnieszka as a narrative device to facilitate the unfolding of the story. It follows that Ms Coutinho is not responsible for any of the views or opinions expressed by the character of Agnieszka in the book.[71]

The encounters that led to Browne's book were shaped by Peterborough's attraction as a destination for Polish migrants in two periods: the years immediately following the Second World War, and since Poland's accession to the EU in 2004. Krystyna's husband Alfons Porsz had moved to Scotland in 1940 as part of the first independent Polish parachute brigade and was later stationed near Peterborough, at an airbase at Stamford. The couple met at a displaced persons' camp in Germany in 1946, went on dance dates and later decided to marry. They moved to Peterborough in 1947, knowing from Alfons's past that there was a Polish community in the city. Krystyna was twenty-six and remembered having been homeless, penniless and unable to speak English. For Chris Porsz, his parents' subsequent stories of work and their contributions to Peterborough society inspire a solidarity with international migrants more generally. In a piece about his parents on 30 January 2017 in his weekly column for the *Peterborough Telegraph*, this time dedicated to Holocaust Memorial Day, Chris's words, interspersed with his mother's phrase 'just be kind', carry extra urgency, having come as they did seven months after the UK's referendum over membership of the EU and the rise in racist and xenophobic hate crimes that occurred during the referendum campaign and afterwards.

> Well I think Peterborough is a great city and the reason for that is in part due to people like my parents. 'JUST BE KIND.' How different from taking our jobs, taking our homes, send them back. Sounds familiar and the same was said about our parents. Who do they think looks after my mother, their mother. As a paramedic, I know when I hand over my patient they will be cared for by the new migrants that make the NHS still the best in the world. It would collapse without them … Intolerance and careless words have consequences and careless words cost lives … Irresponsible media with scare mongering headlines, slick 'sound bites' well-rehearsed and repeated again and again fuel the hatred and load the gun. In this climate of fear 40-year-old Harlow man Arek Jowik was enjoying a pizza and speaking in Polish with friends and then murdered … 'JUST BE KIND.' How different from all this hatred and xenophobia with drowning refugees described as cockroaches and Poles as vermin. Sound familiar? My mother has heard such language before and it led to gas chambers and crematoria. Let us not forget the words of the murdered MP Jo Cox in her maiden speech 'we are far more united and have far more in common than the things that divide us'.[72]

Krystyna Porsz's first role at the Embassy Theatre was as a cashier, and by the time she retired she had become assistant manager. She was proud to have met many of the stars who passed through, including the Beatles. Alfons Porsz worked at Peterborough's major centres of manufacturing, its brickyards and then Perkins engineering. He was also the table tennis champion both of Peterborough and Northamptonshire. Yet in the story told by his wife he faced a 'send the Poles home' campaign in the period after the war, with slogans claiming Polish people were 'taking jobs from British workers' that were strongly resonant with sentiments expressed during and after the UK's 2016 referendum over EU membership.[73]

There is an intense emotionality to the book as it stretches its story across space and time. It includes detailed and harrowing stories of Ravensbrück concentration camp, where Krystyna Porsz remembered doing forced labour 'digging roads and filling trucks with rubble' and being piled into overcrowded rodent-ridden accommodation at night: 'We lay there like knives and forks in a cutlery drawer'.[74] Browne breaks up the otherwise relentless horror of the camps by returning attention to Peterborough. She has the fictionalised version of the narrator Agnieszka Coutinho turn to the window of the flat where she lived:

> Out there was a city that took its freedom for granted, in a land that prized democracy. It was colourful, rich and cosmopolitan; but the images in my mind were starkly different.[75]

Tragically Alfons Porsz developed early-onset dementia at the age of forty-eight and died after fifteen years in an asylum. Both he and Krystyna had experienced various forms of confinement in their lives. During my interview with Krystyna in 2012, Chris Porsz asked her why she did not like the door of her room being closed, and she responded, 'Because it reminds me of the concentration camp.' The story related in *Being Krystyna* in fact turns on how Krystyna Lewandowska was a name she assumed when the Nazis forced Jews into the Warsaw ghetto, and how she ran away and adopted a Polish Catholic identity. Her birth name was Dorca Szafir. As Krystyna Lewandowska she had joined the Polish resistance and had been in Ravensbrück – 'originally intended as a labour camp for dissidents'[76] – as a Pole but not as a Jew.

Krystyna's mother Sarah, sister Rega and niece, Rega's daughter Lilian, all died as Jews in Majdanek concentration camp. Chris Porsz found out that his mother had been Jewish only towards the end of the 1990s and believed she had hidden her Jewish origins with the aim of protecting her children because she feared that the Holocaust could happen again.

Being Krystyna offers an explicit message for the current times, one which, as already mentioned, Chris Porsz drew on in his newspaper article for Holocaust Memorial Day 2017. Krystyna herself is quoted as saying that if she had a message for readers it would be: 'be kind to each other. If we all do that, we shall have a better world. Just be kind.' Browne extends this through the voice of Agnieszka Coutinho as her narrator:

> Fascist or fundamentalist, there are many people who preach hatred against other people because they have a different nationality, religion, race or sexuality … But there is hope. We can and must learn from the past. We can celebrate our differences rather than use them as an excuse to start wars … And one way to do this is to make sure that stories like Krystyna's are never forgotten.[77]

Conclusion

Understanding the processes through which these four books were created illuminates how they all both channelled and produced cultural change in and beyond the places where they were made. I have engaged with these processes by interweaving discussion of the books with my own interactions with the authors before and after their publication, using the *Workers* film project as a sub-plot. Elements of the four books themselves emerge as having lives beyond the book form (for example in exhibitions, cookery shows and media coverage). It may be a coincidence that they appeared at the same time. But taken together, they reveal what might otherwise have been largely unnoticed creativity in a particular city that national organisations have suggested is lacking in the arts. Beyond this, each book in its different way deals with the more universal theme of loss, actual or imagined, either of people or of place.

In more or less subtle language, the books make their voices heard in the struggle over, to adopt Doreen Massey's question, what Peterborough stands for. Each connects with, and is produced, through connection with both Peterborough and many places elsewhere – including the destinations of the original subjects of Chris Porsz's reunion photographs, Bradford and Kashmir in Parveen Ashraf's cookbook, London and the many places of origin of the people who made recordings for Jessie Brennan or contributed writings to her book, and Poland and Germany in *Being Krystyna*. Moreover, at the national scale, in their engagement with time as well as place, all of the books contribute to debates over what England and the UK stand for in the current conjuncture.

Yasmin Gunaratnam states near the start of her book *Death and the Migrant* that she hopes 'to derail dominant ideas and narratives about migrants by showing something of our singular differences and our humanity'.[78] The book that Gunaratnam co-authored with Hannah Jones and several others, *Go Home? The Politics of Immigration Controversies*, is said by the authors to be a plea 'to recognise our common humanity'.[79] In Massey's terms, these four books are not *about* Peterborough but rather arise *from* it.[80] I have drawn on them here to argue for understandings of the city that both value vernacular and pro-am creativity in provincial places, and avoid the tendency of our times to separate 'migrants' and 'locals' into binary categories, in the process setting up tropes like 'white working class' that have the effect of dividing us, allowing the worst depradations of capitalism to continue unchallenged and enabling what some have referred to as 'creeping fascism' to creep still closer. There is hope in all four books, and I will return to the politics of hope in dark times at the end of the next and final chapter.

Notes

1 Caroline lived in Kent for the first sixteen years of her life before moving to the north of England.
2 Robert Minto, 'A smuggling operation: John Berger's theory of art', *Los Angeles Review of Books*, 2 January 2017, available online at: https://lareviewofbooks.org/article/a-smuggling-operation-john-bergers-theory-of-art/#! (accessed April 2019).
3 Harriet Hawkins, *Creativity* (London: Routledge, 2017), pp. 115 and 127.
4 Tim Edensor *et al.* (eds), *Spaces of Vernacular Creativity: Rethinking the Cultural Economy* (London: Routledge, 2010).
5 Doreen Massey, *World City* (Cambridge: Polity Press, 2007).
6 Known as the 'Take Me To' project, this work was initiated by the Citizen Power Peterborough programme set up by Peterborough City Council and the Royal Society of Arts (see Chapter 4).
7 Karen Olson and Linda Stopes, 'Crossing boundaries, building bridges: doing oral history among working-class women and men', in Sherna Berger Gluck and Daphne Patai (eds), *Women's Words: The Feminist Practice of Oral History* (London and New York: Routledge, 1991), p. 193.

8 Alessandro Portelli, 'What makes oral history different', in Robert Perks and Alistair Thomson (eds), *The Oral History Reader* (third edition, London: Routledge, 2016), p. 52.
9 On the poll tax, see Nick Higham, 'National Archives: Thatcher's poll tax miscalculation', *BBC News*, 30 December 2016, available online at: www.bbc.co.uk/news/uk-38382416 (accessed March 2019).
10 Ben Rogaly and Kaveri Qureshi, 'Diversity, urban space and the right to the provincial city', *Identities: Global Studies in Culture and Power*, 20:4 (2013), 423–437.
11 John Berger, 'Revolutionary undoing: on Max Raphael's *The Demands of Art*', *Landscapes: John Berger on Art*, ed. Tom Overton (London: Verso, 2016), p. 51.
12 Hawkins, *Creativity*, p. 114, emphasis added.
13 See Jay Gearing and Ben Rogaly, '"Workers": life, creativity and resisting racial capitalism', *The Sociological Review Blog*, 8 March 2019, available online at: www.thesociologicalreview.com/blog/workers-life-creativity-and-resisting-racial-capitalism.html (accessed April 2019).
14 Across the UK, people of colour and people who were visibly identified as Muslim faced heightened racisms, including open calls for them to 'go home', regardless of whether they were born in the UK or had British citizenship. EU nationals, especially people from central or eastern European countries or the Baltic states, reported increased xenophobia and hostility as well as nervousness about their future rights and status in the UK. There was also a rise in anti-Semitic attacks.
15 Satnam Virdee and Brendan McGeever, 'Racism, crisis, Brexit', *Ethnic and racial studies*, 41:10 (2017), 1802–1819.
16 Hawkins, *Creativity*, p. 112.
17 In 2018 Fiona Onasanya was convicted for lying about a driving offence and served one month in prison. She was expelled from the Labour Party and removed as an MP following a recall petition. In the byelection that followed on 8 June 2019, Labour retained the seat in spite of a strong challenge from the newly formed Brexit Party led by Nigel Farage, a key ally of far-right leaders in several EU countries. Just two weeks earlier, the Brexit Party had achieved the highest vote share in elections to the EU Parliament.
18 John Berger, *And Our Faces, My Heart, Brief as Photos* (London: Writers and Readers, 1984), p. 31.
19 Charles Leadbeater and Paul Miller, *The Pro-Am Revolution: How Enthusiasts are Changing Our Economy and Society* (London: DEMOS, 2004).
20 The fourth argument applies this general Massey-inspired approach to place to one particular kind of place, the workplace, specifically food factories and warehouses (see Chapter 3).

21 The meeting with Jay and me went ahead but he eventually decided not to make a film with us.

22 Massey, *World City*; Doreen Massey, *Landscape/Space/Politics: An Essay* (2011), available online at: http://thefutureoflandscape.wordpress.com/landscapespacepolitics-an-essay/ (accessed January 2019).

23 Massey, *World City*, p. 10.

24 John Harris, 'If eastern Europeans leave Britain after Brexit, what happens? – video', *The Guardian*, 2 February 2017, available online at: www.theguardian.com/commentisfree/video/2017/feb/02/if-eastern-europeans-leave-britain-after-brexit-what-happens-video (accessed March 2019).

25 See n. 17 above.

26 Michele Lobo, 'Reframing the creative city: fragile friendships and affective art spaces in Darwin, Australia', *Urban studies*, 55:3 (2017), 627.

27 Ibid., p. 628.

28 I have written elsewhere about Chris Porsz and other Peterborough-based photographers' care and support during my research. See Ben Rogaly, '"Don't show the play at the football ground, nobody will come": the micro-sociality of co-produced research in an English provincial city', *Sociological review*, 64:4 (2016), 657–680.

29 At this stage I had not yet begun to work with Jay Gearing, director of *Workers*, who also came up with the title for the film.

30 See Chris Porsz, 'Nene Park project', in *Chris Porsz – Street Photography*, available online at: www.chrisporsz.com/nene-park-project.html (accessed March 2019).

31 Chris Porsz, *New England: The Culture and People of an English New Town during the 1970s and 1980s* (Peterborough: Chris Porsz, 2012). With Chris Porsz's kind permission, the cover of *Stories from a migrant city* is based on the photograph 'Marie 4 Martin' originally published in his *New England*.

32 Chris Porsz, *Reunions* (Peterborough: Chris Porsz, 2016), pp. 86, 88 and 90.

33 Ibid., p. 169.

34 Ibid., pp. 202, 208 and 238.

35 Ibid., p. 274.

36 Les Back, *The Art of Listening* (London: Bloomsbury Academic, 2007), p. 104.

37 Ibid., p. 108.

38 A popular lights festival that runs for several months each year in the coastal resort of Blackpool in Lancashire, England.

39 Hawkins, *Creativity*, p. 174.

40 Parveen Ashraf, *Parveen the Spice Queen: Authentic Indian Cooking* (n.p.: FCM Publishing, 2016), p. 7.

41 Ibid., p. 10.
42 See Chapter 1.
43 As part of the 'Creative Interruptions' project: see https://creativeinterruptions.com (accessed March 2019).
44 The workshop was entitled 'Migrant cartographies: cities, circuits and circulations' and organised by Caroline Knowles at Goldsmiths, University of London, on 12 May 2017.
45 Ashraf, *Parveen the Spice Queen*, p. 79.
46 Ibid., p. 9.
47 Ibid., p. 105.
48 Ibid., p. 83.
49 Ibid., p. 141.
50 Ibid., p. 143.
51 Back, *The Art of Listening*.
52 Ashraf, *Parveen the Spice Queen*, pp. 99–101.
53 Ibid., p. 7.
54 Ibid., p. 35.
55 Rogaly and Qureshi, 'Diversity, urban space and the right to the provincial city'.
56 Hawkins, *Creativity*, p. 20.
57 Jessie Brennan, 'Introduction', in Jessie Brennan (ed.), *Re: Development: Voices, Cyanotypes and Writings from The Green Backyard* (London: Silent Grid, 2016), pp. 25–26.
58 In Brennan (ed.), *Re: Development*, p. 106.
59 Dougald Hine, 'Spelling it out', in Jessie Brennan (ed.), *Re: Development: Voices, Cyanotypes and Writings from The Green Backyard* (London: Silent Grid, 2016), p. 60.
60 Rebecca Solnit's praise for John Berger's *Portraits: John Berger on Artists*, ed. Tom Overton (London Verso, 2016), printed inside the cover of the companion collection of writing by Berger, *Landscapes: John Berger on Art*, ed. Tom Overton (London: Verso, 2016).
61 Sophie Antonelli, 'Digging for our lives', in Jessie Brennan (ed.), *Re: Development: Voices, Cyanotypes and Writings from The Green Backyard* (London: Silent Grid, 2016), pp. 29–32.
62 Anna Minton, 'The Green Backyard and the right to the city', in Jessie Brennan (ed.), *Re: Development: Voices, Cyanotypes and Writings from The Green Backyard* (London: Silent Grid, 2016), pp. 49–50.
63 See Ben Rogaly, 'Contesting neo-liberal common sense: bottom-up history and the struggle over urban space', in Jessie Brennan (ed.), *Re: Development: Voices, Cyanotypes and Writings from The Green Backyard* (London: Silent Grid, 2016), p. 51.
64 Coutinho mentions this fact in a short piece about her life in Peterborough ('Peterborough together: why have I stayed?', *The Moment*

Magazine, November 2018, available online at: www.themoment-magazine.com/community/peterborough-together-i-stayed/ (accessed December 2018)).

65 Ibid.

66 Available online at: https://vimeo.com/290264914 (accessed December 2018).

67 Coutinho, 'Peterborough together'.

68 Browne, *Being Krystyna*, p. 5.

69 The interview took place in English on 20 March 2012.

70 Although with typical modesty in a short contribution to the preface of *Being Krystyna* Chris Porsz refers to his writings as 'notes I had taken over the years whenever I questioned my mother about her wartime experiences' (Carol Browne, *Being Krystyna: A Story of Survival in WWII* (n.p.: Dilliebooks, 2016), p. 6). *The Three Beauties* is available on request from Chris Porsz at http://www.chrisporsz.com.

71 Browne, *Being Krystyna*, p. 5.

72 In a critique of responses to Jo Cox's murder, Hannah Jones echoes the implication of Chris Porsz's piece, arguing that although the killer's 'violent misogynist white supremacy was extreme and unregulated, it was not out of step with wider patterns' in politics and society. Hannah Jones, 'More in common: the domestication of misogynist white supremacy and the assassination of Jo Cox', *Ethnic and racial studies* (2019), available online (early view) at: doi.org/10.1080/01419870.2019.1577474 (accessed June 2019).

73 Browne, *Being Krystyna*, p. 52.

74 Ibid., pp. 66, 64.

75 Ibid., p. 72.

76 Ibid., p. 71.

77 Ibid., pp. 100–101.

78 Yasmin Gunaratnam, *Death and the Migrant: Bodies, Borders and Care* (London: Bloomsbury Academic, 2013), p. 8.

79 Hannah Jones *et al.*, *Go Home? The politics of Immigration Controversies* (Manchester: Manchester University Press, 2017), p. 150.

80 Massey, *World City*, p. 12.

Conclusion: the immigration debate and common anger in dangerous times

> We put [politics beyond exceptionalism] into practice when we stand alongside others and act according to the egalitarian maxim. I fight for my own liberation precisely because I fight for that of the stranger.[1]

Through the lens of a small provincial city in Brexit-era England, this book has used people's stories to reimagine and reconceptualise what the commonly used terms 'migrant', 'immigrant', 'migration' and 'immigration' mean, and to whose bodies they become attached. It is written at a time when these notions have frequently been drawn on to frame an 'Other' responsible for society's ills to be contrasted with the 'local' or 'native' person. Writings that suggest that 'native' people have lost out to immigrants and immigration have received strong backing from a large publishing company (Penguin Random House) and promotion in the mainstream media.[2] Such rhetoric is strongly racialised. In the UK and elsewhere in the Global North, some white supremacists claim that 'white' people are being 'replaced' by darker-skinned people and in particular Muslims.[3] One brutal consequence of white supremacist ideology was the murder of nine African Americans at Emanuel African Methodist Episcopal Church in Charleston, South Carolina, in June 2015. Versions of white supremacism portray diaspora

Jews as responsible for promoting universalist notions of rights and belonging. When eleven people were killed in another terrorist atrocity in October 2018 at the Tree of Life Synagogue in Pittsburgh, Pennsylvania, the ideology of hatred towards Muslims was directly linked to anti-Semitism, with the synagogue's participation in the Hebrew Immigrant Aid Society cited by the perpetrator as a reason for the attack.[4] The motivation behind the terrorist massacre of Muslim worshippers in the Al-Noor mosque in Christchurch, Aotearoa/New Zealand, in March 2019 was attributed by many to the way Islamophobia (or, conversely, denial of Islamophobia's existence) had been made publicly acceptable, even hegemonic, by significant parts of the corporate-owned news media.[5] Islamophobia was (and at the time of writing still is) prevalent on social media and being enabled via the algorithms used by companies such as YouTube.[6]

The immigration debate in white-dominated and settler colonial societies of the Global North has long been racialised. In the UK, one legacy of the movement of New Commonwealth citizens from former colonies in South Asia, the Caribbean and elsewhere was that not only those who had themselves moved to the UK since the 1940s, but their descendants too, became known as 'immigrants'. The word 'immigrant' is hard to separate in UK public discourse from black and brown residents, whether or not they have been born in the UK and whatever their citizenship status. Yet the UK also has a long history of anti-immigrant mobilisation aimed at 'white' people including Jews in the late nineteenth and early twentieth centuries,[7] and, as experienced by Chris Porsz's father Alfons and referred to in Chapter 5, of Polish people after the Second World War.[8] The Leave campaign in the UK's 2016 referendum focused intensively on freedom of movement within the EU. It was argued that the arrival of large numbers of EU nationals in the UK (especially after the enlargement of the EU in 2004) lowered wages for British workers,[9] brought rapid large-scale 'cultural change' to areas of the country that were not accustomed to it and led to overcrowded doctors' surgeries and shortages of primary school places.[10] However, this discourse ran alongside a hyping-up of the idea that freedom of movement within the EU represented a danger to the whiteness and nominal Christian majority culture of Britain because it risked allowing in large numbers of mainly brown-skinned,

Muslim men and (in smaller number) women and children who had made their way to the EU from countries in the Middle East, South Asia and sub-Saharan Africa, with particularly large numbers fleeing the Syrian civil war in 2015. Added to this was the false claim that Turkey was on the verge of joining the EU – a point that was meant to awaken fears of greater numbers of Muslims entering the UK.[11] Since the referendum, far-right parties in some other EU countries have ramped this up further by arguing that climate change will lead to large-scale immigration from the Global South and is, for this reason, a major threat to the continued prosperity of the Global North.[12] This narrative ignores the racial injustice entailed in the far greater damage being done by climate change to livelihoods in the Global South.[13] In contrast to the internationalism of some advocates of a 'green new deal',[14] it represents the emergence of a white supremacist approach to the question of who should be allowed to survive ecological catastrophe, a kind of eco-fascism.[15]

Following in the footsteps of other authors,[16] I have tried to debunk some key myths about immigration and about the notion of a pure,[17] native, 'white' working-class to whom 'immigration' represents a threat. Class is central to this discussion. Neoliberalist policies from the 1980s had led to deindustrialisation, deregulation of labour markets and the decimation of trade union power. I write this as the austerity policies that were implemented so brutally in the UK by the 2010–15 Conservative–Liberal Democrat coalition government and continued to be meted out by subsequent Conservative governments cut increasingly deeply into people's lives, especially affecting women and working-class people, and often cutting deeper still for racialised minorities and recent international migrants within the working class.[18] Alongside the 'hostile environment' policy aimed at international migrants,[19] the effects of these recent Conservative-led government policies include a decade-long decline in average real wages, increasing in-work poverty, job insecurity and intensification of workplace regimes. As David Harvey has argued, neoliberalism implemented by the state was a victory for the power of a corporate capitalist class.[20]

The book's two key questions about place, 'what does this place stand for?' and 'to whom does this place belong?', derive from the work of Doreen Massey. As we have seen throughout the book, the answers to these questions are complex for four reasons. First, places are contested; secondly, places exist at multiple scales, for example as buildings, workplaces, streets, neighbourhoods, towns, cities, nations (when territorialised as states) and continents; thirdly, places are made and imagined through their relations to other places which they may influence and/or be shaped by; and fourthly, places change over time in relation both to their own pasts and to the pasts of places elsewhere.

Thinking about place in this way makes space for attempts to understand struggles over the nation-state and what *it* stands for through the lens of a particular place within its territory. The Brexit era in England is characterised by austerity, legacies of colonialism and ideological battles over migration, 'race' and the country's relation to other countries in the UK and above all to the EU.[21] The English provincial city of Peterborough is a microcosm, experiencing all of these contestations as part of its particular trajectory, on top of the sediment of its own history. There are battles over what Peterborough stands for as a city; most relevant to this book are differences of view over the arrival and settlement of international migrants as well as over their rights and representation. Given that the UK maintains a hierarchy of citizenship statuses including the status of being undocumented, to what extent should a city seek to promote an *urban citizenship* applying equally to all residents?

Below the city scale, contests have occurred and are ongoing over specific areas in Peterborough. As we learned in Chapter 4, for example, the establishment in 2005 of New Link, a reception service for newly arrived international migrants, was opposed by an organised group of mainly white British residents in the Millfield and New England neighbourhoods. These residents were concerned about the number of non-British EU nationals renting in homes of multiple occupancy in these areas and about the proportion of properties owned by landlords with South Asian (mostly Pakistani Muslim) heritage there. In what can be seen as a local prefiguring of a national position expressed in the 2016 campaign for the UK to leave the EU, arguments that 'indigenous' white British people had 'legitimate grievances' about levels of immigration from central and eastern Europe gave renewed energy, as Umut Erel has shown, to those who believed there could be too many brown and black people and too many Muslims.[22]

The idea that Peterborough's white British population is 'indigenous' at all is spurious, whether indigeneity is considered at the national or local scale. At the national scale it denies the multiple histories of immigration by 'white' people and the ways in which some international migrants and their descendants were not initially treated as white but became so over time.[23] Locally, while some families have histories of residence going back many generations, any association of indigeneity with whiteness and Britishness is given the lie by the large-scale migration by white British people from London to Peterborough in the 1970s and 1980s (as well as from elsewhere in England and other countries of the UK). In the late 1960s Peterborough was a market town with an Anglican cathedral. The building of New Town areas was masterminded by the Peterborough Development Corporation set up in 1968 as part of a national strategy of housing provision – one in which London exerted major influence as the main source of new residents; of experts who came to run the Development Corporation and other new initiatives in the city;[24] and of capital investments in new businesses there. Many such changes were contested at the time. While the Development Corporation provided tours for existing Peterborough residents of areas of new housing, shops and schools that were under construction, some residents felt bitter. Among them were people whose homes or business premises had been compulsorily purchased and demolished.

This book began with the recollections of a white Peterborough-born woman, Fiona Dawson, about the attitudes of new arrivals from London she met while out dancing. Fiona's father died suddenly when she was eighteen. A short time later the Peterborough Development Corporation issued a compulsory purchase order for her house:

Ben: And what's your first memory of people coming to live in the Development Corporation housing that was being built?

Fiona: Well that's a very vivid memory because I was working at the Education Office by this time … and I was an administrator and the teachers used to come in for interviews and I remember so well that if they got the job … they had to come into reception and I had a heap of forms with

> numbers on and those numbers represented a Development Corporation house. So you can imagine, I'd had to move, compulsory purchase moved and my dad's dead and I've had to find a house for my mum and it's been, blurgh! ... They knew it came with a house but it was such a big thing for you coming from London or wherever you were coming from and I don't know their situation but I guess it was quite a difficult one but suddenly to get a job and guarantee a Development Corporation house must have been such a big thing. So yes, that's what I remember ... you know everybody has different situations and mine was a very unique situation, so I never said anything about it but I did used to think, 'Hmh!' ... There was this big incentive if you worked in Peterborough and you got a job, that often on the advert it would say, 'The successful applicant will be offered a Development Corporation house.' ... We've got all these new people and all this expansion and lots of people got work.

Sean Brennan, who, like Fiona, was born in Peterborough, spoke of the resentment that existing residents had towards the newcomers when they started moving into the New Town houses, and a sense of powerless in relation to the allocation decisions being made:

Ben: When you were a teenager a lot of new people came in and you were talking about the people who came from London, you said there was tension between them and local people?

Sean: There was tension because people couldn't get the houses. There were these houses being built in Westwood, Ravensthorpe, Bretton, all Development Corporation houses and of course a lot of the Londoners were, 'They're our houses', and that didn't go down very well. And local kids and I was one of them as well, we couldn't get a house.

Ben: Did you protest?

Sean: Well everybody protested but it's like talking to a bloody brick wall and then you got fed up and that was it.

This book has drawn on such stories to insist on making strange what for some is a familiar, taken-for-granted, equivalence of white Britishness with indigeneity both nationally, in England as a whole, and locally, in Peterborough. This poses a challenge to the often racialised common usage of 'immigration' and 'migration'. At the same time the biographical approach to recording people's stories in a single city reveals a binary division of people into categories of 'local' and 'migrant' to be problematic. Moreover, when combined with an analysis of the working of structural inequalities, this approach also challenges the sometimes automatic association of people who move with privilege, and of those who stay put in the place they grew up in as lacking the resources to do otherwise.

Listening to people speak about their whole lives is inevitably partial: only so much can be said in a few hours of interview, and how narrators tell these parts of their life histories reflects where and when the interviews take place, how they view the person doing the interviewing and how they decide they want to come across to them.[25] However, even partial biographies are more likely to escape the confines of social categorisation and allow histories of mobility *and* fixity to emerge in the life of the same person than interviews solely focused on the present. Individual biographies of Peterborough residents also reveal shorter-distance residential moves within and out of the city, as well as mobilities associated with employment, education and ways of life that involve coming and going between places. Yet, while residential mobility and migration are seen to be experienced by white British people as much as by racialised minorities and international migrants, fixity, staying in a place, is part of the biographies of people who might be seen by others as 'immigrants' or 'migrants'.

In Chapter 2 I emphasised how racisms, class-based inequalities and gender shaped the biographies of three men with South Asian heritage, including their decisions over migration and staying put. Moving is not necessarily privileged as some anti-immigration arguments imply:[26] it can be that people have little choice but to move. Equally, staying put can be, and often is, a choice.[27] Massey drew attention to differences in power between people in a position to choose mobility or fixity, and others who were forced either to move or to remain where they were. She highlighted the potential for common anger between people experiencing displacement because they have had little choice but to move away from a place that was familiar, and others who experience it because they have not had the resources to move and have witnessed dramatic change in the place around them.[28] The potential for common anger among working-class people with different histories of displacement, for unity across racialised divides, was noticed by Phil Piratin, a Jew and a future Communist Party Member of Parliament, in London's East End in the 1930s. Piratin was transformed by his attendance, incognito, at a meeting and subsequent march led by Oswald Mosley, the leader of the British Union of Fascists, in 1935. He noticed that behind the ranks of uniformed fascists came 'people. About 1,500 men, women (some with babies in arms), and youngsters ... I knew some of these people, some of the men wore trade-union badges ... There were certain latent anti-Semitic prejudices it is true, but above all these people, like most in East London, were living miserable, squalid lives. Their homes were slums, many were unemployed. Those at work were often in low-paid jobs.' He resolved that his party 'should help the people to improve their conditions of life, in the course of which we could show them who was really responsible for their conditions, and get them organised to fight against their real exploiters'.[29] On the barricades that prevented the British Union of Fascists marching down the Cable Street on 4 October 1936 Piratin observed that '[n]ever was there such unity of all sections of the working class ... People whose lives were poles apart, though living within a few hundred yards of each other; bearded Orthodox Jews and rough-and-ready Irish Catholic dockers ... The struggle ... against the fascists had brought them together against their common enemies and their lackeys.'[30]

In early twenty-first-century Peterborough one source of common anger across racialised difference was the intensity of workplace regimes that characterised employment in its warehouses and food factories. Peterborough Development Corporation had closed in 1988 during Margaret Thatcher's premiership, and this led to a period of economic stagnation in the city.[31] With dramatically diminished funding available from central government, Peterborough's economic fortunes were more closely related to capital investment from companies based in other cities and/or other countries. In the 2000s and 2010s Peterborough, along with certain other provincial towns and cities in England such as Doncaster,[32] saw increased investment in logistics and warehouse distribution.[33] In Chapter 3 I showed how the means of recruiting and managing warehouse workers through employment agencies evolved out of the historical practice of hiring gang labour for agricultural production in the city's hinterland. Temporary agency workers were also in demand to staff the retail distribution centres and food factories that supermarkets relied on for their algorithm-based, just-in-time supply chains.

Symptomatic of increasingly skewed capital–labour relations in the UK after a decade of austerity and nearly four decades of neoliberalist policies, large corporations involved in logistics in Peterborough operated harsh workplace regimes that involved the regular ratcheting-up of performance targets for low-paid agency workers and increasing surveillance of work breaks through digital technology. These were enforced by sanctions: a certain number of breaches, however minor, could lead to dismissal. Workers felt disposable. Companies' determination to drive ever higher levels of added value from each worker was evident from their cavalier approach to induction, training and health and safety in the workplace. As one former warehouse manager, Sabina, put it in 2017, 'it is about just getting people in, cheap, I would say, cheap work resources'.

Certain kinds of roles, particularly those involving uncertain numbers of hours or periods of employment, along with low-status, low-paid, fast-paced work, became associated with international migrants rather than British workers. As a result, the people employed to work in these roles became racialised as 'migrants'. As elsewhere in England, this was seen as 'foreigners' work'.[34] In order to push people to work at the pace needed, some supervisors used verbal aggression, shouting instructions at workers. Management played on divisions between workers of different national backgrounds. They took advantage of their power to decide when to carry out threats (such as dismissal) and of the different degrees of knowledge among workers regarding how to try to reach their targets in the least exhausting way. Sabina reported an approach among her fellow managers that meant not intervening when some newer workers strained hard to meet targets that could have been fulfilled more quickly and easily if the workers had known about informal practices such as 'cherry-picking'. Another narrator spoke of instances of double standards used by a supervisor who would vary their speed in bringing workplace conversations among workers to a halt – faster for workers of some nationalities, slower for others. Yet at some sites, the workforce was also divided because it had internalised a racialised hierarchy,[35] or because people employed for 'foreigners' work' brought with them work practices learned through experience elsewhere. For example, we saw in Chapter 3 how Agnieszka Sobieraj viewed her embeddedness in punitive work cultures that she and other colleagues were familiar with in Poland as the main cause of her intensity of work effort in a fruit-processing factory. Several years after the event she narrated this to me almost regretfully, suggesting that she and other young co-nationals and workers who had moved to Peterborough from central or eastern European or Baltic countries tended to work at a speed that locally raised British workers could not keep up with. The effect of this, she now reflected, was potentially to worsen working conditions for all, for example by raising the target required to fulfil the output quota considered equivalent to a day's work.

Yet common anger at particular workplace practices could also *unite* people – even if only momentarily – to contest the divide-and-rule techniques of racial capitalism rather than identifying with narrower national or linguistic groups or allowing themselves to be separated into categories such as white 'natives', established ethnic minorities or recent international migrants. In spite of ongoing racisms and racialised hierarchies, the foundations for coming together to take action were sown by the enjoyment some narrators reported of the multi-ethnic, multi-lingual multi-nationality warehouse and food factory workplaces. This non-elite cosmopolitan disposition emerged for some through experiences at work, for example for Agnieszka Kowalczyk-Wojcik, who spoke with me in 2017 about her relations with other workers in a Peterborough warehouse:

> When I start working at [the warehouse], I couldn't imagine that I can spend my off time during the break with people from Malaysia, we have one guy from New Zealand. It's amazing. I can sit with them and speak. I like it.

Others, like Laura Chłopeka, Azwer Sabir and Judita Grubliene, also appreciated the mix of people at warehouses where they worked. Laura, who moved to the UK from Poland in 2005, met her South American husband in a Peterborough workplace. Azwer, originally from Iraqi Kurdistan and living in the UK since 2002, spoke of his experience working in a warehouse with Polish, Lithuanian, Latvian, Bulgarian and Romanian colleagues and the friendships he and his wife (working at the same warehouse) developed with people of other nationalities there:

> There were so many different communities … Sometimes we sit with English people as well; honestly, it does all depend on individuals. Some of the English people I still have friendships with them.

Judita, who moved to Peterborough from Lithuania in 2009, described a specific moment of resistance where she combined with Turkish, Latvian and other Lithuanian colleagues to challenge what they had experienced as nationality-based discrimination. Like Laura's, her broad employment experience before and after working in a warehouse enabled her to reflect on the specific opportunities such workplaces presented for communicating with others across difference, and for sharing stories. Reflecting on a much earlier instance of capitalist work – in the tobacco fields of colonial Virginia in the seventeenth century – Satnam Virdee shows that, in a harshly exploitative environment, the workforce, made up of indentured labourers from England and African slaves, plotted their escape together, seeking support on occasion from Algonquin people whose land had been expropriated.[36]

Beyond the workplace, the book has also drawn attention to cosmopolitan citizenship acts initiated by international migrants in Peterborough, such as the film club established by Agnieszka Sobieraj and others, and the private party for St Andrew's Day that I attended in a community room hosted by Maria, another Polish woman, in December 2011. As detailed in Chapter 4, the party involved people from multiple national backgrounds, white people and racialised minorities, international migrant couples from different countries – and sometimes continents – of origin who met in Peterborough and a diverse array of culinary practices. But during the EU referendum in June 2016 and subsequently, racist and xenophobic attacks on people in Peterborough (including on racialised minorities and white non-British EU nationals) increased,[37] and the early months of 2019 saw far-right graffiti emerge at several sites in the city including an image of Hitler, swastikas and the slogan 'bring slavery back'. In the long-drawn-out process of negotiating Brexit within the UK and between the UK and the EU and after more than a decade of austerity, including savage cuts to public services across the board, to council funding and in turn to voluntary organisations, these were dangerous times.[38]

While 'immigration' in its current usage serves to racialise people and further divide us according to differential citizenship status, nationality and migration history, hope for equal status and rights for all residents of any UK city is likely to remain elusive. Yet, in the words of the activist and academic Angela Davis, reflecting on what she felt was the missed opportunity of the Occupy movement in 2011, 'sometimes we have to do the [preparatory] work' so as to be organised when the chance to push for a changed narrative comes, 'even though we don't yet see a glimmer on the horizon that it's actually going to be possible'.[39] One important step towards changing the racialising effects of the terms of the immigration debate is to listen out for bottom-up, non-elite cosmopolitanism practices and for memories of past ones. This means rejecting the narrative that cosmopolitanism is necessarily a disposition of (or solely practised by) a metropolitan elite. This notion was a key part of the speech given by the UK Prime Minister Theresa May at the Conservative Party conference in 2016 and is central to the arguments of writers who urge understanding and accommodation of populist (white) nationalism and thus 'close off any possibility that the prevailing order might be challenged by people coming together in their difference to work towards common goals'.[40]

Indeed, elites who travel widely and with ease may not be cosmopolitan at all in that they may be dismissive, racist, even deliberately sowing division. Conversely, as the stories in this book have shown, provincial and non-elite cosmopolitanisms are alive and well in spite of racisms, austerity policies and a hugely skewed distribution of wealth and income. Like those of other provincial cities, Peterborough's cultural productions usually go unnoticed. Yet as we saw in the case of the four Peterborough books discussed in Chapter 5, they confound the condescension of the metropolitan middle-classes towards provincial and predominantly working-class places. At the same time, they positively reflect the city's migrant heritage (while also respecting people who have never, or only very rarely, moved residence). These books, together with the biographical oral histories quoted from throughout *Stories from a migrant city*, are part of Peterborough's gift to the rest of the UK and to the world. Collectively, through their portrayal of universal human experiences of loss, absence and death, they provide a vision of common humanity and thus make their own contribution, however small, to preparing the ground for future struggles against all forms of racism, class and gender inequalities, workplace exploitation and climate injustice.

Notes

1 Asad Haider, *Mistaken Identity: Race and Class in the Age of Trump* (London: Verso, 2018), pp. 110–111.

2 Eric Kaufman, *Whiteshift: Populism, Immigration and the Future of White Majorities* (London: Allen Lane, 2018); Roger Eatwell and Matthew Goodwin, *National Populism: The Revolt Against Liberal Democracy* (London: Pelican, 2018).

3 The idea that Muslims and Islam are threats to mainly white European countries and white-dominated former settler colonies, such as the USA, is not new (see Ben Rogaly and Becky Taylor, *Moving Histories of Class and Community: Identity, Place and Belonging in Contemporary England* (Basingstoke: Palgrave Macmillan, 2009), pp. 208–210). However, the idea was promoted by mainstream news outlets and politicians in the wake of terrorist atrocities carried out in the name of Islamist extremist organisations such as Al-Qaeda and Daesh (Sayeeda Warsi, *The Enemy Within: A Tale of Muslim Britain* (London and New York: Allen Lane, 2017).

4 Historical evidence for the intertwining of Islamophobia and anti-Semitism (as well as instances of their separate development) is expertly compiled in Ben Gidley and James Renton (eds), *Antisemitism and Islamophobia in Europe: A Shared Story?* (London: Palgrave Macmillan, 2017).

5 See, for example, Imran Awan, 'Christchurch attacks show Islamophobia is real, deadly and spreading around the world', *The Conversation*, 20 March 2019, available online at: http://theconversation.com/christchurch-

attacks-show-islamophobia-is-real-deadly-and-spreading-around-the-world-113786 (accessed April 2019).

6 According to the chair of the UK parliament's Home Affairs Select Committee, Yvette Cooper. See Alex Hern, 'MPs criticise social media firms for failure to report criminal posts', *The Guardian*, 24 April 2019, available online at: www.theguardian.com/media/2019/apr/24/mps-criticise-tech-giants-for-failure-to-report-criminal-posts-twitter-facebook-google-youtube (accessed April 2019).

7 Satnam Virdee, *Racism, Class and the Racialized Outsider* (Basingstoke: Palgrave Macmillan, 2014), p. 48.

8 See www.polandinexile.com/polishresettlement.htm (accessed April 2019).

9 An expansion of low-wage employment, one of the most deregulated labour markets in the Organization for Economic Cooperation and Development and low productivity caused average real wages to decline in the UK in the years following the 2007–08 financial crisis. Valentina Romei, 'How wages fell in the UK while the economy grew', *Financial Times*, 2 March 2017, available online at: www.ft.com/content/83e7e87e-fe64–11e6–96f8–3700c5664d30 (accessed April 2019). A review of studies conducted over a similar time period found little impact of immigration on the average wages of UK workers with a small negative impact in the short term for the lowest-paid, who are themselves likely to be international migrants. The effect of immigration on wages in the longer term was predicted to be positive as demand for goods and services increased with the net growth in population. See Martin Ruhs and Carlos Vargas-Silva, 'The labour market effects of immigration', *Migration Observatory Briefing*, Centre on Migration, Policy and Society, University of Oxford, UK, December 2018.

10 On the contrary, international migrants were critical to improving 'overall health' in the UK, and many have been key workers in 'health, educational, social and care services'. Danny Dorling, *Peak Inequality: Britain's Ticking Time Bomb* (Bristol: Policy Press, 2018), p. 70. In areas where health, education and other services have not been expanded in response to relatively large-scale or rapid net inward migration, any resulting squeeze experienced by existing residents (such as longer waits for appointments with general practitioners or greater competition for admission to local state schools) represents failure by the government to adequately target resources, a consequence, it can be argued, of the ending of the Migration Impacts Fund (MIF) in 2010. A new 'Controlling Migration Fund' was launched in England in 2016, part of which, in spite of the new fund's name, has a similar objective. See 'Commons Library Briefing: The New Controlling Migration Fund

(England)', available online at: https://researchbriefings.parliament.uk/ResearchBriefing/Summary/CBP-7673 (accessed April 2019).

11 Kathy Burrell *et al.*, 'Brexit, race and migration', *Environment and planning C: Politics and space*, 37:1 (2019), 3–40.

12 Kate Aronoff, 'The European far right's environmental turn', *Dissent*, 31 May 2019, available online at: https://www.dissentmagazine.org/online_articles/the-european-far-rights-environmental-turn (accessed June 2019).

13 Zamzam Ibrahim and Laura Clayson, 'Gogreen 19: climate change is a racist issue', *People and Planet*, 11 February 2019, available online at: https://peopleandplanet.org/blog/2019–02–11/gogreen19-climate-change-racist-issue (accessed April 2019); Leon Sealey-Huggins, '"The climate crisis is a racist crisis": structural racism, inequality and climate change', in Azeezat Johnson, Remi Joseph-Salisbury and Beth Kamunge (eds), *The Fire Now: Anti-Racist Scholarship in Times of Explicit Racial Violence* (London: Zed, 2018), pp. 99–116.

14 Chris Saltmarsh, 'An internationalist Green New Deal', *The Ecologist*, 23 April 2019, available online at: https://theecologist.org/2019/apr/23/internationalist-green-new-deal (accessed April 2019).

15 Sarah Manavis, 'Eco-fascism: the ideology marrying environmentalism and white supremacy thriving online', *New Statesman*, 21 September 2018, available online at: www.newstatesman.com/science-tech/social-media/2018/09/eco-fascism-ideology-marrying-environmentalism-and-white-supremacy (accessed April 2019).

16 Such as Akala, *Natives: Race and Class in the Ruins of Empire* (London: Two Roads, 2018); Robbie Shilliam, *Race and the Undeserving Poor: From Abolition to Brexit* (Newcastle upon Tyne: Agenda Publishing, 2018); Aurelien Mondon and Aaron Winter, 'Whiteness, populism and the racialisation of the working-class in the United Kingdom and the United States', *Identities: Global Studies in Culture and Power*, available online (early view, 2018), DOI: 10.1080/1070289X.2018.1552440 (accessed April 2019).

17 See Mohsin Hamid, 'In the land of the pure, no one is pure enough', *The Guardian*, January 2018, available online at: www.theguardian.com/books/2018/jan/27/mohsin-hamid–exit-west-pen-pakistan (accessed April 2019).

18 Ruth Pearson, 'A feminist analysis of neoliberalism and austerity policies in the UK', *Soundings*, 71 (2019), 28–39.

19 Although generally not at wealthy, white ones.

20 David Harvey, *A Brief History of Neoliberalism* (Oxford: Oxford University Press, 2005).

21 Fintan O'Toole, *Heroic Failure: Brexit and the Politics of Pain* (London: Head of Zeus, 2018).

22 Umut Erel, 'Complex belongings: racialization and migration in a small English city', *Ethnic and racial studies*, 34:12 (2011), 2048–2068.

23 Alastair Bonnett, *White Identities: An Historical and International Introduction* (London: Routledge, 2000); Robert Young, *The Idea of English Ethnicity* (Chichester: Wiley-Blackwell, 2007).

24 Mark Roberts, 'Communication breakdown: understanding the role of policy narratives in conflict and consensus', *Critical policy studies*, 12:1 (2016), 82–102.

25 Lynn Abrams, *Oral History Theory* (second edition, London: Routledge, 2016).

26 Anti-immigrant sentiment is 'the thread that links the vast array of Europe's right-wing populists'. In this narrative, immigration is one of the 'global forces' threatening both cultural identity and economic prosperity. Far-right groups are framed 'as underdogs, bravely fighting more powerful forces'. Manuela Achilles, Kyrill Kunakhovich and Nicole Shea, 'Nationalism, nativism and the revolt against globalization', *Europe Now*, 1 February 2018, available online at: www.europenowjournal.org/2018/01/31/nationalism-nativism-and-the-revolt-against-globalization/ (accessed April 2019).

27 For evidence that the proportion of people migrating across international borders internationally declined between 1960 and 2000, see Mathias Czaika and Hein de Haas, 'The globalization of migration: has the world become more migratory?', *International migration review*, 48:2 (2015), 296.

28 Doreen Massey, *Landscape/Space/Politics: An Essay*, available online at: https://thefutureoflandscape.wordpress.com/landscapespacepolitics-an-essay/ (accessed April 2019); Ben Rogaly and Kaveri Qureshi, 'Diversity, urban space and the right to the provincial city', *Identities: global studies in culture and power*, 20:4 (2013), 423–437.

29 Phil Piratin, *Our Flag Stays Red* (1948; third edition, London: Lawrence and Wishart, 2006), p. 18.

30 Ibid., pp. 23–24.

31 Peter Tyler, Emil Evenhuis and Ron Martin, 'Case study report: Peterborough', Structural Transformation, Adaptability and City Economic Evolutions, Working Paper 10 (UK Economic and Social Research Council, Urban Transformations Initiative, 2018), p. 3, available online at: www.cityevolutions.org.uk/working-paper-peterborough-case-study/ (accessed January 2019).

32 John Harris, 'Amazon v the high street: how Doncaster is fighting back', *The Guardian*, 11 October 2018, available online at: www.theguardian.com/uk-news/2018/oct/11/amazon-v-the-high-street-how-doncaster-is-fighting-back (accessed April 2019).

33 Tyler, Evenhuis and Martin, 'Case study report: Peterborough', p. 16.

34 James Bloodworth, *Hired: Six Months Undercover in Low-Wage Britain* (London: Atlantic Books, 2018).

35 Ben Rogaly and Kaveri Qureshi, '"That's where my perception of it all was shattered": oral histories and moral geographies of food sector workers in an English city region', *Geoforum*, 78 (2017), 189–198.

36 Satnam Virdee, 'Racialized capitalism: an account of its contested origins and consolidation', *The sociological review*, 67:1 (2019), 11–12. Virdee's example adds to the seminal attempt by Peter Linebaugh and Marcus Rediker to 'recover some of the lost history of the multi-ethnic class that was essential to the rise of capitalism' between the early seventeenth century and the middle of the nineteenth. This class, they show, was made up of 'variously designated dispossessed commoners, transported felons, indentured servants, religious radicals, pirates, urban laborers, soldiers, sailors, and African slaves.' Peter Linebaugh and Marcus Rediker, *The Many-Headed Hydra: Sailors, Slaves, Commoners, and the Hidden History of the Revolutionary Atlantic* (London: Verso, 2000), pp. 4–7.

37 Just as they did in many parts of England. See Jon Burnett, *Racial Violence and the Brexit State* (London: Institute of Race Relations, 2016).

38 And still are at the time of writing this conclusion. During the byelection in Peterborough in June 2019, the newly formed Brexit Party was assisted in its city centre campaigning by the far-right anti-Muslim activist and journalist Katie Hopkins. Labour narrowly held the seat through a well-organised grassroots campaign.

39 Angela Davis, *Freedom is a Constant Struggle: Ferguson, Palestine and the Foundations of a Movement* (Chicago: Haymarket Books, 2016), p. 29.

40 Daniel Trilling, 'I'm not racist, but ...', review of Eric Kaufman, *Whiteshift* and Roger Eatwell and Matthew Goodwin, *National Populism*, *London Review of Books*, 18 April 2019, available online at: www.lrb.co.uk/v41/n08/daniel-trilling/im-not-racist-but- (accessed April 2019).

Acknowledgements

My thanks to all who took part in the research that led to this book and especially to the oral history narrators, artists, activists and fellow academics who collaborated directly in one of the two projects funded by the UK Arts and Humanities Research Council, 'Places for All?' (2011–13) and 'Creative Interruptions' (2016–19), on which the book draws. My greatest debt is to Kaveri Qureshi, who worked flat out during three months of residential fieldwork in Peterborough and co-authored three academic publications with me. Kaveri's sharpness and integrity as an academic are matched only by her generosity of spirit. She repeatedly told me I should be the sole author of this book and has been a continuous source of encouragement and insightful comments.

Thanks to Tom Dark of Manchester University Press for believing in the book, and for his patience, persistence and wise counsel throughout; as well as to his colleagues Robert Byron and Lianne Slavin and MUP's reviewers, who have improved the book through contributing valuable time, thoughts and suggestions.

I owe much to historian Becky Taylor for the oral history work we did together in Norwich and the thinking on migration and mobility that emerged from that, which formed part of our joint book *Moving Histories of Class and Community: Identity, Place and Belonging in*

Contemporary England (Palgrave Macmillan, 2009). Huge gratitude to the rest of the 'Places for All?' team including Mukul Ahmed, Teresa Cairns, Denis Doran, Donna Hetherington, Liz Hingley, Raminder Kaur, Keely Mills and Jabeen Maqbool; and to Sarita Malik, for her skilful and supportive leadership of the 'Creative Interruptions' project, and the rest of the team, especially Daisy Hasan, Churnjeet Mahn, Michael Pierse, Anandi Ramamurthy, Jasber Singh and Photini Vrikki.

In 2017 and 2018 I worked closely as researcher and co-producer with the film director Jay Gearing on *Workers*. Many insights from our collaboration have come into this book. I owe an enormous amount to Jay and to everyone who contributed to *Workers* as well as to many other friends in Peterborough – in particular Sophie Antonelli, Parveen Ashraf, Zain Awan, Mam Bandali, Agnieszka and Weslly Coutinho, Alison and Mostyn Davies, Jabeen Maqbool, Chris Porsz and Anna Siekacz. Special thanks to Chris and Jay for helping me to search for a suitable cover photograph from Chris's extensive collection; to Jay for proposing this one and even making a mock-up of what it could look like as the cover for me to pitch to MUP; and to Chris for generously giving me permission to use it. The photograph was originally published in Chris's iconic first book *New England: The Culture and People of an English New Town during the 1970s and 1980s*. Alison and Mostyn generously gave me a permanent invitation to stay at their house, which became a second home to me just outside the city. I felt equally at home in Anna and Miles Bunten's house on the many occasions when I stayed in Peterborough with them. Big thanks to all four of you. I was lucky enough to be offered a residency at Metal Peterborough in 2016 and remain a Writer-in-Residence there at the time of completing this manuscript. Thank you to Ruth Campbell, Sarah Haythornthwaite and Mark Richards at Metal for your generosity and encouragement. Special thanks also for inspiration from beyond Peterborough to Bridget Anderson, Moushumi Bhowmik, Jessie Brennan, Reetika Khera, Churnjeet Mahn, Clare Rishbeth and Becky Taylor, to my mentor Barbara Harriss-White and to Les Back for encouraging me to keep listening for hope.

This book has been much improved by the astute comments on the whole manuscript by Anoop Nayak and on various parts of the book by Kirat Randhawa, Khem Rogaly, Simran Rogaly, Harald Bauder,

Gurminder Bhambra, Amy Clarke, Tom Dark, Jonathan Darling, Alison and Mostyn Davies, Madhumita Dutta, Jay Gearing, Katy Hawkins, Mark Richards, Ron Singh, Becky Taylor and Katie Walsh. I am grateful to all of them and also to Debbie Samaniego for assistance with formatting the endnotes and the bibliography, Fiona Little for expert copy-editing and Tanya Izzard for the index.

Massive thanks to colleagues at the University of Sussex, especially to Debbie Humphry and Aya Nasser for teaching the second-year Social Geography module at times when I was busy researching or writing this book; to Amy Clarke for helping me put together the first iteration of the third-year Class, Community, Nation module; and to all the other colleagues who discussed the ideas in the book with me or helped in other ways – big or small – to bring it to fruition, including Gurminder Bhambra, Grace Carswell, Michael Collyer, Priya Deshingkar, Evelyn Dodds, Francisco Dominguez, Fae Dussart, Meike Fechter, Tony Fielding, Carl Griffin, Elizabeth Harrison, Malcolm James, Margaretta Jolly, Russell King, Anna Laing, Claire Langhamer, Eleftheria Lekakis, Alan Lester, Chris McDermott, JoAnn McGregor, Geoffrey Mead, Katie Meek, Geert de Nève, Ceri Oeppen, Tanya Palmer, Clionadh Raleigh, Naaz Rashid, Clare Rogers, Simon Rycroft, Cathérine Senger, Sarah Scuzzarello, Cath Senker, Ron Skeldon, Bal Sokhi-Bulley, Paul Statham, Charlotte Taylor, Rachel Thomson, Divya Tolia-Kelly, Maya Unnithan, Katie Walsh, Alice Wilson, Martin Wingfield and Tahir Zaman. Thanks too to the amazing doctoral researchers with whom I had many discussions about my work-in-progress when I should have been discussing theirs, including Julius Baker, Suryamayi Clarence-Smith, Amy Clarke, Sally Daly, Debbie Humphry, Josie Jolley, Etienne Joseph, Deeptima Massey, Mimi McGann, Emilia Melossi, Suravee Nayak, Alexa Neale, Saskia Papadakis, Debbie Samaniego and Donna Simpson; and to my undergraduate thesis supervisees and students on the Social Geography and Class, Community, Nation modules for their insights and some inspiring conversations.

Thanks above all to the three people who will be the most relieved to see this book completed and who have contributed in ways beyond measure: my partner Kirat Randhawa, and our daughter Simran and son Khem. All gave freely of their thoughts, ideas, feedback and much else too from the conception of the book to its completion. I would also like to thank my sisters Sarah Rogaly, Rachel Dunkerley and Jessica Rogaly and their families for their interest in this project and their love and support throughout as well as my parents-in-law Jagir Singh and Gian Kaur, and all my brothers and sisters-in-law, especially Mike Fountain, who was born in Peterborough and kindly agreed to share his memories of growing up in the city, and Dan Gooch, who talked the early ideas for the book through with me on a long walk.

In addition, I am deeply grateful to Gladstone Community Association, Jack Hunt School, National Life Stories (British Library), Penguin Transcription, Peterborough Archive Services, Peterborough Racial Equality Council and West Town Primary Academy and to the following people for their direct or indirect contributions to this book and/or to sustaining me while I wrote it: Rehana Ahmed, Sundari Anitha, Sameena Aziz, Jane Bartlett, Michaela Benson, Rina Biswas, Richard Black, Rahul Bose, Kate Botterill, Tina Bramhill, Kath Browne, Michelle Buckley, Peter Budakiewicz, Kamil and Sinem Buer, Dan Bulley, Kathy Burrell, Stephen Bushell, Binal Cadieu, Indira Chowdhury, Karenjit Clare, Graeme Clark, Kerry Cliffe, Erica Consterdine, Andrea Cornwall, Phil Crang, Jocelyn Cunningham, Ivan Cutting, Meena Dhanda, Siobhán Duggan, Barbara Einhorn, Jay Emery, Cemre Erciyes, Umut Erel, Chris Erskine, Rosalind Eyben, David Feldman, Anne-Marie Fortier, Ben Gidley, David Glenn, Gary Grubb, Arjan de Haan, Suzanne Hall, Natasha Herriott, Steven High, Hye-Eun Hills, Peter Hopkins, Richard Hunt, Muzammal Hussain, Maggie Ibrahim, Yasmin Ilahi, Emma Jackson, Esther Johnson, Susan Johnson, Hannah Jones, Joe Kennedy, Stacey Kennedy, Jawaid Khan, Shumaisa Khan, Pamela Kilbey, Mahebub Ladha, Gosia Lasota, Anita Lucchesi, Abdullah Majid, Kate Marsh, Leonie McCarthy, Siobhán McGrath, Sam McLean, Siobhán McPhee, Elspeth Millar, Kirsty Millward, E.-J. Milne, Edwin Mingard, Martyn Moore, Paul Oestreicher, Shannon O'Floinn, Jeanne Openshaw, Luke Payn, Ruth Pearson, Rob Perks, Mythri Prasad, Abdur Rafique, Paige Raibmon, Sayeed Rana, Shamima Rehman, Phil Ritchie, Mark Roberts, Fiona Samuels, Hannah Saunders, Amrita Sengupta, Anna Sexton, Ghulam Shabbir, Polina Shepherd, Dorothy Sheridan, Pritam Singh, Emily Steele, Alison Stenning, Angharad Closs Stephens, Mary Stewart, Joanna and Krzysztof Szczepaniak, Susan Thieme, Alistair Thomson, Kasia Tomasiewicz, Sivamohan Valluvan, Primitivo Viray, Satnam

Virdee, Julie Vullnetari, Danyal and Katrin Wahbi, Louise Waite, John Watters, Helen Wilson and Ulala Yamamoto.

None of the people named above are responsible for any of the book's faults nor for the views expressed in it.

Thanks to Sage Publications for its permission to include a revised version of my article 'Disrupting migration stories: reading life histories through the lens of mobility and fixity' (in *Environment and planning D: Society and space*, 2015) and to draw on my short piece 'Brexit writings and the war of position over migration, "race" and class' (in *Environment and planning C: Politics and space*, 2019); and to Manchester University Press for permission to include a revised version of my chapter 'Rescaling citizenship struggles in provincial urban England' (in Jonathan Darling and Harald Bauder (eds), *Sanctuary Cities and Urban Struggles: Rescaling Migration, Citizenship and Rights*, 2019).

Bibliography

Abrams, L., *Oral History Theory* (2010; revised edition, London: Routledge, 2016).

Achilles, M., K. Kunakhovich and N. Shea, 'Nationalism, nativism and the revolt against globalization', *Europe Now* 1 February 2018, available online at: www.europenowjournal.org/2018/01/31/nationalism-nativism-and-the-revolt-against-globalization/ (accessed April 2019).

Adey, P., 'If mobility is everything then it is nothing: towards a relational politics of (im)mobilities', *Mobilities*, 1:1 (2006), 75–94.

Adey, P., *Mobility* (London: Routledge, 2010).

Ahmad, A., 'Gender and generation in Pakistani migration: a critical study of masculinity', in L. Ryan and W. Webster (eds), *Gendering Migration: Masculinity, Femininity and Ethnicity in Post-War Britain* (Aldershot, Hants: Ashgate, 2008), pp. 155–169.

Ahmed, S., C. Castañeda, A. Fortier and M. Sheller, 'Introduction: uprootings/regroundings: questions of home and migration', in S. Ahmed, C. Castañeda, A. Fortier and M. Sheller (eds), *Uprootings/Regroundings* (Oxford: Berg, 2003), pp. 1–22.

Akala, *Natives: Race and Class in the Ruins of Empire* (London: Two Roads, 2018).

Alexander, C. and H. Kim, 'South Asian youth cultures', in J. Chatterji and D. Washbrook (eds), *Routledge Handbook of the South Asian Diaspora* (London: Routledge, 2013), pp. 350–362.

Allen, D., 'Foreword', in I. Young, *Justice and the Politics of Difference* (second edition, Princeton: Princeton University Press, 2011), pp. ix–x.

Amin, A., *Land of Strangers* (Cambridge: Polity Press, 2012).

Anderson, B., *Imagined Communities: Reflections on the Origins and Spread of Nationalism* (1983; revised edition, London: Verso, 2016).

Anderson, B., *Us and Them? The Dangerous Politics of Immigration Control* (Oxford: Oxford University Press, 2013).

Anderson, B., and V. Hughes, 'Introduction', in B. Anderson and V. Hughes (eds), *Citizenship and its Others* (Basingstoke: Palgrave Macmillan, 2015), pp. 1–9.

Anderson, B. and B. Rogaly, 'Forced labour and migration to the UK', study prepared by Centre on Migration, Policy and Society in collaboration with the Trades Union Congress, 2005, available online at: www.compas.ox.ac.uk/wp-content/uploads/PR-2007-Forced_Labour_TUC.pdf (accessed February 2019).

Anderson, B., M. Ruhs, S. Spencer and B. Rogaly, *Fair Enough? Central and Eastern European Migrants in the Low Wage Employment in the UK*, Centre on Migration, Policy and Society Research Report (London: Joseph Rowntree Foundation, 2006), available online at: www.compas.ox.ac.uk/2006/pr-2006-changing_status_fair_enough/ (accessed January 2019).

Andrucki, M. and J. Dickinson, 'Rethinking centers and margins in geography: bodies, life course, and the performance of transnational space', *Annals of the Association of American Geographers*, 105:1 (2015), 203–218.

Anitha, S. and R. Pearson, *Striking Women: Struggles and Strategies of South Asian Women Workers from Grunwick to Gate Gourmet* (London: Lawrence & Wishart, 2018).

Anthias, F., 'Social stratification and social inequality: models of intersectionality and identity', in F. Devine, M. Savage, J. Scott and R. Crompton (eds), *Rethinking Class: Culture, Identities and Lifestyle* (Basingstoke: Palgrave Macmillan, 2005), pp. 24–45.

Antonelli, S., 'Digging for our lives', in Jessie Brennan (ed.), *Re: Development: Voices, Cyanotypes and Writings from The Green Backyard* (London: Silent Grid, 2016), pp. 29–32.

Antonsich, M. and T. Matejskova, 'Conclusion: nation and diversity – a false conundrum', in T. Matejskova and M. Antonsich (eds), *Governing through Diversity: Migration Societies in Post-Multiculturalist Times* (Basingstoke: Palgrave Macmillan, 2015), pp. 201–209.

Anushka, A. with C. Cadwalladr and E. Wiseman, 'Arron Banks: the man who bankrolled Brexit', podcast, *The Guardian*, 2018, available online at: www.theguardian.com/news/audio/2018/nov/09/arron-banks-man-who-bankrolled-brexit-podcast-today-in-focus (accessed January 2019).

Aronoff, K., 'The European far right's environmental turn', *Dissent*, 31 May 2019, available online at: https://www.dissentmagazine.org/online_articles/the-european-far-rights-environmental-turn (accessed June 2019).

Ashraf, P., *Parveen the Spice Queen: Authentic Indian Cooking* (n.p.: FCM Publishing, 2016).

Askins, K., 'Emotional citizenry: everyday geographies of befriending, belonging and intercultural encounter', *Transactions of the Institute of British Geographers*, 41:4 (2016), 515–527.

Imran, A., 'Christchurch attacks show Islamophobia is real, deadly and spreading around the world', *The Conversation*, 20 March 2019, available online at: http://theconversation.com/christchurch-attacks-show-islamophobia-is-real-deadly-and-spreading-around-the-world-113786 (accessed April 2019).

Back, L., *New Ethnicities and Urban Culture: Racisms and Multiculture in Young Lives* (London: University College London Press, 1996).

Back, L., *The Art of Listening* (London: Bloomsbury Academic, 2007).

Back, L., 'Researching community and its moral projects', *21st century society*, 4:2 (2009), 201–214.

Back, L. and S. Sinha with C. Bryan, V. Baraku and M. Yemba, *Migrant City* (London: Routledge, 2018).

Bagelman, J., 'Sanctuary artivism: expanding geopolitical imaginations', in J. Darling and H. Bauder (eds), *Sanctuary Cities and Urban Struggles: Rescaling Migration, Citizenship and Rights* (Manchester: Manchester University Press, 2019), pp. 131–164.

Balibar, E., 'The "impossible" community of the citizens: past and present problems', *Environment and Planning D: Society and space*, 30 (2012), 437–449.

Barnett, M., 'Organising Amazon', *Tribune Magazine*, November 2018, available online at: https://tribunemag.co.uk/2018/11/organising-amazon (accessed January 2019).

Bauböck, R., 'Reinventing urban citizenship', *Citizenship studies*, 7:2 (2003), 139–160.

Bauder, H., 'Domicile citizenship, human mobility and territoriality', *Progress in human geography*, 38:1 (2014), 91–106.

Benvegnù, C., B. Haidinger and D. Sacchetto, 'Restructuring labour relations and employment in the European logistics sector: unions' responses to a segmented workforce', in V. Doellgast, N. Lillie and V. Pulignano (eds), *Reconstructing Solidarity: Labour Unions, Precarious Work and the Politics of Institutional Change in Europe* (Oxford: Oxford University Press, 2018), pp. 83–103.

Berger, J., *And our faces, my heart, brief as photos* (London: Writers and Readers, 1984).

Berger, J., *Portraits: John Berger on Artists*, ed. Tom Overton (London: Verso, 2015).

Berger, J., 'Revolutionary undoing: on Max Raphael's *The Demands of Art*', in *Landscapes: John Berger on Art*, ed. Tom Overton (London: Verso, 2016), pp. 44–53.

Berger, J. and J. Mohr, *A Seventh Man: A Book of Images and Words about the Experiences of Migrant Workers in Europe* ([1975] London: Verso, 2010).

Beynon, H., 'Beyond Fordism', in S. Edgell, H. Gottfried and E. Granter (eds), *The SAGE Handbook of the Sociology of Work and Employment* (London: Sage, 2015), pp. 306–328.

Bhambra, G. K., 'Brexit, the Commonwealth, and exclusionary citizenship', *Open Democracy*, 8 December 2016, available online at: www.opendemocracy.net/gurminder-k-bhambra/brexit-commonwealth-and-exclusionary-citizenship (accessed April 2019).

Bhambra, G. K., 'Brexit, Trump, and 'methodological whiteness': on the misrecognition of race and class', *The British journal of sociology*, 68:S1 (2017), S214–S232.

Bhambra, G. K., 'Viewpoint: Brexit, class and British 'national' identity', *Discover Society*, 5 July 2016, available online at: https://discoversociety.org/2016/07/05/viewpoint-brexit-class-and-british-national-identity/ (accessed February 2019).

Bhambra, G. K. and J. Narayan, 'Introduction: a new vision of Europe: learning from the south', in G. K. Bhambra and J. Narayan (eds), *European Cosmopolitanism: Colonial Histories and Postcolonial Societies* (London: Routledge, 2017), pp. 1–14.

Bhambra, G. K. and J. Narayan (eds), *European Cosmopolitanism: Colonial Histories and Postcolonial Societies* (London: Routledge, 2017).

Bhattacharyya, G., *Rethinking Racial Capitalism: Questions of Reproduction and Survival* (London: Rowman & Littlefield International, 2018).

Bhopal, K., *White Privilege: The Myth of a Post-Racial Society* (Bristol: Policy Press, 2018).

Binnie, J., T. Edensor, J. Holloway, S. Millington and C. Young, 'Editorial: mundane mobilities, banal travels', *Social and cultural geography*, 8:2 (2007), 165–174.

Bloch, A., S. Neal and J. Solomos, *Race, Multiculture and Social Policy* (Basingstoke: Palgrave Macmillan, 2013).

Bloemraad, I., and A. Sheares, 'Understanding membership in a world of global migration: (How) does citizenship matter?', *International migration review*, 51:4 (2017), 823–867.

Bloodworth, J., *Hired: Six Months Undercover in Low-Wage Britain* (London: Atlantic Books, 2018).

Blunt, A., 'Cultural geographies of migration: mobility, transnationality and diaspora', *Progress in Human Geography*, 31:5 (2007), 684–694.

Bonnett, A., *White Identities: Historical and International Perspectives* (London: Routledge, 2000).

Botterill, K., 'Rethinking "community" relationally: Polish communities in Scotland before and after Brexit', *Transactions of the Institute of British Geographers*, 43:4 (2018), 540–554.

Brah, A., *Cartographies of Diaspora: Contesting Identities* (London: Routledge, 1996).

Brandon, D. and J. Knight, *Peterborough Past: The City and the Soke* (Chichester: Phillimore, 2001).

Braverman, H., *Labor and Monopoly Capital: The Degradation of Work in the Twentieth Century* (New York: Monthly Review Press, 1974).

Brennan, J., 'Introduction', in Jessie Brennan (ed.), *Re: Development: Voices, Cyanotypes and Writings from The Green Backyard* (London: Silent Grid, 2016), pp. 17–28.

Brennan, J. (ed.), *Re: Development: Voices, Cyanotypes and Writings from The Green Backyard* (London: Silent Grid, 2016).

Brickell, K. and A. Datta, 'Introduction: translocal geographies', in K. Brickell and A. Datta (eds), *Translocal Geographies: Spaces, Places, Connections* (Aldershot, Hants: Ashgate, 2011), pp. 3–22.

Browne, C., *Being Krystyna: A Story of Survival in WWII* (n.p.: Dilliebooks, 2016).

Bulat, A., 'The rights of non-UK EU citizens living here are not a "done deal". This is why', *LSE Brexit Blog*, 27 February 2018, available online at: https://blogs.lse.ac.uk/brexit/2018/02/27/the-rights-of-non-uk-eu-citizens-living-here-are-not-a-done-deal-this-is-why/ (accessed April 2019).

Burawoy, M., *Manufacturing Consent: Changes in the Labor Process under Monopoly Capitalism* (Chicago: University of Chicago Press, 1979).

Burnett, J., *The New Geographies of Racism: Peterborough* (London: Institute of Race Relations, 2012).

Burnett, J., *Racial Violence and the Brexit State* (London: Institute of Race Relations, 2016).

Burrell, K., P. Hopkins, A. Isakjee, C. Lorne, C. Nagel, R. Finlay, A. Nayak, M. Benwell, R. Pande, M. Richardson, K. Botterill and B. Rogaly, 'Brexit, race and migration', *Environment and planning C: Politics and space*, 37:1 (2019), 3–40.

Burrell, K. and P. Panayi (eds), *Histories and Memories: Migrants and their History in Britain* (London: Tauris, 2006).

Cameron, J., 'Postwar European integration: how did a brick shortage change Peterborough?' (MA thesis, Birkbeck College, University of London, 2012).

Canepari, E., and Rosa, E., 'A quiet claim to citizenship: mobility, urban spaces and city practices over time', *Citizenship studies*, 21:6 (2017), 657–674.

Castles, S. and G. Kosack, *Immigrant Workers and Class Structure in Western Europe* (Oxford: Oxford University Press, 1985).

Chatterjee, P., 'Nationalism, internationalism and cosmopolitanism: some observations from modern Indian history', *Comparative studies of South Asia, Africa and the Middle East*, 36:2 (2016), 320–334.

Cheng, Y., 'Educated non-elites' pathways to cosmopolitanism: the case of private degree students in Singapore', *Social & cultural geography*, 19:2 (2018), 151–170.

Christophers, B., R. Lave, J. Peck and M. Werner (eds), *The Doreen Massey Reader* (Newcastle upon Tyne: Agenda Publishing, 2018).

Clarke, A., 'National lives, local voices: boundaries, hierarchies and possibilities of belonging' (PhD dissertation, University of Sussex, 2018).

Clarke, J., 'Finding place in the conjuncture: a dialogue with Doreen', in M. Werner, J. Peck, R. Lave and B. Christophers (eds), *Doreen Massey: Critical Dialogues* (Newcastle-upon-Tyne: Agenda, 2018), pp. 201–213.

Collins, E. J. T., 'Migrant labour in British agriculture in the nineteenth century', *Economic history review*, 29:1 (1976), 38–59.

Collins, F., 'Transnational mobilities and urban spatialities: notes from the Asia-Pacific', *Progress in human geography*, 36:3 (2012), 316–335.

'Commons Library Briefing: The New Controlling Migration Fund (England)', available online at: https://researchbriefings.parliament.uk/ResearchBriefing/Summary/CBP-7673 (accessed April 2019).

Coutinho, A., 'Peterborough together: why have I stayed?', *The Moment Magazine*, November 2018, available online at: www.themomentmagazine.com/community/peterborough-together-i-stayed/ (accessed December 2018).

'Creative Interruptions: grass-roots creativity, state structures, and disconnection as a space for "radical openness"', available online at: www.creativeinterruptions.com (accessed April 2019).

Cresswell, T., 'Towards a politics of mobility', *Environment and planning D: Society and space*, 28:1 (2010), 17–31.

Cresswell, T. and P. Merriman, 'Introduction: geographies of mobilities – practices, spaces, subjects', in T. Cresswell and P. Merriman (eds), *Geographies of Mobilities: Practices, Spaces, Subjects* (Aldershot, Hants: Ashgate, 2011), pp. 1–15.

Crewe, T., 'The strange death of municipal England', *London review of books*, 38:24 (2016), 6–10.

Czaika, M. and H. de Haas, 'The globalization of migration: has the world become more migratory?', *International migration review*, 48:2 (2015), 283–323.

Darling, J., 'Acts, ambiguities and the labour of contesting citizenship', *Citizenship studies*, 21:6 (2017), 727–736.

Darling, J., 'Sanctuary, presence and the politics of urbanism', in Jonathan Darling and Harald Bauder (eds), *Sanctuary Cities and Urban Struggles: Rescaling Migration, Citizenship and Rights* (Manchester: Manchester University Press, 2019), pp. 242–264.

Davies, A., 'Tradition and transformation: Pakistani-heritage young people explore the influences upon their educational progress', *Race ethnicity and education* (2019), available online (early view), DOI: 10.1080/13613324.2017.1395320 (accessed June 2019).

Davis, A., *Freedom is a Constant Struggle: Ferguson, Palestine and the Foundations of a Movement* (Chicago: Haymarket Books, 2016).

Day, A., *Believing in Belonging: Belief and Social Identity in the Modern World* (Oxford: Oxford University Press, 2011).

Delanty, G., 'The cosmopolitan imagination: critical cosmopolitanism and social theory', *The British journal of sociology*, 57:1 (2016), 25–47.

Delanty, G., 'Cultural diversity, democracy and the prospects of cosmopolitanism: a theory of cultural encounters', *The British journal of sociology*, 62:4 (2011), 633–656.

Devine, F., M. Savage, J. Scott and R. Crompton (eds), *Rethinking Class: Culture, Identities and Lifestyle* (Basingstoke: Palgrave Macmillan, 2005).

Digital, Culture, Media and Sport Committee, report, 29 July 2018, available online at: https://publications.parliament.uk/pa/cm201719/cmselect/cmcumeds/363/36302.htm (accessed January 2019).

Dorling, D., *Peak Inequality: Britain's Ticking Time Bomb* (Bristol: Policy Press, 2018).

Dorling, D. and S. Tomlinson, *Rule Britannia: Brexit and the End of Empire* (London: Biteback, 2019).

Eatwell, R. and M. Goodwin, *National Populism: The Revolt Against Liberal Democracy* (London: Pelican, 2018).

Eddo-Lodge, R., *Why I'm No Longer Talking to White People about Race* (London: Bloomsbury, 2017).

Edensor, T., 'Reconsidering national temporalities: institutional times, everyday routines, serial spaces and synchronicities', *European journal of social theory*, 9:4 (2006), 525–545.

Edensor, T., D. Leslie, S. Millington and N. Rantisi (eds), *Spaces of Vernacular Creativity: Rethinking the Cultural Economy* (London: Routledge, 2010).

Ehrkamp, P., 'Geographies of migration II: the racial-spatial politics of immigration', *Progress in human geography*, 43:2 (2019), 363–375.

Emejulu, A., 'On the hideous whiteness of Brexit: "Let us be honest about our past and our present if we truly seek to dismantle white supremacy"', *Verso*, 28 June 2016, available online at: www.versobooks.com/blogs/2733-on-the-hideous-whiteness-of-brexit-let-us-be-honest-about-our-past-and-our-present-if-we-truly-seek-to-dismantle-white-supremacy (accessed January 2019).

Emery, J., 'Belonging, memory and history in the north Nottinghamshire coalfield', *Journal of historical geography*, 59 (2018), 77–89.

Emery, J., 'Geographies of de-industrialization and the working-class: industrial ruination, legacies, and affect', *Geography compass*, 2018, available online (early view) at: doi/pdf/10.1111/gec3.12417 (accessed April 2019).

Erel, U., 'Complex belongings: racialization and migration in a small English city', *Ethnic and racial studies*, 34:12 (2011), 2048–2068.

Esch, E. and D. Roediger, '"One symptom of originality": race and the management of labor in US history', in D. Roediger, *Class, Race and Marxism* (London: Verso, 2017), 115–155.

'Fact check: how high were interest rates in the eighties?', *Channel 4 News*, 22 September 2008, available online at: www.channel4.com/news/articles/politics/domestic_politics/factcheck+how+high+were+interest+rates+in+the+eighties/2470357.html (accessed March 2019).

Faist, T., 'The mobility turn: a new paradigm for the social sciences?', *Ethnic and racial studies*, 36:11 (2013), 1637–1646.

Fanon, F., *The Wretched of the Earth*. trans. Richard Philcox (1961; New York: Grove Press, 2005).

Featherstone, D., *Solidarity: Hidden Histories and Geographies of Internationalism* (London: Zed, 2012).

Fitzgerald, I. and R. Smoczynski, 'Anti-Polish migrant moral panic in the UK: rethinking employment insecurities and moral regulation', *Czech sociological review*, 51:3 (2015), 339–361.

Fortier, A., 'Migration studies', in P. Adey, D. Bissell, K. Hannam, P. Merriman and M. Sheller (eds), *The Routledge Handbook of Mobilities* (London: Routledge, 2014), pp. 64–73.

Gardner, K., *Age, Narrative and Migration: The Life Course and Life Histories of Bengali Elders in London* (Oxford: Berg, 2002).

Gearing, J. and B. Rogaly, '"Workers": life, creativity and resisting racial capitalism', *The Sociological Review Blog*, 8 March 2019, available online at: www.thesociologicalreview.com/blog/workers-life-creativity-and-resisting-racial-capitalism.html (accessed April 2019).

Gidley, B., 'Landscapes of belonging, portraits of life: researching everyday multiculture in an inner city estate', *Identities: Global studies in culture and power*, 20:4 (2013), 361–376.

Gidley, B., 'Sivanandan's pessimistic hope in a degraded age', *The Sociological Review Blog*, 10 February 2018, available online at: www.thesociologicalreview.com/blog/sivanandan-s-pessimistic-hope-in-a-degraded-age.html (accessed April 2019).

Gidley, B. and J. Renton (eds), *Antisemitism and Islamophobia in Europe: A Shared Story?* (London: Palgrave Macmillan, 2017).

Gidwani, V. K., 'Subaltern cosmopolitanism as politics', *Antipode*, 38:1 (2006), 7–21.

Gill, N., J. Caletrio and V. Mason, 'Introduction: mobilities and forced migration', *Mobilities*, 6:3 (2011), 301–316.

Gilmore, R. W., 'Abolition geography and the problem of innocence', in G. T. Johnson and A. Lubin (eds), *Futures of Black Radicalism* (London and New York: Verso, 2017), pp. 225–226.

Gilroy, P., *After Empire: Multiculture or Postcolonial Melancholia* (London: Routledge, 2004).

Gilroy, P., *The Black Atlantic: Modernity and Double Consciousness* (Cambridge, MA: Harvard University Press, 1993).

Gilroy, P., 'Cosmopolitanism and conviviality in an age of perpetual war', in N. G. Schiller and A. Irving (eds), *Whose Cosmopolitanism? Critical Perspectives, Relationalities and Discontents* (Oxford: Berghahn, 2015), pp. 232–244.

Gilroy, P., *There Ain't No Black in the Union Jack* (Chicago: University of Chicago Press, 1987).

Go, J., 'Fanon's postcolonial cosmopolitanism', *European journal of social theory*, 16:2 (2013), 208–225.

Goodhart, D., *The Road to Somewhere: The Populist Revolt and the Future of Politics* (London: Hurst and Company, 2017).

Greiner, C. and P. Sakdapolrak, 'Translocality: concepts, applications and emerging research perspectives', *Geography compass*, 7:5 (2013), 373–384.

Griffin, C., *The Rural War: Captain Swing and the Politics of Protest* (Manchester: Manchester University Press, 2012).

Grosvenor, I., 'A different reality: education and the racialization of the black child', *History of education*, 16:4 (1987), 299–308.

Guarnizo, L., 'The fluid, multi-scalar, and contradictory construction of citizenship', in M. Smith and M. McQuarrie (eds), *Remaking Urban Citizenship:*

Organizations, Institutions and the Right to the City (New Brunswick and London: Transaction, 2012), pp. 11–38.

Gunaratnam, Y., *Death and the Migrant: Bodies, Borders and Care* (London: Bloomsbury Academic, 2013).

Guthman, J., *Agrarian Dreams: The Paradox of Organic Farming in California* (second edition, Berkeley: University of California Press, 2014).

Haider, A., *Mistaken Identity: Race and Class in the Age of Trump* (London: Verso, 2018).

Halfacree, K. and P. Boyle, 'The challenge facing migration research: the case for a biographical approach', *Progress in human geography*, 17:3 (1993), 333–358.

Hall, S., 'The great moving right show', in *Selected Political Writings: The Great Moving Right Show and Other Essays*, ed. Sally Davison, David Featherstone, Michael Rustin and Bill Schwarz (1979; London: Lawrence & Wishart, 2017), pp. 172–186.

Hall, S., 'The neo-liberal revolution', *Cultural studies*, 25:6 (2011), 705–728.

Hall, S., *Selected Political Writings: The Great Moving Right Show and Other Essays*, ed. S. Davison, D. Featherstone, M. Rustin and B. Schwarz (1979; London: Lawrence & Wishart, 2017).

Hall, S., C. Critcher, T. Jefferson, J. Clarke and B. Roberts, *Policing the Crisis: Mugging, the State and Law and Order* (1978; second edition, Basingstoke: Palgrave Macmillan, 2013).

Hall, S., D. Massey, and M. Rustin, *After Neoliberalism? The Kilburn Manifesto* (London: Lawrence & Wishart, 2015).

Hall, S., in conversation with Pnina Werbner, 'Cosmopolitanism, globalization and diaspora', in P. Werbner (ed.), *Anthropology and the New Cosmopolitanism: Rooted, Feminist and Vernacular Perspectives* (Oxford and New York: Berg, 2008), pp. 345–360.

Hamid, M., *Exit West* (New York: Penguin, 2018).

Hamid, M., 'In the land of the pure, no one is pure enough', *The Guardian*, January 2018, available online at: www.theguardian.com/books/2018/jan/27/mohsin-hamid–exit-west-pen-pakistan (accessed April 2019).

Hannam, K., M. Sheller and J. Urry, 'Editorial: mobilities, immobilities and moorings', *Mobilities*, 1:1 (2006), 1–22.

Harris, J., 'Amazon v the high street: how Doncaster is fighting back', *The Guardian*, 11 October 2018, available online at: www.theguardian.com/uk-news/2018/oct/11/amazon-v-the-high-street-how-doncaster-is-fighting-back (accessed April 2019).

Harris, J., 'If eastern Europeans leave Britain after Brexit, what happens? – video', *The Guardian*, 2 February 2017, available online at: www.theguardian.com/commentisfree/video/2017/feb/02/if-eastern-europeans-leave-britain-after-brexit-what-happens-video (accessed March 2019).

Hart, G., 'Becoming a geographer: Massey moments in a spatial education', in Marion Werner, Jamie Peck, Rebecca Lave and Brett Christophers (eds), *Doreen Massey: Critical Dialogues* (Newcastle upon Tyne: Agenda Publishing, 2018), 75–88.

Harvey, D., *A Brief History of Neoliberalism* (Oxford: Oxford University Press, 2005).

Harvey, D., *Cosmopolitanism and the Geographies of Freedom* (New York: Columbia University Press, 2009).

Harvey, D., *Social Justice and the City* (1973; revised edition, Atlanta: University of Georgia Press, 2009).

Harvey, D., 'Three myths in search of a reality in urban studies', *Environment and planning D: Society and space*, 5:4 (1987), 367–376.

Hastings, T. and D. MacKinnon, 'Re-embedding agency at the workplace scale: workers and labour control in Glasgow call centres', *Environment and planning A*, 49:1 (2016), 104–120.

Hawkins, H., *Creativity* (London: Routledge, 2017).

Herbert, J., *Negotiating Boundaries in the City: Migration, Ethnicity, and Gender in Britain* (Aldershot, Hants: Ashgate, 2008).

Herbert, J. and R. Rodger, 'Frameworks: testimony, representation and interpretation', in R. Rodger and J. Herbert (eds), *Testimonies of the City: Identity, Community and Change in a Contemporary Urban World* (Aldershot, Hants: Ashgate, 2007), pp. 1–19.

Hern, A., 'MPs criticise social media firms for failure to report criminal posts', *The Guardian*, 24 April 2019, available online at: www.theguardian.com/media/2019/apr/24/mps-criticise-tech-giants-for-failure-to-report-criminal-posts-twitter-facebook-google-youtube (accessed April 2019).

Hesse, B. and S. Sayyid, 'Narrating the postcolonial political and the immigrant imaginary', in N. Ali, V. S. Kalra and S. Sayyid (eds), *A Postcolonial People: South Asians in Britain* (London: Hurst, 2006), pp. 13–31.

Higham, N., 'National Archives: Thatcher's poll tax miscalculation', *BBC News*, 30 December 2016, available online at: www.bbc.co.uk/news/uk-38382416 (accessed March 2019).

Hine, D., 'Spelling it out', in Jessie Brennan (ed.), *Re: Development: Voices, Cyanotypes and Writings from The Green Backyard* (London: Silent Grid, 2016), pp. 58–60.

Hodkinson, D., *Safe as Houses: Private Greed, Political Negligence and Housing Policy after Grenfell* (Manchester: Manchester University Press, 2019).

Hoekstra, M., 'Diverse cities and good citizenship: how local governments in the Netherlands recast national integration discourses', *Ethnic and racial studies*, 38:10 (2015), 1798–1814.

Holmes, S. M., '"Oaxacans like to work bent over": the naturalization of social suffering among berry farm workers', *International migration*, 45:3 (2007), 39–68.

Hudson, G., 'City of hope, city of fear: sanctuary and security in Toronto, Canada', in Jonathan Darling and Harald Bauder (eds), *Sanctuary Cities and Urban Struggles: Rescaling Migration, Citizenship and Rights* (Manchester: Manchester University Press, 2019), pp. 77–104.

Humphry, D., 'Moving on? Experiences of social mobility in a mixed-class north London neighbourhood' (PhD thesis, University of Sussex, 2014).

Ibrahim, Z. and L. Clayson, 'Gogreen 19: climate change is a racist issue', *People and Planet*, 11 February 2019, available online at: https://peopleandplanet.org/blog/2019–02–11/gogreen19-climate-change-racist-issue (accessed April 2019).

Jackson, E. and H. Jones, 'Conclusion: creeping familiarity and cosmopolitan futures', in H. Jones and E. Jackson (eds), *Stories of Cosmopolitan Belonging: Emotion and Location* (London: Earthscan, 2014), pp. 196–202.

James, D., *Doña María's Story: Life History, Memory, and Political Identity* (Durham, NC: Duke University Press, 2000).

Jazeel, T., 'Postcolonial geographies of privilege: diaspora space, the politics of personhood and the Sri Lankan Women's Association', *Transactions of the Institute of British Geographers*, New Series, 31:1 (2006), 19–33.

Jazeel, T., 'Review essay: spectres of tolerance: living together beyond cosmopolitanism', *Cultural geographies*, 14:4 (2007), 617–624.

Johnson, A., R. Joseph-Salisbury and B. Komunge (eds), *The Fire Now: Anti-Racist Scholarship in Times of Explicit Racial Violence* (London: Zed, 2018).

Jonas, A., 'Local labour control regimes: uneven development and the social regulation of production', *Journal of regional studies*, 30:4 (1996), 323–338.

Jones, H., 'More in common: the domestication of misogynist white supremacy and the assassination of Jo Cox', *Ethnic and racial studies* (2019), available online (early view) at: doi.org/10.1080/01419870.2019.1577474 (accessed June 2019).

Jones, H., *Negotiating Cohesion, Inequality and Change: Uncomfortable Positions in Local Government* (Bristol: Policy Press, 2013).

Jones, H., 'Uncomfortable positions: how policy practitioners negotiate difficult subjects' (PhD dissertation, Goldsmiths, University of London, 2011).

Jones, H., Y. Gunaratnam, G. Bhattacharyya, W. Davies, S. Dhaliwal, K. Forkert, E. Jackson and R. Saltus, *Go Home? The Politics of Immigration Controversies* (Manchester: Manchester University Press, 2017).

Jones, R., and C. Fowler, 'Placing and scaling the nation', *Environment and planning D: Society and space*, 25 (2007), 332–354.

Kalra, V., *From Textile Mills to Taxi Ranks: Experiences of Migration, Labour and Social Change* (Aldershot, Hants: Ashgate, 2000).

Kaufman, E., *Whiteshift: Populism, Immigration and the Future of White Majorities* (London: Allen Lane, 2018).

Kelley, R. D., 'Foreword', in Cedric J. Robinson, *Black Marxism: The Making of the Black Radical Tradition* (1983; revised edition, Chapel Hill: University of North Carolina Press, 2000), pp. xi–xxvi.

Kelly, P., 'Migration, transnationalism and the spaces of class identity', *Philippine studies: historical and ethnographic viewpoints*, 60:2 (2012), 153–185.

Kennedy, J., *Authentocrats: Culture, Politics and the New Seriousness* (London: Repeater, 2018).

Khan, O. and F. Shaheen, 'Minority report: race and class in post-Brexit Britain' (London: Runnymede, 2017).

Kothari, U., 'Global peddlers and local networks: migrant cosmopolitanisms', *Environment and planning D: society and space*, 26:3 (2008), 500–516.

Kuge, J., 'Uncovering sanctuary cities: between policy, practice and politics', in J. Darling and H. Bauder (eds), *Sanctuary Cities and Urban Struggles: Rescaling Migration, Citizenship and Rights* (Manchester: Manchester University Press, 2019), pp. 50–76.

Kunz, S., 'Expatriate, migrant? The social life of migration categories and the polyvalent mobility of race', *Journal of ethnic and migration studies* (2019), available online (early view), DOI: 10.1080/1369183X.2019.1584525 (accessed April 2019).

Kushner, T. and K. Knox, *Refugees in an Age of Genocide* (London: Routledge, 2001).

Lawson, V., 'Arguments within geographies of movement: the theoretical potential of migrants' stories', *Progress in human geography*, 24:2 (2000), 173–189.

Leadbeater, C. and P. Miller, *The Pro-Am Revolution: How Enthusiasts are Changing Our Economy and Society* (London: DEMOS, 2004).

Linebaugh, P. and Marcus Rediker, *The Many-Headed Hydra: Sailors, Slaves, Commoners, and the Hidden History of the Revolutionary Atlantic* (London: Verso, 2000).

Lobo, M., 'Reframing the creative city: fragile friendships and affective art spaces in Darwin, Australia', *Urban studies*, 55:3 (2017), 623–638.

Lowe, L., *The Intimacies of Four Continents* (Durham, NC: Duke University Press, 2015).

Lowkey, 'Grenfell: from micro to macro and back again', lecture given at the University of Sussex, March 2019, available online at: www.youtube.com/watch?v=JLyZ8QVEBco, accessed April 2019.

Lugosi, P., H. Janta and B. Wilczek, 'Work(ing) dynamics of migrant networking among Poles employed in hospitality and food production', *The sociological review*, 64:4 (2016), 894–911.

Manavis, S., 'Eco-fascism: the ideology marrying environmentalism and white supremacy thriving online', *New Statesman*, 21 September 2018, available online at: www.newstatesman.com/science-tech/social-media/2018/09/eco-fascism-ideology-marrying-environmentalism-and-white-supremacy (accessed April 2019).

Massey, D., 'A global sense of place', *Marxism Today*, June 1991, 24–29.

Massey, D., *Landscape/Space/Politics: An Essay* (2011), available online at: http://thefutureoflandscape.wordpress.com/landscapespacepolitics-an-essay/ (accessed January 2019).

Massey, D., 'Power geometry and a progressive sense of place', in J. Bird *et al.* (eds), *Mapping the Futures: Local Cultures, Global Change* (London: Routledge, 1993), pp. 59–69.

Massey, D., 'Questions of locality', *Geography*, 78:2 (1993), 142–149.

Massey, D., *Space, place and gender*. (Minneapolis: University of Minnesota Press, 1994).

Massey, D., *Spatial Divisions of Labour: Social Structures and the Geography of Production* (1984; revised edition, New York: Routledge, 1995).

Massey, D., *World City* (Cambridge: Polity Press, 2007).

May, T., Conservative Party Conference Speech, October 2016, *International Business Times*, available online at: www.ibtimes.co.uk/brits-are-well-travelled-open-minded-global-citizens-damn-brexiteers-that-want-change-us-1587348 (accessed January 2019).

McDowell, L., 'Thinking through work: complex inequalities, constructions of difference and trans-national migrants', *Progress in human geography*, 32:4 (2008), 491–507.

McMorran, C., 'Mobilities amid the production of fixities: labour in a Japanese inn', *Mobilities*, 10:1 (2015), 83–99.

Medland, L., 'Working for social sustainability: insights from a Spanish organic production enclave', *Agroecology and sustainable food systems*, 40:10 (2016), 1133–1156.

Migration Advisory Committee, *Migrant Seasonal Workers: The Impact on the Horticulture and Food Processing Sectors of Closing the Seasonal Agricultural Workers Scheme and the Sectors Based Scheme* (London: Home Office, 2013).

Miles, R., *Racism and Migrant Labour: A Critical Text* (London: Routledge, 1982).

Minto, R. 'A smuggling operation: John Berger's theory of art', *Los Angeles Review of Books*, 2 January 2017, available online at: https://lareviewofbooks.org/article/a-smuggling-operation-john-bergers-theory-of-art/#! (accessed April 2019).

Minton, A., 'The Green Backyard and the right to the city', in Jessie Brennan (ed.), *Re: Development: Voices, Cyanotypes and Writings from The Green Backyard* (London: Silent Grid, 2016), pp. 49–50.

Mitchell, K., 'Difference', in R. Lee, N. Castree, R. Kitchin, V. Lawson, A. Paasi, C. Philo, S. Radcliffe, S. Roberts and C. Withers (eds), *The SAGE Handbook of Human Geography* (London: Sage, 2014), pp. 69–93.

Mondon, A. and A. Winter, 'Whiteness, populism and the racialisation of the working-class in the United Kingdom and the United States', *Identities: global studies in culture and power*, available online (early view, 2018), DOI: 10.1080/1070289X.2018.1552440 (accessed April 2019).

Moore, P., 'On work and machines: a labour process of agility', *Soundings*, 69:69 (2018), 15–31.

Nayak, A., 'Purging the nation: race, conviviality and embodied encounters in the lives of British Bangladeshi Muslim young women', *Transactions of the Institute of British Geographers*, 42:2 (2017), 289–302.

Neal, S., K. Bennett, A. Cochrane and G. Mohan, *Lived Experiences of Multiculture: The New Social Relations of Diversity* (London: Routledge, 2017).

Newsome, K., 'Value in motion: labour and logistics in the contemporary political economy', in K. Newsome, P. Taylor, J. Bair and A. Rainnie (eds),

Putting Labour in its Place: Labour Process Analysis and Global Value Chains (London: Palgrave, 2015), pp. 29–44.

Newsome, K., P. Taylor, J. Bair and A. Rainnie (eds), *Putting Labour in its Place: Labour Process Analysis and Global Value Chains* (London: Palgrave, 2015).

Noble, G., 'Cosmopolitan habits: the capacities and habitats of intercultural conviviality', *Body & society*, 19:2–3 (2013), 162–185.

Noble, G., 'Everyday Cosmopolitanism and the Labour of Intercultural Community', in A. Wise and S. Velayutham (eds), *Everyday Multiculturalism* (Basingstoke: Palgrave Macmillan, 2009), pp. 46–65.

O'Carroll, L., 'Farmers tell Gove: lack of migrant workers now 'mission critical'', *The Guardian*, 20 February 2018, available online at: www.theguardian.com/politics/2018/feb/20/farmers-tell-gove-lack-of-migrant-workers-now-mission-critical (accessed February 2018).

O'Toole, F., *Heroic Failure: Brexit and the Politics of Pain* (London: Head of Zeus, 2018).

Office for National Statistics, *2011 Census Analysis: Ethnicity and the Labour Market, England and Wales* (13 November 2014), available online at: www.ons.gov.uk/peoplepopulationandcommunity/culturalidentity/ethnicity/articles/ethnicityandthelabourmarket2011censusenglandandwales/2014-11-13 (accessed March 2018).

Olson, K. and L. Stopes, 'Crossing boundaries, building bridges: doing oral history among working-class women and men', in Sherna Berger Gluck and Daphne Patai (eds), *Women's Words: The Feminist Practice of Oral History* (London and New York: Routledge, 1991), pp. 189–204.

Oosterlynck, S., M. Loopmans, N. Schuermans, J. Vandenabeele and S. Zemni, 'Putting flesh on the bone: looking for solidarity in diversity, here and now', *Ethnic and racial studies*, 39:5 (2016), 764–782.

Pastore, F., and I. Ponzo (eds), *Inter-Group Relations and Migrant Integration in European Cities: Changing Neighbourhoods* (London: Springer Open, 2016).

Peach, C., 'Demographics of BrAsian settlement, 1951–2001', in N. Ali, V. S. Kalra and S. Sayyid (eds), *A Postcolonial People: South Asians in Britain* (London: Hurst, 2006), pp. 168–181.

Pearson, R., 'A feminist analysis of neoliberalism and austerity policies in the UK', *Soundings*, 71 (2019), 28–39.

Peck, J., *Work-Place: The Social Regulation of Labor Markets* (New York: Guilford Press, 1996).

Peck, J., M. Werner, R. Lave and B. Christophers, 'Out of place: Doreen Massey, radical geographer', in B. Christophers, R. Lave, J. Peck and M. Werner (eds), *The Doreen Massey Reader* (Newcastle upon Tyne: Agenda Publishing, 2018), pp. 1–38.

Phizacklea, A. and R. Miles, *Labour and Racism* (London: Routledge, 1980).

Piratin, P., *Our Flag Stays Red* (1948; third edition, London: Lawrence and Wishart, 2006).

'Places for all? A multi-media investigation in an English city', available online at: www.placesforall.co.uk (accessed March 2019).

Porsz, C., *New England: The Culture and People of an English New Town during the 1970s and 1980s* (Peterborough: Chris Porsz, 2012).

Porsz, C., *Reunions* (Peterborough: Chris Porsz, 2016).

Porsz, C., 'Nene Park project', in *Chris Porsz – Street Photography*, available online at: www.chrisporsz.com/nene-park-project.html (accessed March 2019).

Portelli, A., 'What makes oral history different', in Robert Perks and Alistair Thomson (eds), *The Oral History Reader* (third edition, London: Routledge, 2016), pp. 48–58.

Qureshi, K., 'Pakistani labour migration and masculinity: industrial working life, the body and transnationalism', *Global networks*, 12:4 (2012), 485–504.

Rajkowska, J., and M. Humm, '*The Peterborough Child* and Joanna Rajkowska: themes, influences, art', in D. Shaw and M. Humm (eds), *Radical Space: Exploring Politics and Practice* (London: Rowman and Littlefield, 2016), pp. 3–20.

Ramazani, J., '"Cosmopolitan sympathies": poetry of the First Global War', *Modernism/modernity*, 23:4 (2016), 855–874.

Reid-Musson, E., 'Intersectional rhythmanalysis: Power, rhythm, and everyday life', *Progress in Human Geography*, 42:6 (2018), pp. 881–897.

Rex, J., *Race, Colonialism and the City* (Oxford: Oxford University Press, 1973).

Rishbeth, C. and B. Rogaly, 'Sitting outside: conviviality, self-care and the design of benches in urban public space', *Transactions of the Institute of British Geographers*, 43:2 (2018), 284–298.

Roberts, M., 'Communication breakdown: understanding the role of policy narratives in conflict and consensus', *Critical policy studies*, 12:1 (2016), 82–102.

Robinson, C. J., *Black Marxism: The Making of the Black Radical Tradition* (London: Zed, 1983).

Roediger, D., *Class, Race and Marxism* (London: Verso, 2017).

Rogaly, B., 'Brexit writings and the war of position over migration, "race" and class', *Environment and planning C: Politics and space*, 37:1 (2019), 28–33.

Rogaly, B., 'Class, spatial justice and the production of not-quite citizens', in B. Anderson and V. Hughes (eds), *Citizenship and Its Others* (Basingstoke: Palgrave Macmillan, 2015), pp. 157–176.

Rogaly, B., 'Contesting neo-liberal common sense: bottom-up history and the struggle over urban space', in Jessie Brennan (ed.), *Re: Development: Voices, Cyanotypes and Writings from The Green Backyard* (London: Silent Grid, 2016), pp. 51–54.

Rogaly, B., '"Don't show the play at the football ground, nobody will come": the micro-sociality of co-produced research in an English provincial city', *Sociological review*, 64:4 (2016), 657–680.

Rogaly, B., 'Intensification of workplace regimes in British horticulture: the role of migrant workers', *Population, space and place*, 14:6 (2008), 497–510.

Rogaly, B. and D. Coppard, '"They used to go to eat, now they go to earn": the changing meanings of seasonal migration from Puruliya District in West Bengal, India', *Journal of agrarian change*, 3:3 (2003), 395–433.

Rogaly, B. and K. Qureshi, 'Diversity, urban space and the right to the provincial city', *Identities: global studies in culture and power*, 20:4 (2013), 423–437.

Rogaly, B. and K. Qureshi, '"That's where my perception of it all was shattered": oral histories and moral geographies of food sector workers in an English city region', *Geoforum*, 78 (2017), 189–198.

Rogaly, B. and B. Taylor, *Moving Histories of Class and Community: Identity, Place and Belonging in Contemporary England* (Basingstoke: Palgrave Macmillan, 2009).

Rogaly, B. and B. Taylor, '"They called them communists then … what d'you call 'em now? Insurgents?" Narratives of British military expatriates in the context of the new imperialism', *Journal of ethnic and migration studies*, 36:8 (2010), 1335–1351.

Rogaly, B. and S. Thieme, 'Experiencing space-time: the stretched lifeworlds of migrant workers in India', *Environment and planning A*, 44:9 (2012), 2086–2100.

Rogaly, J., *Grunwick* (London: Penguin, 1977).

Romei, V., 'How wages fell in the UK while the economy grew', *Financial Times*, 2 March 2017, available online at: www.ft.com/content/83e7e87e-fe64–11e6–96f8–3700c5664d30 (accessed April 2019).

Ruhs, M. and C. Vargas-Silva, 'The labour market effects of immigration', *Migration Observatory Briefing*, Centre on Migration, Policy and Society, University of Oxford, UK, December 2018.

Rutter, J., *Moving Up and Getting On: Migration, Integration and Social Cohesion in the UK* (Bristol: Policy Press, 2015).

Sacchetto, D. and D. Perrotta, 'Migrant farmworkers in southern Italy: ghettoes, caporalato and collective action', *Workers of the world: international journal on strikes and social conflicts*, 1:5 (2014), 58–74.

Saltmarsh, C., 'An internationalist Green New Deal', *The Ecologist*, 23 April 2019, available online at: https://theecologist.org/2019/apr/23/internationalist-green-new-deal (accessed April 2019).

Sayer, A., 'Behind the locality debate: deconstructing geography's dualisms', *Environment and planning A*, 23:2 (1991), 283–308.

Schiller, N. G., 'Whose cosmopolitanism? And whose humanity?', in N. G. Schiller and A. Irving (eds), *Whose Cosmopolitanism? Critical Perspectives, Relationalities and Discontents* (Oxford: Berghahn, 2015), pp. 31–33.

Schiller, N. G. and A. Irving, 'Introduction: what's in a word? What's in a question?', in N. G. Schiller and A. Irving (eds), *Whose Cosmopolitanism? Critical Perspectives, Relationalities and Discontents* (Oxford: Berghahn, 2015), pp. 1–22.

Schiller, N. G. and A. Irving (eds), *Whose Cosmopolitanism? Critical Perspectives, Relationalities and Discontents* (Oxford: Berghahn, 2015).

Schiller, N. G. and N. Salazar, 'Regimes of mobility across the globe', *Journal of ethnic and migration studies* 39 (2013), 183–200.

Sealey-Huggins, L., '"The climate crisis is a racist crisis": structural racism, inequality and climate change', in A. Johnson, R. Joseph-Salisbury and B. Kamunge (eds), *The Fire Now: Anti-Racist Scholarship in Times of Explicit Racial Violence* (London: Zed, 2018), pp. 99–116.

Seymour, R., 'Nigel Farage is the most dangerous man in Britain', *New York Times*, 28 May 2019, available online at: www.nytimes.com/2019/05/28/opinion/nigel-farage-brexit.html, (accessed June 2019).

Shilliam, R., *Race and the Undeserving Poor: From Abolition to Brexit* (Newcastle upon Tyne: Agenda Publishing, 2018).

Shukla, N. (ed.), *The Good Immigrant* (London: Unbound, 2016).

Sivanandan, A., 'Poverty is the new black', *Race and class*, 43:2 (2001), 1–6.

Skeldon, R., 'Interlinkages between internal and international migration and development in the Asian region', *Population, space and place*, 12:1 (2006), 15–30.

Smith, A., M. Barbu, L. Campling, J. Harrison and B. Richardson, 'Labor regimes, global production networks and European trade union policy: labor standards and export production in the Moldovan clothing industry', *Economic geography*, 94:5 (2018), 550–574.

Smith, N., 'Dangers of the empirical turn: some comments on the CURS initiative', *Antipode*, 19:1 (1987), 59–68.

Söderström, O., S. Randeria, D. Ruedin, G. D'Amato and F. Panese, 'Of mobilities and moorings: critical perspectives', in O. Söderström, S. Randeria, D. Ruedin, G. D'Amato and R. Panese (eds), *Critical Mobilities* (Lausanne: EPFL Press, 2013), pp. v–xxv.

de Sousa Santos, B., 'Beyond neoliberal governance: the world social forum as subaltern cosmopolitan politics and legality', in B. de Sousa Santos and C. Rodriguez-Gravito (eds), *Law and Globalization from Below* (Cambridge: Cambridge University Press, 2005), pp. 29–63.

Staeheli, L., P. Ehrkamp, H. Leitner and C. Nagel, 'Dreaming the ordinary: daily life and the complex geographies of citizenship', *Progress in human geography*, 36:5 (2012), 628–644.

Stephens, A. C., 'National atmospheres and the "Brexit" revolt', *Society and Space Blog*, 23 August 2016, available online at: https://societyandspace.org/2016/08/23/national-atmospheres-and-the-brexit-revolt-angharad-closs-stephens/ (accessed March 2019).

Stoler, A., 'On degrees of imperial sovereignty', *Public culture*, 18:1 (2006), 125–146.

Taylor, B. and M. Sliwa, 'Polish migration: moving beyond the iron curtain', *History workshop journal*, 71:1 (2011), 128–146.

Thompson, P., 'Family myth, models, and denials in the shaping of individual life paths', in D. Bertaux and P. Thompson (eds), *Between Generations:*

Family Models, Myths and Memories. International Yearbook of Oral History and Life Stories II (Oxford: Oxford University Press, 1993), pp. 13–38.

Thomson, A., 'Moving stories: oral history and migration studies', *Oral history*, 27:1 (1999), 24–37.

Tilley, L. and R. Shilliam, 'Raced markets: An introduction', *New political economy*, 23:5 (2017), 534–543.

Trades Union Congress, 'Insecure work and ethnicity' (London, 2017), available online at: www.tuc.org.uk/research-analysis/reports/insecure-work-and-ethnicity (accessed January 2019).

Travis, A., 'Number of eastern EU nationals in UK workforce falls by 5%', *The Guardian*, 21 February 2018, available online at: www.theguardian.com/uk-news/2018/feb/21/number-of-western-eu-nationals-in-uk-workforce-falls-by-5-percent (accessed February 2018).

Traynor, I. *et al.*, 'David Cameron blocks EU treaty with veto, casting Britain adrift in Europe', *The Guardian*, available online at: https://www.theguardian.com/world/2011/dec/09/david-cameron-blocks-eu-treaty (accessed June 2019).

Trilling, D., 'I'm not racist, but …', review of Eric Kaufman, *Whiteshift* and Roger Eatwell and Matthew Goodwin, *National Populism*, *London Review of Books*, 18 April 2019, available online at: www.lrb.co.uk/v41/n08/daniel-trilling/im-not-racist-but- (accessed April 2019).

Tyler, K., 'The suburban paradox of conviviality and racism in postcolonial Britain', *Journal of ethnic and migration studies*, 43:11 (2017), 1890–1906.

Tyler, P., E. Evenhuis and R. Martin, 'Case study report: Peterborough', Structural Transformation, Adaptability and City Economic Evolutions, Working Paper 10 (UK Economic and Social Research Council Urban Transformations Initiative, 2018), available online at: www.cityevolutions.org.uk/working-paper-peterborough-case-study/ (accessed January 2019)..

Valluvan, S., 'Conviviality and multiculture: a post-integration sociology of multi-ethnic interaction', *Young*, 24:3 (2016), 204–221.

Valluvan, S., 'Cosmopolitanism and intelligibility', in N. G. Schiller and A. Irving (eds), *Whose Cosmopolitanism? Critical Perspectives, Relationalities and Discontents* (Oxford: Berghahn, 2015), pp. 74–82.

Valluvan, S., 'The uses and abuses of class: left nationalism and the denial of working class multiculture', *The sociological review*, 67:1 (2019), 36–46.

Verdon, N., 'The employment of women and children in agriculture: a reassessment of agricultural gangs in nineteenth-century Norfolk', *Agricultural history review*, 49:1 (2001), 41–55.

Verdon, N., *Working the Land: A History of the Farmworker in England from 1850 to the Present Day* (London: Palgrave Macmillan, 2017).

Virdee, S., 'Racialized capitalism: an account of its contested origins and consolidation', *The sociological review*, 67:1 (2019), 3–27.

Virdee, S., *Racism, Class and the Racialized Outsider* (New York: Palgrave Macmillan, 2014).

Virdee, S. and B. McGeever, 'Racism, crisis, Brexit', *Ethnic and racial studies*, 41:10 (2017), 1802–1819.

Visser, A. and S. Simpson, 'Understanding local government's engagement in immigrant policy making in the US', in Jonathan Darling and Harald Bauder (eds), *Sanctuary Cities and Urban Struggles: Rescaling Migration, Citizenship and Rights* (Manchester: Manchester University Press, 2019), pp. 165–190.

Walker, P. and P. Lewis, 'Nigel Farage discussed fronting far-right group led by Steve Bannon', *The Guardian*, available online at: www.theguardian.com/politics/2019/may/22/nigel-farage-discussed-fronting-far-right-group-led-by-steve-bannon (accessed June 2019).

Warsi, S., *The Enemy Within: A Tale of Muslim Britain* (London and New York: Allen Lane, 2017).

Warsi, S., 'Tory peer accuses Boris Johnson of making "hate crime more likely"', 2018, available online at: www.theguardian.com/politics/2018/aug/08/tory-peer-accuses-boris-johnson-of-making-hate-more-likely (accessed January 2019).

Waters, J., "Mobilities", in, R. Lee, N. Castree, R. Kitchin, V. Lawson, A. Paasi, C. Philo, S. Radcliffe, S. Roberts and C. Withers (eds), *The SAGE Handbook of Human Geography* (London: Sage, 2014), pp. 22–44.

Watson, S., 'Making multiculturalism', *Ethnic and racial studies*, 40:5 (2017), 2635–2652.

Werbner, P., 'Global pathways: working class cosmopolitans and the creation of transnational ethnic worlds', *Social anthropology*, 7:1 (1999), 17–35.

Werbner, P. (ed.), *Anthropology and the New Cosmopolitanism: Rooted, Feminist and Vernacular Perspectives* (Oxford and New York: Berg, 2008).

Werner, M., K. Strauss, B. Parker, R. Orzeck, K. Derickson and A. Bonds, 'Feminist political economy in geography: why now, what is different, and what for?', *Geoforum*, 79:1 (2017), 1–4.

Wise, A., 'Becoming cosmopolitan: encountering difference in a city of mobile labour', *Journal of ethnic and migration studies*, 42:14 (2016), 2289–2308.

Wise, A., 'Convival labour and the "joking relationship": humour and everyday multiculturalism at work', *Journal of intercultural studies*, 37:5 (2016), 481–500.

Wise, A. and G. Noble, 'Convivialities: an orientation', *Journal of intercultural studies*, 37:5 (2016), 423–431.

Wise, A. and S. Velayutham, 'Conviviality in everyday multiculturalism: some brief comparisons between Singapore and Sydney', *European journal of cultural studies*, 17:4 (2014), 406–430.

Young, R., *The Idea of English Ethnicity* (Chichester: Wiley-Blackwell, 2007).

Zeng, M., 'Subaltern cosmopolitanism: concept and approaches', *The sociological review*, 62:1 (2014), 137–148.

Index